The Instant Handbook of

# Boat Handling, Navigation, and Seamanship

300
330
0
30
60

# Boat Handling, Navigation, and Seamanship

## A Quick Reference for Sail and Power

Nigel Calder
Richard Clinchy
Bill Gladstone
Peter Nielsen
John Rousmaniere
Bob Sweet
Charlie Wing

International Marine / McGraw-Hill
Camden, Maine • New York • Chicago • San Francisco • Lisbon • London • Madrid • Mexico City • Milan • New Delhi • San Juan • Seoul • Singapore • Sydney • Toronto

The McGraw·Hill Companies

2 3 4 5 6 7 8 9 CTP/CTP 0 9



Library of Congress Control Number: 2007928466

ISBN 978-0-07-149910-1
MHID 0-07-149910-5

Questions regarding the content of this book should be addressed to
International Marine
P.O. Box 220
Camden, ME 04843
www.internationalmarine.com

Questions regarding the ordering of this book should be addressed to
The McGraw-Hill Companies
Customer Service Department
P.O. Box 547
Blacklick, OH 43004
Retail customers: 1-800-262-4729
Bookstores: 1-800-722-4726

All art courtesy the authors unless otherwise noted:
Rick Barrentine/Corbis: 17; Ed Bohon/Corbis: 143; Dana Bowden: 18; FEMA: 228 (second from top); Christian Février, Bluegreen Pictures: 159; Pip Hurn: 133–38, 140–41 (illustrations only); www.mirtoart.com: 162 (bottom), 167 (bottom), 168 (bottom), 171 (top), 192–96, 197 (top and middle), 198–99, 203, 204 (top), 205 (top); Maptech: 44 (top); Nick Noyes: 161 (bottom); Ritchie Navigation: 60 (bottom), 62; Hal Roth: 162 (top), 171 (bottom), 172; Fritz Seegers: 180 (top), 181 (bottom), 221; David Shuler: 1, 191, 197 (bottom); Tom Upham: 224 (top); USCG: 204 (bottom two); Volvo: 175; West Marine: 63, 95, 111, 207; Yanmar: 176.

# CONTENTS



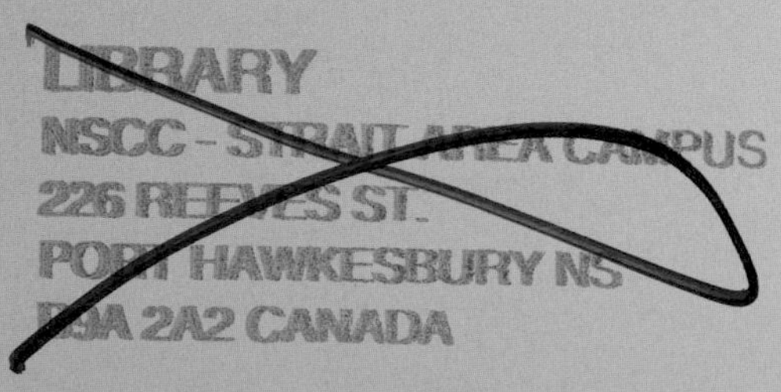

# PREFACE

On the water, when questions arise, there is often no time to spend searching through an exhaustive manual. *The Instant Handbook of Boat Handling, Navigation, and Seamanship* provides all the answers you need—fast.

Each of these chapters has been written by a leading expert (see pages 223–24 for a list of the contributors), and every page is designed to impart vital information with maximum ease and efficiency. We feel confident in saying that there has never been another seamanship book as authoritative and at the same time accessible as this one.

With the sole exception of Chapter 3, each of these chapters is also available as a stand-alone Quick Guide—a foldout, accordion-style, heavily laminated resource that is waterproof and virtually indestructible. We present the full product lineup below. With a folded size of just 4 inches by 9 inches, the Quick Guides are perfect for onboard use. They are available as Captain's Quick Guides from marine stores, from online book and marine retailers, from the U.S. Power Squadrons, and from www.internationalmarine.com. They are also available as West Marine Quick Guides from West Marine's stores, catalog, and website.

We hope *The Instant Handbook of Boat Handling, Navigation, and Seamanship* makes your time on the water more enjoyable, more rewarding, and safer.

—the editors of International Marine

CHAPTER 1

# Boat Handling Under Power

Bob Sweet

# Know Your Boat

Every boat under power moves in reaction to the thrust of water discharged from its propeller. When the discharge stream is directed astern, the boat moves ahead, and vice versa.

① The operator of an outboard, sterndrive (inboard/outboard or I/O), or jet-drive boat steers by directing the discharge stream from side to side—and that makes these boats highly maneuverable as long as the engine is engaged.

② In boats powered by a conventional inboard gas or diesel engine, the propeller is mounted on a fixed shaft, so the boat must be steered solely by means of a rudder. Add a second engine, however, and the engines and steering working in concert make the boat highly maneuverable, as we'll see.

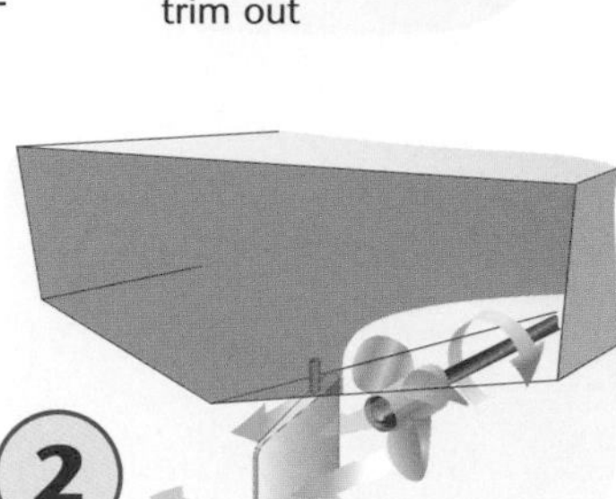

The following table is for comparative purposes. Any production boat will handle sufficiently well provided you adapt your handling techniques to your boat's tendencies rather than trying to fight them.

| Type of Propulsion | Outboard or Sterndrive (I/O) | Jet Drive | Single-Engine Inboard | Twin-Engine Inboard | Sailboat Auxiliary |
|---|---|---|---|---|---|
| **Directional Control** | Directed thrust propeller(s) | Directed thrust nozzle(s) | Rudder | Rudders + Engines | Large rudder |
| **Low-Speed Handling** | | | | | |
| Forward | Very good[1] | Very good | Good | Excellent | Fair/Good |
| Reverse | Good | Fair/Good | Poor | Good | Poor/Fair |
| Maneuvers | Very good | Very good | Good | Excellent | Fair |
| Turn in place | Fair/Good | Fair/Good | Fair | Excellent | Poor |
| Propeller Side thrust | Moderate | None | Significant | None[2] | Significant |
| **Docking** | | | | | |
| Forward | Very good | Very good | Good | Excellent | Fair/Good |
| Backing in | Fair/Good | Fair/Good | Poor/Fair | Very good | Poor |
| **Cruise-Speed Handling** | | | | | |
| Turns | Excellent | Excellent | Very good | Excellent | Good |
| Trim Front-to-back | Drive trim, Trim tabs | Trim tabs | Trim tabs | Trim tabs | None |
| Side-to-side | Trim tabs | Trim tabs | Trim tabs | Trim tabs | None |

Excellent · Very good · Good · Fair · Poor · None

1. with engine in gear—does not respond to helm when engine is in neutral
2. with both engines engaged ahead or astern

# Slow-Speed Maneuvering

A powerboat turns on a center of rotation that is typically about one-third of the way from the bow to the stern (1A).

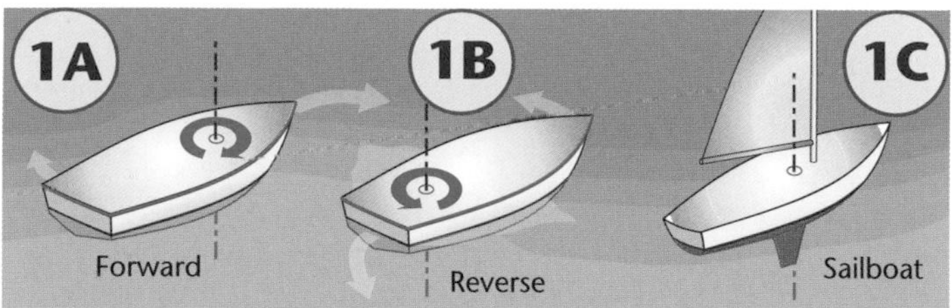


In effect, your boat's propulsion system pushes the stern *away* from the turn so the bow will rotate *into* it, and the stern swing is wider than the bow swing. Also, due to its momentum, your boat *slides* into a turn rather than carving it like a car on a curve ②.

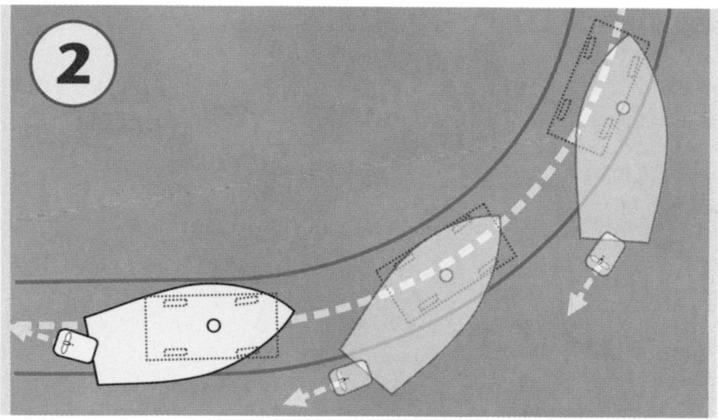


You need to be aware of these effects or you are likely to strike with your stern the very boat or dock you turned your bow away from ③. In time you will learn what clearances your boat requires for turns at various speeds and in various conditions of wind and current.

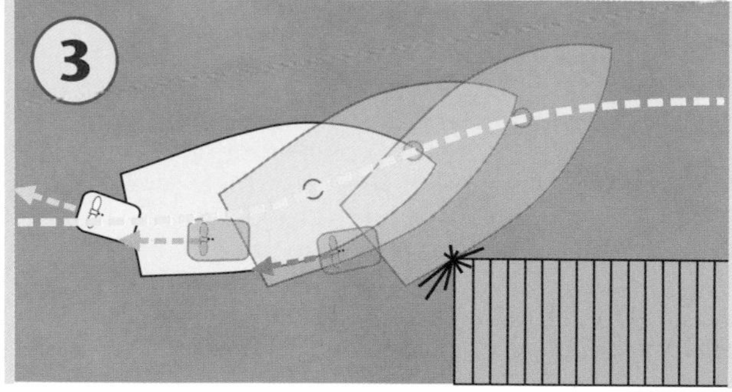


In reverse, a powerboat's pivot point typically moves to about two-thirds of the way from the bow to the stern, so the bow now swings more widely (1B).

The pivot point on a sailboat is more nearly amidships (1C).

## Single-Engine Inboard

A single-engine (single-screw) inboard powerboat depends on its rudder for steering. When the engine is in forward gear, the rudder turns the boat by deflecting the prop discharge (often called "wash") as well as the current created by the boat's motion. At slow speeds the boat depends heavily on prop wash for steering control; the smaller the rudder, the more true this is.

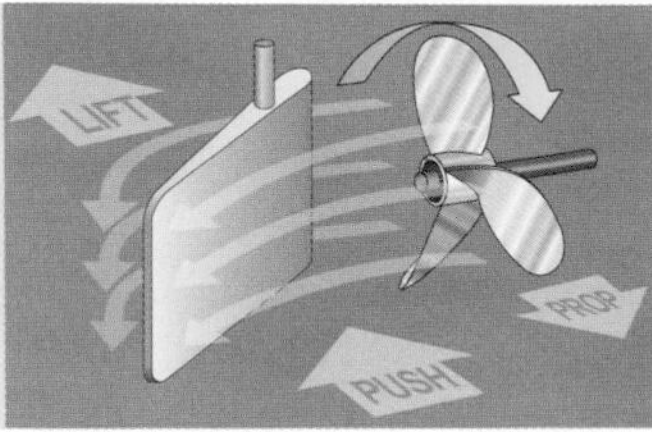


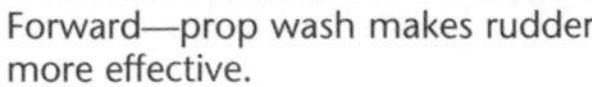

Forward—prop wash makes rudder more effective.

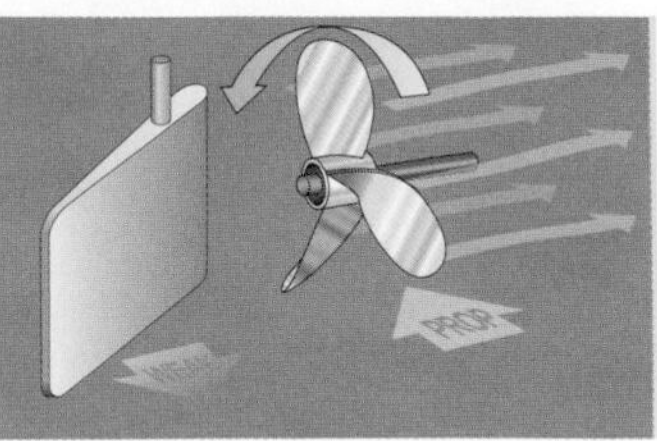


Reverse—no prop wash.

The propeller also produces a small side thrust that pushes the stern to port or starboard. Most boats use a "right-handed" prop, which turns clockwise in forward gear when viewed from astern, pushing the stern to starboard. Take your cue from the direction the blades are moving at the top of the swing; that's the direction of this so-called prop walk. Prop walk will give your boat a tighter turn to port than to starboard in forward gear.

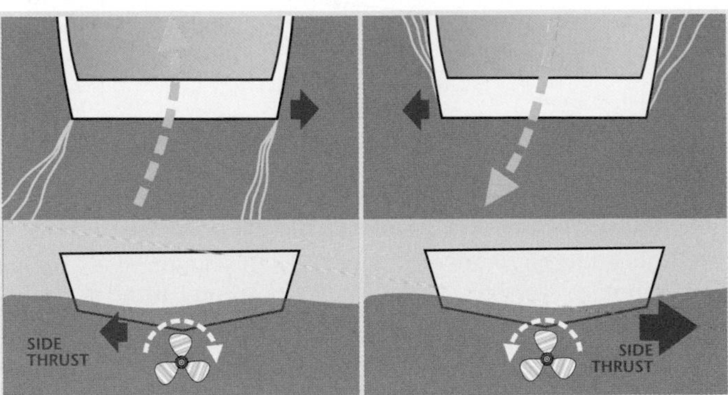


Side thrust in forward pushes stern to starboard.

Side thrust in reverse pushes stern to port.

When you put the single engine in reverse, however, the direction of side thrust also reverses, and the impact is greater in reverse than in forward since the propeller is not as efficient in reverse. To compound the problem with a single-screw inboard, in reverse there is no prop wash on the rudder to help with steering. To counter the stern moving to port, briefly shift the engine from reverse to forward and apply a brief burst of power while you steer hard to port. Then shift back to reverse. You won't make any forward headway, but the stern will kick over to starboard.

You can use prop walk to help you make a slow close-quarters turn to starboard. First turn the wheel hard to starboard and apply a brief burst of power ①. This should turn the boat 20 degrees or more. When you start to make forward progress, apply a brief burst of reverse power ②. The resultant side thrust "walks" the stern to port, continuing the turn while slowing your forward motion. Repeat the process ③ until your turn is completed. With practice, you'll be able to turn a clockwise circle within the boat's length.

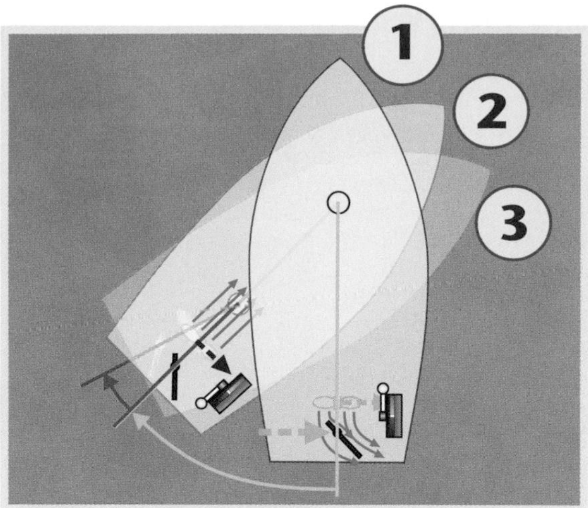


Turning counterclockwise is more difficult because prop walk—while it aids the turn in forward—opposes it in reverse.

## Twin-Engine Inboard

Twin inboard engines with a rudder behind each prop make a highly maneuverable boat. Usually the starboard propeller will be right-handed and the port prop will be left-handed , so that their side thrusts cancel when both engines are in forward ① or reverse ②. A twin-engine boat will therefore back straight when you center the rudders (absent wind or current) and is steerable at low backing speeds.

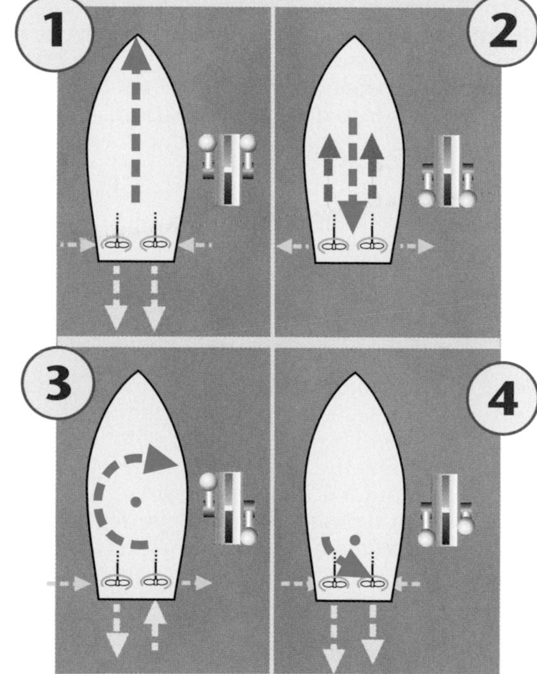


When one engine is in forward while the other is reversed ③, the side thrusts combine to make a turn even tighter. When rudder action is added, the boat can even spin within its own length.

You can often maneuver with engines alone. E.g., backing with more throttle on the port engine turns the stern to starboard ④.

On some boats, you can even slide the boat sideways. Try putting the starboard engine in reverse and the port engine ahead with left rudder.

## Outboard and Sterndrive (I/O)

Single-engine outboards and sterndrives steer by turning the propeller so as to direct its discharge current. These boats permit easier steering in reverse and tighter turns than you can possibly get from a single-engine inboard.

Without a rudder, however, there is little steerage with an outboard or I/O if the propeller is not engaged. This means it's more difficult to approach a dock with the engine in neutral. Also, most outboard- and sterndrive-powered hulls are designed for planing, not slow speeds. But you soon learn how to use throttle and helm to handle the boat.

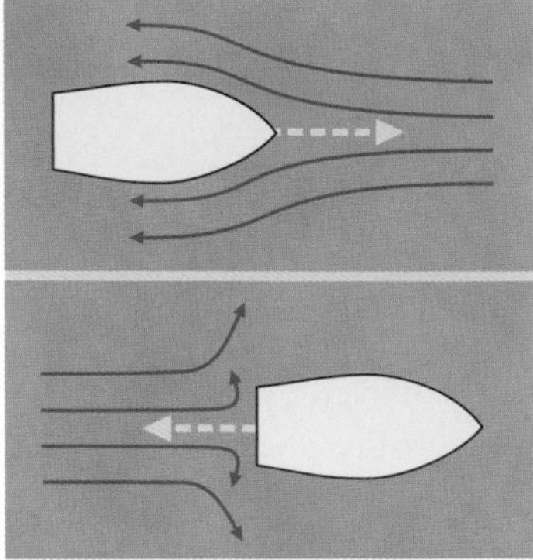

Planing hulls are designed to go fast, and track better going forward than in reverse.

Twin outboards or sterndrives offer some of the same handling benefits as twin inboard engines, but not to the same degree, since the propellers tend to be much closer together and farther aft from the boat's center of rotation than inboard props.

## Jet Drives

A jet drive has no external propeller. Instead an internal impeller mounted in a tube sucks water in through a grate in the hull bottom and forces it out toward the rear to produce thrust much like a jet aircraft. Steerage is accomplished by turning a nozzle to direct the discharge. When it's time to back up, a deflector shield swings down over the nozzle outlet, directing the discharge thrust forward. This produces a small and relatively ineffective reverse that can be steered for directional control.

Jet drives operate like outboards or sterndrives with nearly instantaneous response. However, the jet drive has no steerage without power applied.

## Auxiliary Sailboats

A sailboat's larger rudder makes it slightly more steerable in reverse when the boat is moving than a single-engine inboard powerboat. The sailboat's keel or centerboard will help it track through turns and provides a pivot point fixed nearer amidships. That means the stern kicks out less in a turn ahead, and the bow kicks out less in a turn astern.

However, a typical lack of horsepower imposes restraints. Prop walk is likely to be significant, especially in reverse. Adapting the approaches for single-engine inboards as a starting point, experiment in open water to see how your boat turns and backs. Do not expect great maneuverability under power from a boat designed primarily for sailing. Maneuver upwind or upcurrent when possible and avoid situations that might demand more precise handling than your boat can deliver.

# Docking

Docking techniques depend on current and wind. Current affects all boats equally, but wind has a greater influence on a light boat with high topsides and cabin structures and a shallow underbody that offers little resistance to leeway, which describes a typical planing cruiser.

Before you dock, look at flags or ripples on the water to determine wind strength and direction. Note which way moored boats are pointing in response to current and wind—especially boats similar to yours. Or simply stop your boat at a convenient location, observe which way it drifts, and plan your docking maneuvers accordingly.

Deploy lines and fenders in advance, briefing the crew on your intentions and their roles. Leave yourself an escape route in case other boats invade your path or your approach goes awry.

The angle of your approach will depend upon the direction of the wind. For a wind blowing off the dock, you will need to increase the angle.

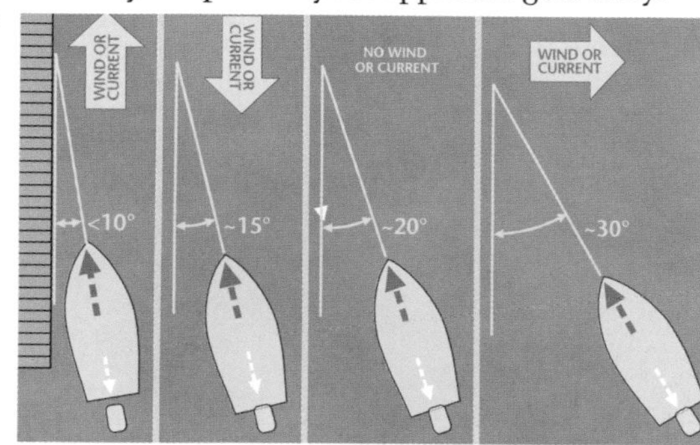


## Single-Engine Inboard Powerboat or Auxiliary Sailboat

A port-side-to landing is most convenient, especially if you have a right-handed prop. If wind and current are negligible, approach at roughly 20 degrees, slow to bare steerageway, and just before touching turn parallel with the dock and apply a touch of reverse power. The resultant prop walk will nudge your port quarter into the dock. Have your crew step onto the dock with docklines (inboard ends cleated in advance).

When there is a significant wind or current parallel to the dock, approach into the wind (or current) if you can ①. Pass a bow line or forward spring line to a dockside helper, who will tie off the line forward of the boat ②. (If a crewmember takes the line ashore, he or she should step—not leap—onto the dock.) As the boat is pushed back by the wind or current, the line will come taut and the stern will settle in toward the dock ③.

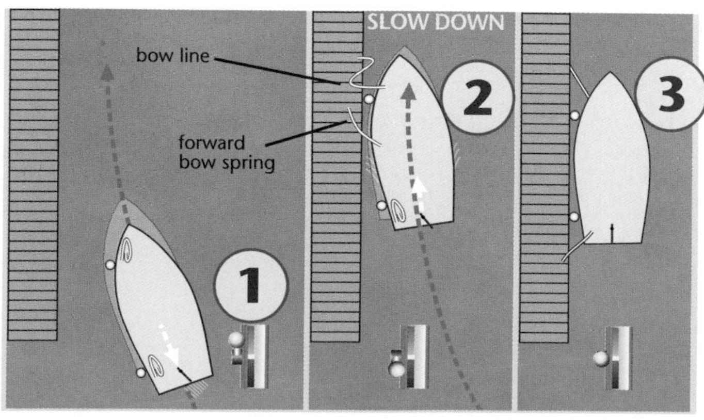

If the wind is blowing toward the dock, turn parallel when farther out than usual and let the breeze nudge you in.

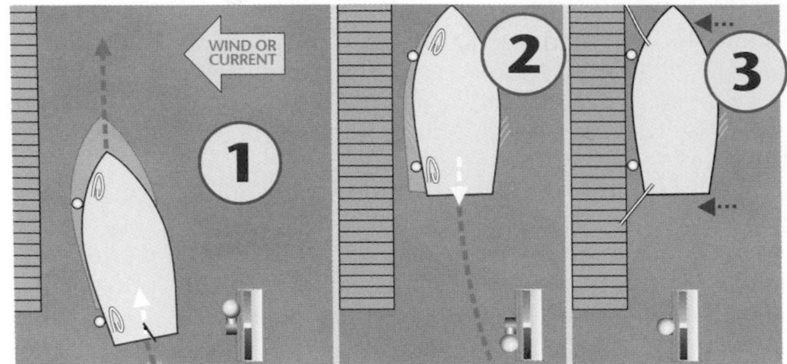


If there is a strong wind blowing off the dock, or if the available dock space is not much longer than your boat, approach at a steeper-than-normal angle and have an after spring line ready—i.e., free to run, with one end cleated at or slightly forward of amidships ①. As your bow quarter approaches the dock, have the spring line led back to a dock cleat or bollard near the "aft" end of the available space and attached there without slack ②. Now when you turn your helm away from the dock and apply gentle forward power, the resultant forces against the spring line will "warp" the boat into the dock ③.

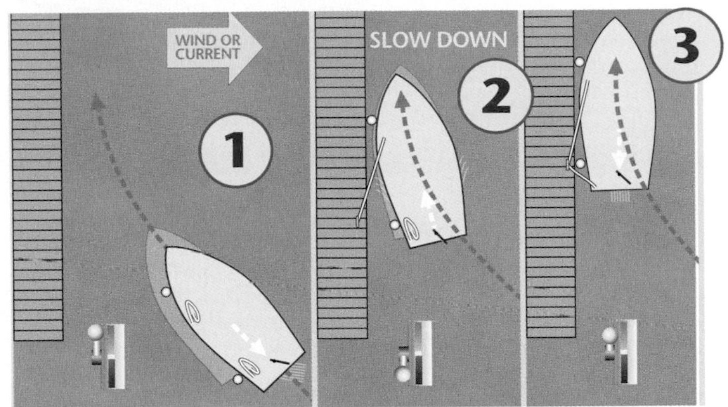


If forced to dock with wind or current behind you, approach at a shallow angle ① and get your stern line or after spring line fast to the dock quickly ②. Gentle forward power with starboard helm (assuming a port-side landing) will hold the stern against the dock while you get the other lines ashore ③.

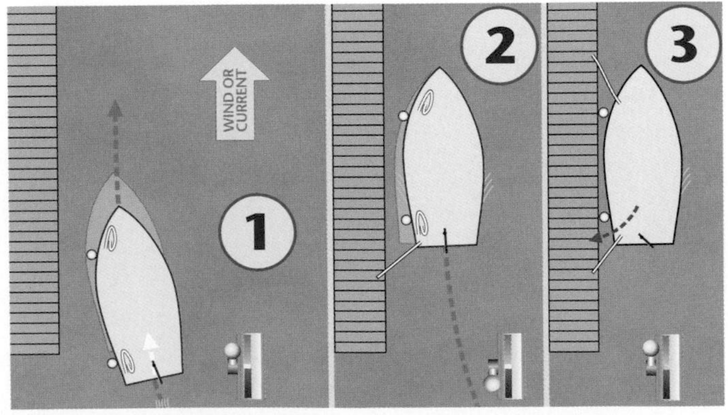

## Outboard and Sterndrive (I/O) Boats

Generally you can use the single-engine inboard docking techniques just described. There is an additional technique with the wind off the dock or when fitting your boat into a short space. As your bow approaches the dock ①, apply a little reverse power while turning the wheel toward the dock to stop your forward motion ②. Now lead a bow line fast to the dock. Backing against the bow line with the wheel to port will move the stern in ③.

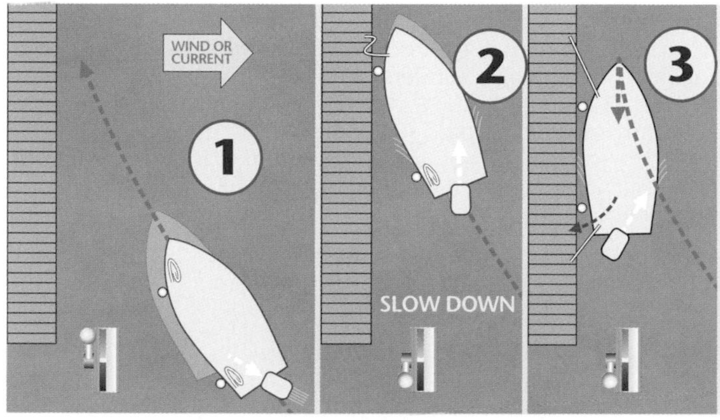


When docking with wind or current from behind ①, hold the boat in a fixed position by applying just the right power in reverse ②. The bow will simply point downwind or downcurrent, and steering gently toward the dock moves the boat sideways to its destination ③.

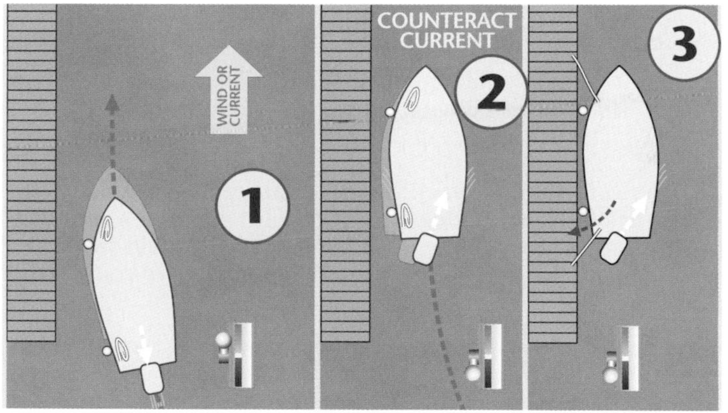


## Twin-Engine Inboard

Adapt the twin-engine techniques described earlier to the docking techniques for a single-engine inboard. A twin-engine boat is more maneuverable and thus easier to dock, and the absence of propeller side thrust means you can land on your port or starboard side with equal ease. You can dock using engines alone to maneuver your boat, but rudders may help.

# Departing the Dock—All Boats

In the absence of wind or current and with plenty of room ahead, simply ease forward and away from the dock, turning gently so as not to clip it with your stern quarter.

If the wind or current is ahead of you or off the dock, untie the bow and let it swing clear. Then apply forward power, steering to keep your stern quarter clear.

When the wind or current is directly on the dock, pinning you to it, cast off all docklines except your after-bow spring line ①. Make sure you have fenders in place. Turn your helm toward the dock and apply gentle forward power against the spring line, and your stern should swing away from the dock ②. Now release the spring and you should be able to back clear ③. This method also works when the wind or current is pushing you from behind.

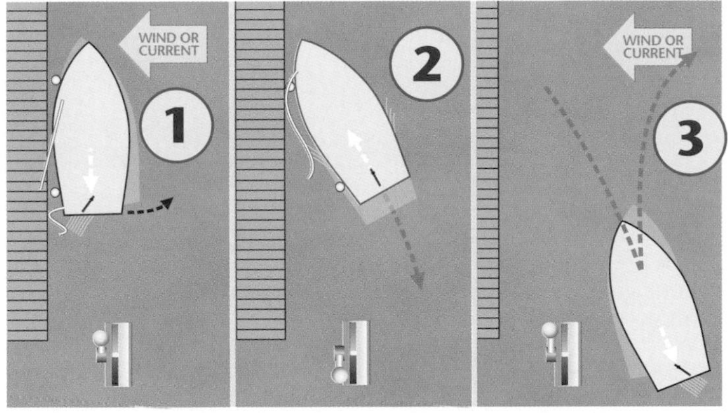


(Hint: If you double the spring line around a dock cleat or bollard, with both ends aboard the boat, you can recover it from the boat simply by releasing one end and pulling in the other.)

To clear a tight berth going ahead rather than astern, back down on a forward quarter spring line with your helm centered ①. The forces working against the restraining line will swing your bow out ②. Then apply forward power, recover your spring line, and proceed ③.

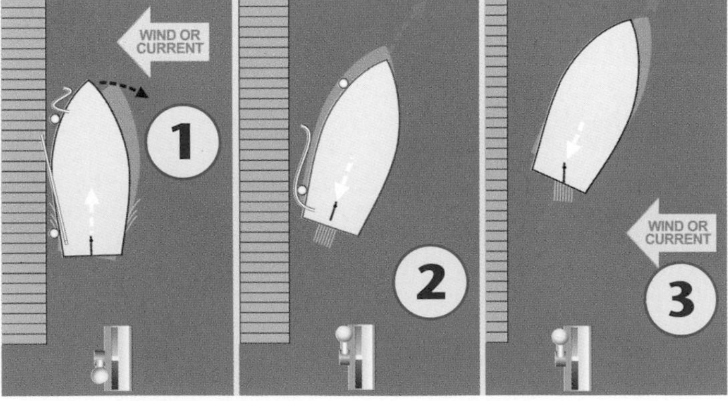

# Docking in a Slip

When entering a slip bow first, aim toward the inner corner with slow steerageway, fenders deployed, until your bow quarter almost kisses the dock ①. Then apply light reverse power to halt your forward progress and get a bow line around a cleat or post at the inner end of the slip ②. Another burst of reverse power with helm toward the dock will pull the stern in ③, either from the directed thrust of an outboard or sterndrive or the prop walk of an inboard. With a twin-engine boat, use the engine away from the dock.

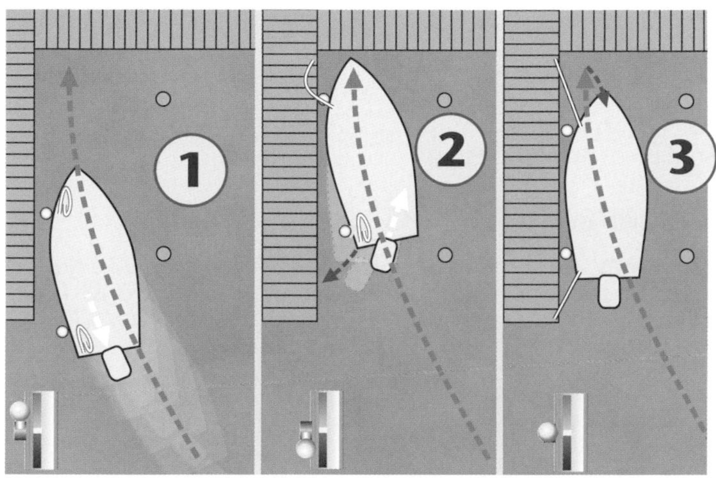


Backing in is more challenging, especially in a single-engine inboard boat or auxiliary sailboat. Get properly aligned in front of the slip. Punctuate your backing with brief bursts of power ahead under port or starboard helm to get back on course without halting sternway. If necessary, pull out and realign your boat for another attempt. Have docklines ready, and don't hesitate to use them to warp yourself in.

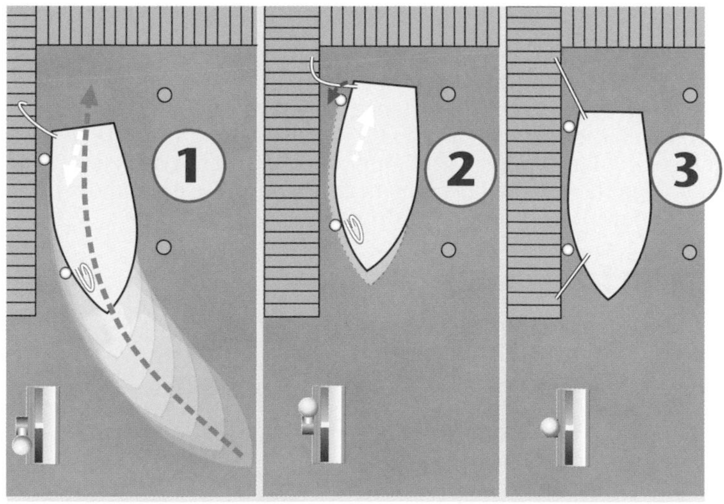


Backing into a slip can be challenging. As soon as you touch, have a crewmember or dockhand tie a stern line, and then use gentle forward power to pull you to the dock.

# Handling at Cruising Speeds

Most boats handle best when running more or less "on their lines"—i.e., parallel with their at-rest waterline. A slight bow-up trim will increase the efficiency of a planing hull, but excessive bow-up trim increases slamming in a chop and impedes visibility ahead. A little bow-down trim can give a more comfortable ride and better steering at slow speeds or in a chop but may also increase spray and might cause "bow steering" or even bury the bow at cruising speeds in following seas.

Neutral trim

## Trimming Your Drives

Outboards and sterndrives typically provide a powered adjustment for the trim angle of the drive unit. When the drive is trimmed "out"—i.e., away from the transom—the bow will rise. When the drive is trimmed "in," the bow falls.

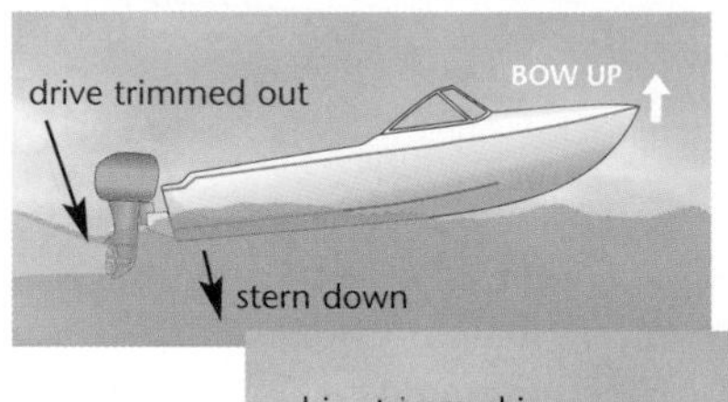


Bow up, drive trimmed out.

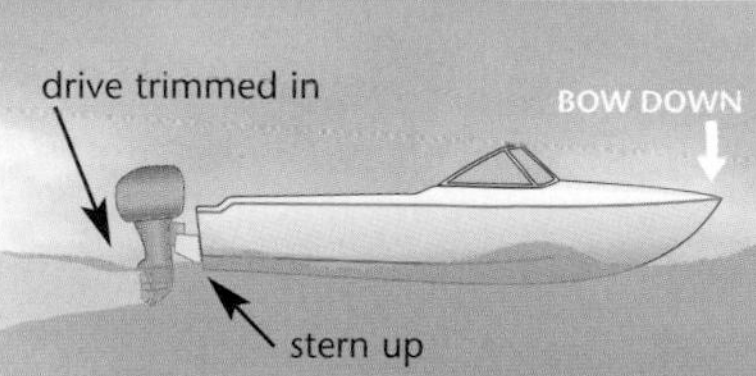


Bow down, drive trimmed in.

Generally you will trim the drive in for steering, visibility, and wave-handling at slower speeds unless you need some "bow-up" trim to counterbalance weight in the bow. Drive-in trim will also help you accelerate to a plane by lifting the stern. Once on plane you will probably want to trim the drive out, but if you go too far, the bow may begin to porpoise up and down. Trim in until the porpoising stops.

## Using Trim Tabs

A trim tab is a hinged plate mounted at each side of the transom's bottom edge. When a tab (or "flap") is in the raised position—flush with the bottom—it has little effect. When it is lowered, it lifts its side of the stern and depresses the opposite bow. The angle of the flap is controlled

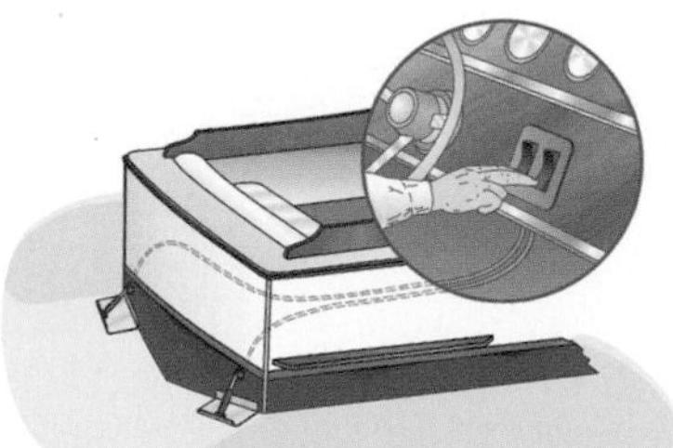

Rocker switches at the helm adjust each trim tab up or down.

hydraulically from a pair of rocker switches at the helm. Since each trim tab can be controlled separately, you can adjust side-to-side as well as fore-and-aft trim.

When both tabs are trimmed down, the stern will rise and the bow will drop. This can be essential for getting an inboard boat to plane and can also augment a trimmed-in outboard or sterndrive. Once on plane, adjust the tabs to suit. Raise them to decrease drag, keep the bow up in a following sea, or fall off plane again; or lower them slightly to maintain planing at a lower speed or to reduce slamming in a chop.

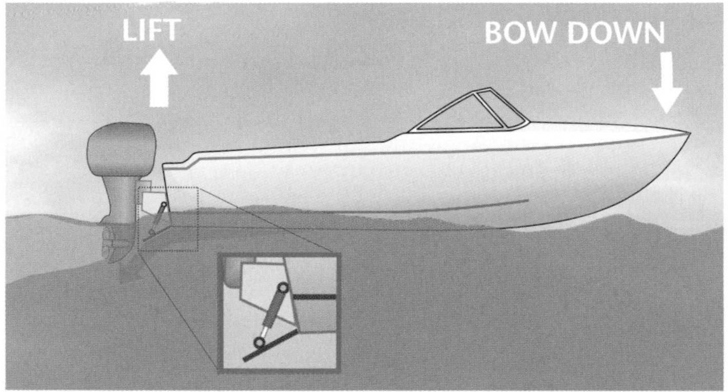


With both trim tabs down, the stern of the boat is lifted, which helps get it on plane. This is particularly helpful with inboard engines. Used in concert with the drive trim on an outboard or I/O, it gives you added flexibility.

If your boat is unevenly loaded, you can level it side-to-side using one trim tab. Similarly, if you're heeling into a crosswind, lower the tab on the side of the boat you want to raise. Do it incrementally. Gauge the effect of the trim before you lower the tab farther.

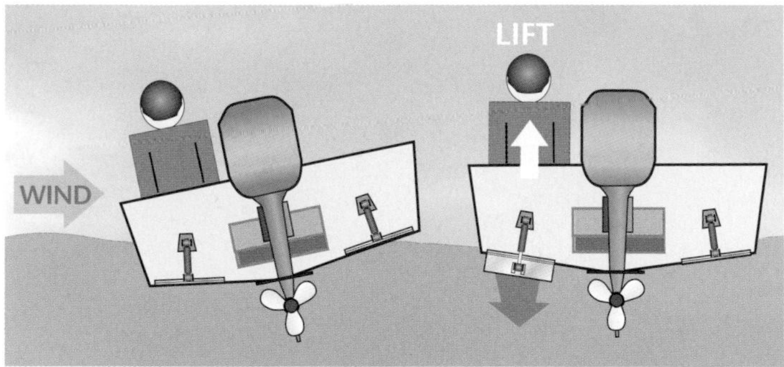


## When the Seas Build

To reduce pounding in a seaway, lower the bow to slice through the waves. Trim tabs will accomplish this while slowing the boat, possibly without falling off plane. Trimming in an outboard or sterndrive will accomplish the same thing without slowing the boat. Be careful not to trim the bow down so far that it buries itself into the back of a following sea or digs into an oncoming one.

# Negotiating Rough Seas and Running Inlets

When the seas surpass what you can handle with trim adjustments alone ①, it's time to slow down and focus on steering and throttle. Treat the waves much like hills that you would rather ski around than over.

## Handling Oncoming Waves

Taking the waves at an angle will increase the effective distance between crests and lessen their slopes ②. Too great an angle, however, might allow your bow to be forced downsea, leaving you broadside to the waves and vulnerable to a capsize ③. The better your boat tracks, the greater the angle you can risk.

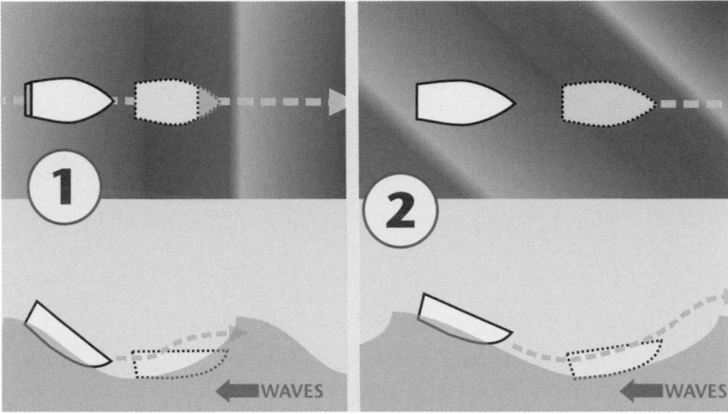


When waves get too steep (left), take them at angle (right).

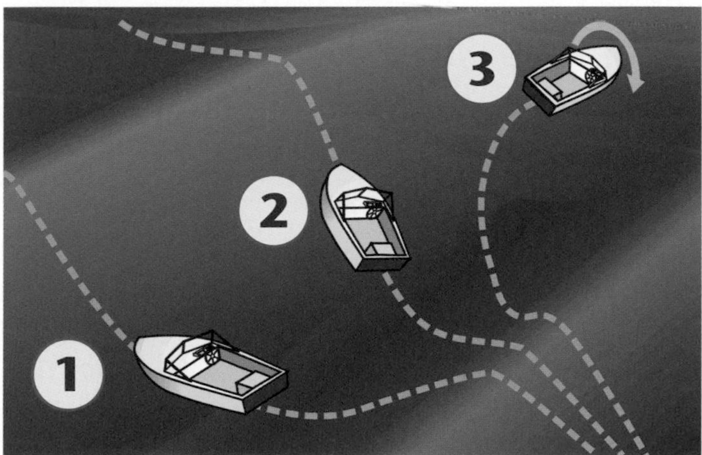


① Head on—waves too steep. ② Ideal angle. ③ Angle too great—possible risk of capsize.

Pick your path through the waves, altering course and speed to avoid steep and breaking seas. A quick burst of throttle will lift the bow to meet a wave; throttle back when you reach the crest to lower the bow and avoid slamming into the next trough.

## Running with the Waves

When running downsea, you could be in danger of digging the bow into the back of the wave ahead ①, which would halt your progress and allow the next following wave to lift your stern or break aboard. In extreme circumstances you might broach (turn broadside to the seas) or even pitchpole (somersault the stern over the bow). For a smoother, safer ride, try to position yourself about a third of the way down the backside of a wave and use your throttle to stay in that position ②.

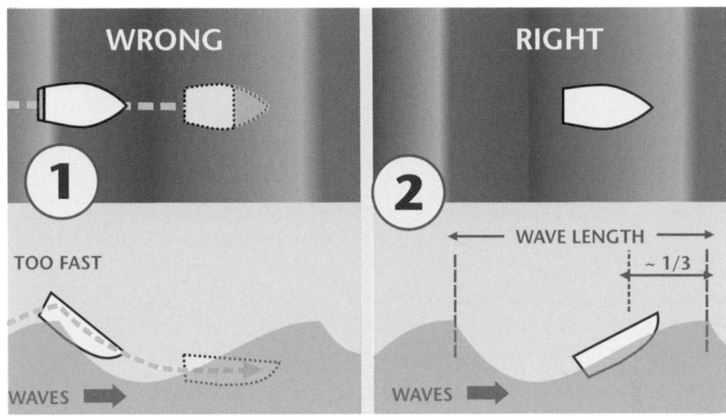


## Running Inlets

Inlets can be treacherous. When an outgoing tide meets an incoming wind, the waves become higher, steeper, and more closely spaced. In a narrow, shallow inlet under the influence of swift tides and a strong onshore wind, the resultant seas can be spectacular.

When possible, wait for slack or flood tide or use a deeper, wider inlet. If you must proceed, make sure everyone is wearing life jackets and use the same techniques as when running with following seas. Using your throttle, stay on the backside of the most benign wave you can find. DO NOT ride over the crest, since that might cause you to broach or swamp, and would certainly leave you no room to maneuver.

To exit an inlet under these conditions, take the waves nearly head on, staying midchannel where the water is deeper, and use your throttle to raise and lower the bow over the waves. This is tense, tricky work. Do not allow your bow to be turned by the oncoming waves, as this will limit your ability to maneuver or even swamp you.

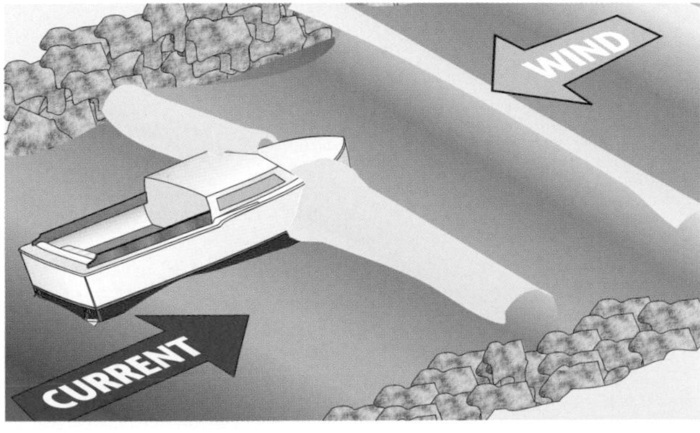

CHAPTER 2

# Sail Trim and Rig Tuning

Bill Gladstone

# About Sails

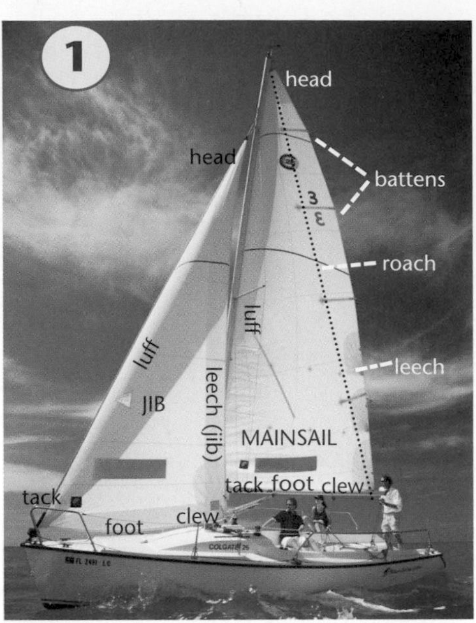


Sails are marvelous things, deceptively simple in appearance but in practice more complex and variable than an airplane wing ①.

The wind on your sails is the *apparent wind*—the sum of the true wind and your boat's forward motion—and this is the wind you must trim to ②.

This wind bends as it approaches your sails, putting the jib in a relative lift and the main in a relative header ③. Thus the jib is trimmed more outboard than the main.

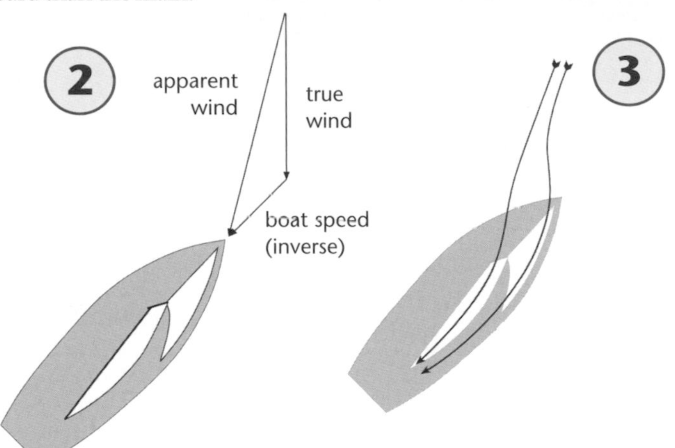


As the apparent wind flows around a sail, for reasons that remain difficult to summarize, the flow over the leeward, convex surface travels faster than the flow over the windward, concave surface. This faster flow exerts less pressure on the leeward (outside) surface than the slower air on the windward (inside) surface. The result is *lift*, which is everywhere perpendicular to the sail surface. Much of this lift is useless, serving only to heel the boat; only a small component drives the boat forward. One goal of your trimming and sail shaping—and of sail design itself—is to improve the ratio of useful (forward) to useless (heeling) forces, often by shifting the maximum

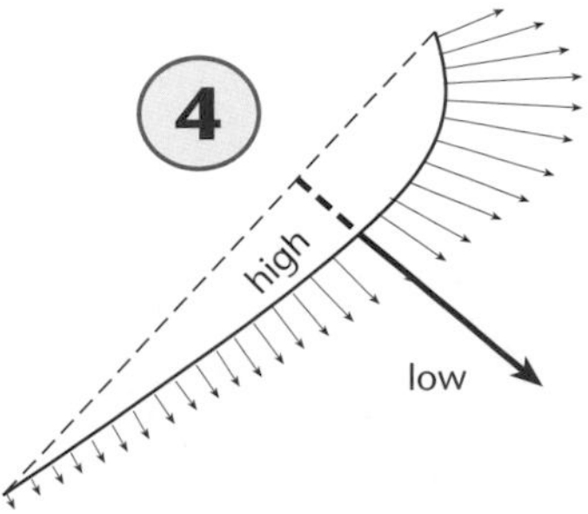

acceleration differences and resultant lift toward the front half of the sail, where the forward component is greater ④.

Even so, the side force of the sails would leave us unable to sail to windward were it not for the keel (or centerboard), which generates an offsetting hydrodynamic lift.

## A Sail Has Three Sources of Power

Proper trim achieves the optimum mix of all three:

**1. Angle of Attack.** This is the angle at which the wind hits the sail. At an angle of zero the sails are luffing. As we trim in sails, move the main traveler to windward, pull the jib lead inboard, or bear away, the angle of attack and the power both increase ⑤.

**2. Shape.** *Depth* is the amount of curve, or camber, in a sail, measured as a proportion of the distance, or *chord length*, from luff to leech. A mainsail with a maximum depth, or draft, of 10% ⑥ is a flat sail, while a draft of 15% would mean a deep or full main. Headsails carry a bit more draft than mains—say, 12% to 20%.

A deep sail provides more power for punching through waves. A flatter sail creates less drag and is faster in smooth water, and also creates a wider angle of attack for closer pointing. A flatter shape is better when a boat is overpowered in heavy air ⑦.

In addition to controlling the *amount* of depth in the sail we can also control its *position*. The usual goal is to put the deepest draft about 40–45% of the way aft from luff to leech in a mainsail, and 30–40% of the way aft in a jib. Moving the draft forward makes for less drag and more forgiving steering in waves, while moving the draft aft enables higher pointing.

**3. Twist.** A sail with lots of twist is open at the upper leech, spilling power aloft. A sail with little twist—i.e., a closed upper leech that is nearly parallel to the lower leech—is more powerful. Some twist is usually necessary because the wind is stronger aloft, which makes the apparent wind angle more open near the top of the sail than down low ⑧.

A sail can be depowered either by easing the sheet to increase twist or by flattening. The former is preferred in a chop, while the latter is better in smooth water.

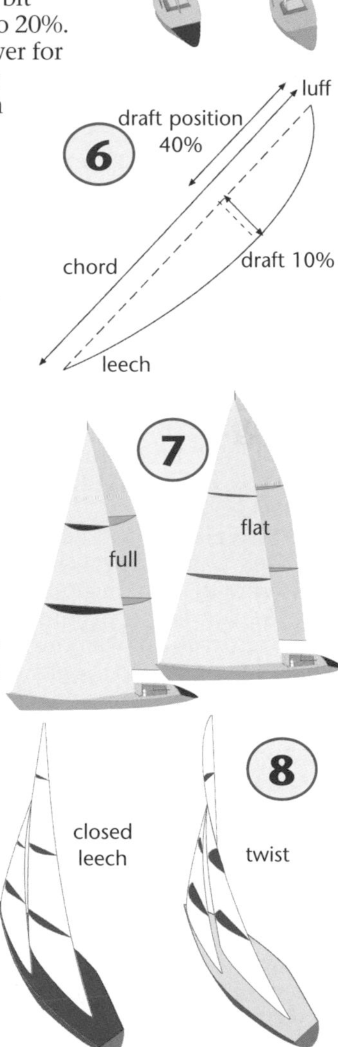

# Mainsail Upwind

Your boat will have some or all of these mainsail controls to work with ①:

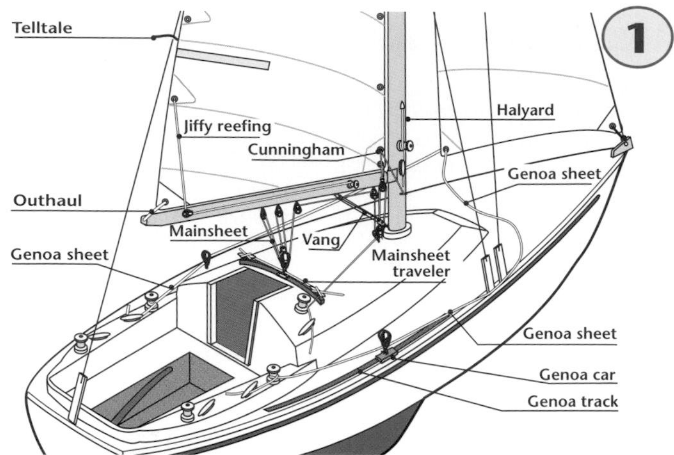


**Mainsheet.** Trimming to close-hauled increases the angle of attack. As the boom nears the centerline, further trim pulls the boom down more than in, reducing the sail's twist and tensioning the leech.

Telltales stream back from the leech when the air flow is smooth ②. When the flow around the outside surface separates, the sail is *stalled,* and the telltales disappear behind the leech ③. For good all-around upwind performance, you want the upper batten parallel with the boom and the leech telltales flowing with just an occasional stall. From there, try further adjustments for specific conditions as on pages 23–25.

**Traveler.** Except when overpowered, adjust the traveler to windward to keep the boom nearly over the centerline, maximizing angle of attack. In overpowering conditions, ease the traveler to leeward to reduce power and relieve weather helm ④. Racers sometimes play the traveler to dump power in puffs.

**Boom Vang.** This is primarily an offwind control. Upwind, remove the slack to help control twist. In light air, leave the vang eased to avoid a closed leech or stalled flow.

**Mast Bend.** After the mainsheet, this is the second most powerful controller of mainsail

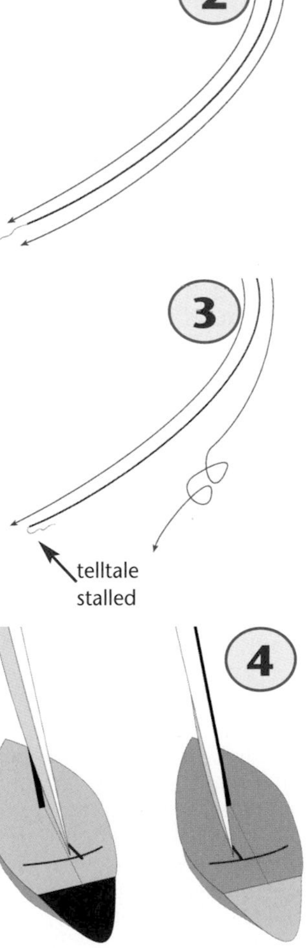

shape. Increasing mast bend flattens the mainsail and reduces its power. The biggest impact is in the middle and upper portions of the sail. Mast bend also adds twist aloft ⑤.

When the boat is fully powered (and only then), adding mast bend can increase speed by reducing heel and weather helm and the drag associated with them.

**Outhaul.** Pull the outhaul tighter as the wind builds to reduce depth in the lower portion of the mainsail, and ease it gently for extra power in light air or chop.

**Halyard and Cunningham.** To hold the draft in its designed position just forward of the middle of the sail, use these controls to tighten the luff as the wind builds. Use the halyard first, and when at full hoist, use the cunningham. When you bend the mast the draft will move aft, so add luff tension as you add mast bend.

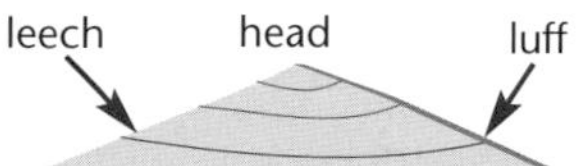


Mainsheet tight for little twist and extra power and pointing.

Mainsheet eased to add twist and spill power.

Mast straight leaves the sail deep and powerful.

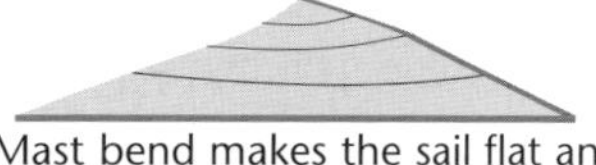

Mast bend makes the sail flat and depowered.

Traveler up for higher angle of attack and more power.

Traveler down reduces angle of attack and power.

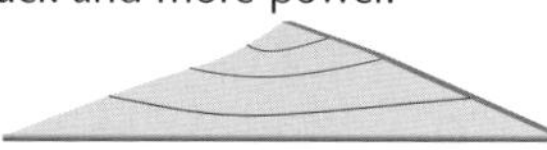

Little luff tension allows the draft to move aft.

Luff tension added with halyard or cunningham pulls the draft foward.

# Headsail Upwind

If you have a choice, select a headsail that matches the wind conditions. Then try any or all of the following sail controls:

**Halyard.** In light air, an overly tight halyard hurts performance. As the wind builds, increase halyard tension to keep the luff firm and the draft in the desired position.

**Sheet.** Trimming to close-hauled adds power by increasing the sail's angle of attack. As the sail nears full trim, the sheet pulls the clew down more than in, which reduces twist and adds further power. For close-hauled trim, the middle leech of the jib should be parallel to the centerline of the boat. The foot of the jib should be a little rounder than the foot of the main, and its overall shape should match the shape of the main ①.

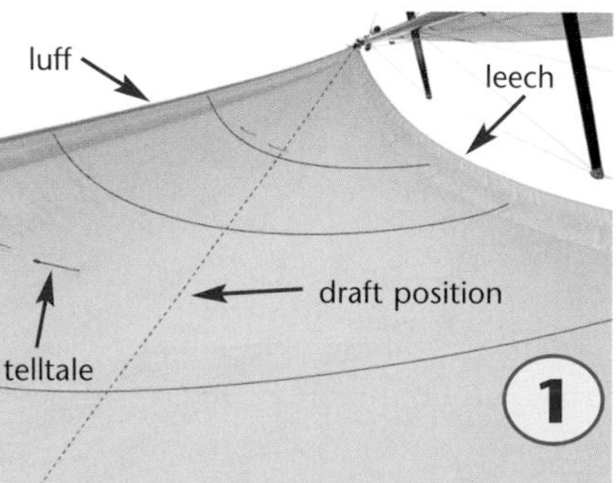

As you trim, pointing will improve, with some loss of speed. When further trim fails to improve pointing, the sheet is overtrimmed. Ease slightly—just a few inches—to optimize trim.

**Headstay Sag.** This can be controlled with an adjustable backstay. A tight headstay flattens the sail, while extra sag adds power. Let the headstay sag in light air, and add tension as the wind builds ②.

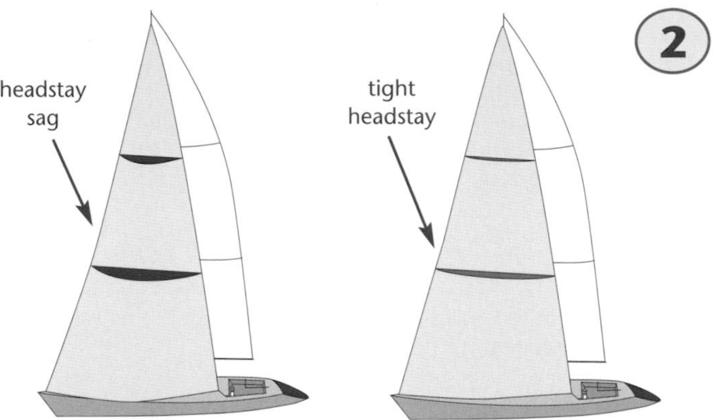


**Genoa Leads.** These change the fore-and-aft sheet position along the genoa tracks. Start by adjusting the lead so the sail luffs along its entire height as you pinch up above close-hauled. From this initial setting, moving the leads forward makes the sail fuller with less twist. Moving them aft makes the sail flatter with more twist ③. See pages 23–25.

3

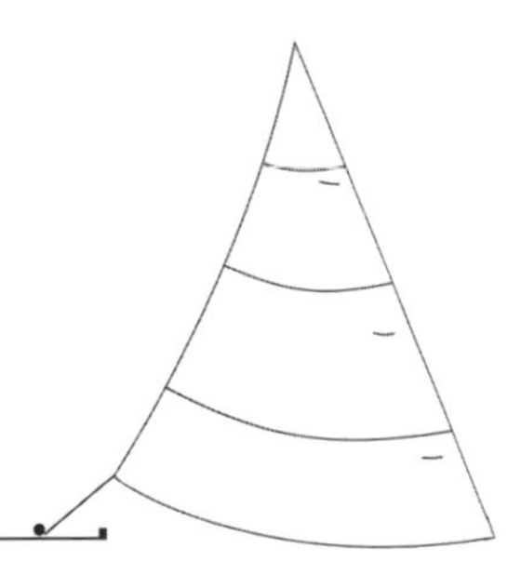

Initial lead position: Genoa shape matches mainsail. Upper telltales break just before lower ones.

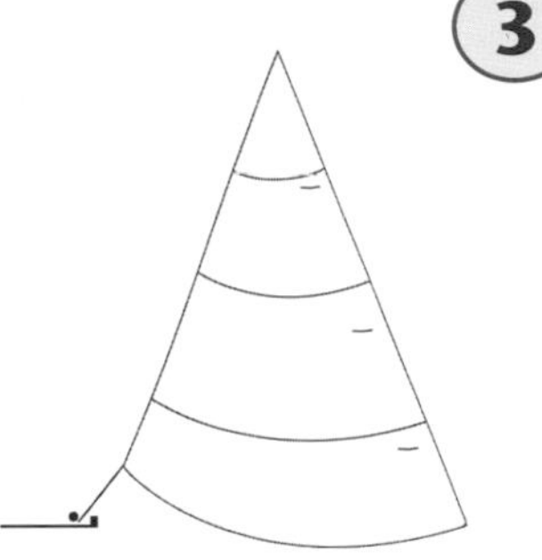

Lead foward: Deeper shape, closed leech.

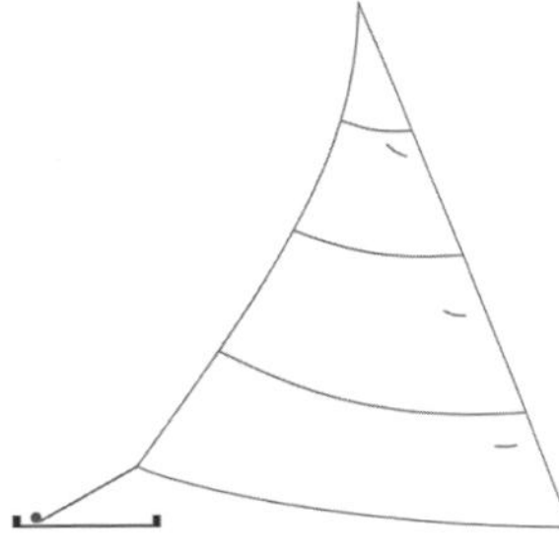

Lead aft: Flatter shape, open leech.

**Leech Cord.** This merely prevents leech flutter, which can quickly stretch the leech of a jib. Tension it just enough to stop flutter, and no more.

# Upwind Sailing

With the jib close-hauled, steer so the lower jib telltales are streaming aft. Head up just short of the point where the inside, or windward, telltales break. The sector you can steer through with the telltales flowing—a range of a few degrees—is the steering groove ①. If you head up too high the inside telltales will break, and soon thereafter the sail will start to luff. But even before that point you will feel the boat starting to lose power and speed. Aim to steer as high as you can in the groove while maintaining full power ②.

If you fall off too far the outside telltales will stall, and you will lose power and speed, not to mention pointing.

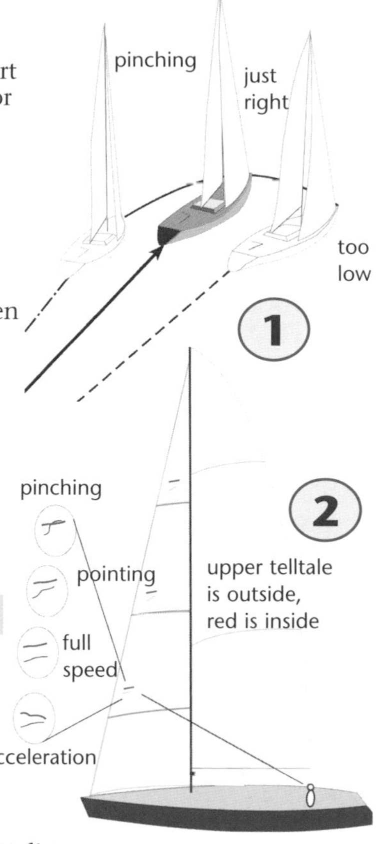


## Moderate-Air Trim

In moderate winds of 8 to 17 knots (the upper limit will be less for some boats), trim for full power and maximum pointing ability. Start as follows:

- Main boom on or near centerline.
- Mainsail twist adjusted with sheet so that telltale at top batten is flowing most of the time but stalling occasionally.
- Mainsail depth adjusted to achieve slight weather helm and a comfortable heel angle.
- Jib trimmed to close-hauled, just shy of a spreader tip or to the point of occasional mainsail backwinding (then steer as described above).
- Jib leads set so that the curve of the leech matches the mainsail shape, and the telltales break evenly from top to bottom. (As you pinch up above closed-hauled, the upper inside telltales should luff *just before* the lower ones.) ③
- Headstay tightened just enough to flatten the jib and improve pointing while still maintaining enough draft and power for a slight weather helm and a comfortable heel angle.

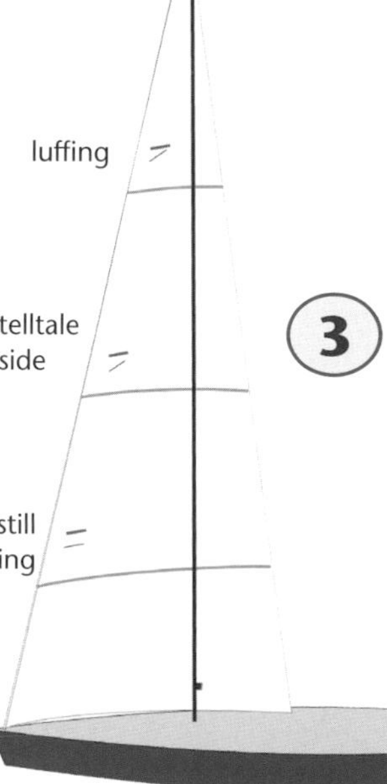

**In Smooth Water**. Try flatter, more closely trimmed sails with less twist for higher pointing. Trim the mainsail until the telltales stall more than half the time. Use more mast bend and a tighter headstay, move the jib leads aft to flatten the jib, and then trim the jibsheet harder to take out the extra twist.

**In Choppy Water.** Straighten the mast, sag the headstay, and move the jib leads forward to add depth and power to punch through the waves. Then ease the jib-sheet a few inches to restore the twist that moving the leads forward removed. You want the twist to prevent stalling and give your pitching boat a wider steering groove. Finally, bear off a couple of degrees to increase the angle of attack ④.

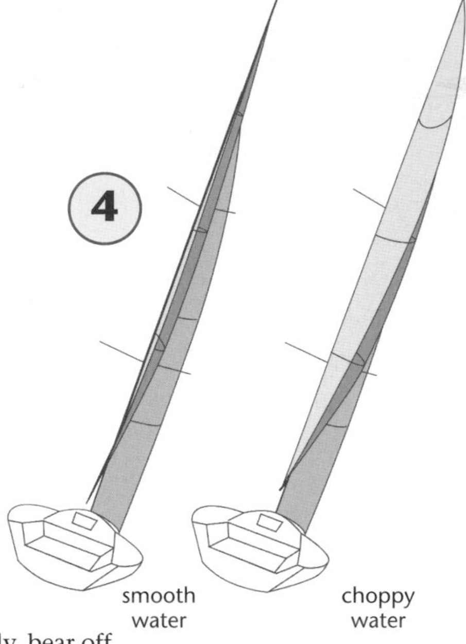


## Light-Air Trim

Speed comes first in light air. Bear off a few degrees from the moderate-air baseline.

You want deep sails, so ease the backstay to straighten the mast and put sag in the headstay. Move the jib leads forward and ease the main outhaul. Make sure your halyards are loose—leave a few wrinkles along the luff of each sail.

Leave enough twist to encourage easy flow. You may have to ease the sheets a foot or more from their moderate-air positions to keep the telltales flowing. Easing the sheets reduces power, but you won't get any power without flow, and overtrimming will stall the sails. Another reason for twist is that in light air the wind at the masthead will be stronger than the wind at the deck, resulting in a wider apparent wind angle aloft.

As your speed builds, head up while trimming to reduce twist and maintain angle of attack ⑤.

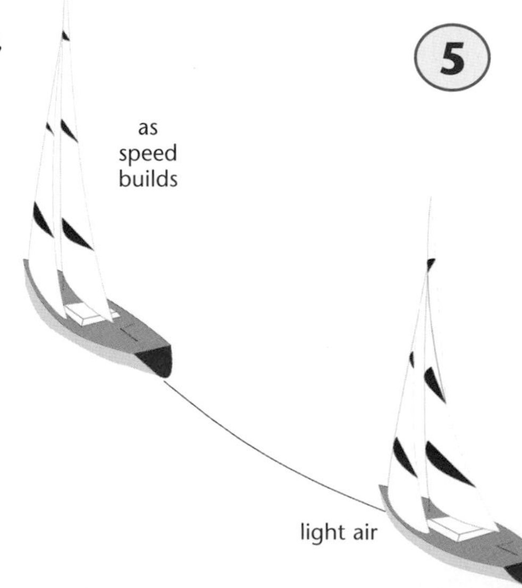

## Heavy-Air Trim

Once a boat is fully powered, performance improvements hinge on the ability to reduce drag. Deep, luffing, or overtrimmed sails are sources of drag in heavy air. Excessive weather helm creates enormous underwater drag, and excessive heel also causes drag. So in a strong wind we need to depower in this sequence:

### Reduce Sail Power

- Reduce power by flattening sails:
  Bend the mast
  Tighten the mainsail outhaul
  Reduce headstay sag
  Move the jib leads aft
- Reduce power by reducing the angle of attack:
  Feather the boat up (head up slightly)
  Lower the traveler
- Reduce power by adding twist:
  Ease sheets a few inches

### Reduce Sail Area

- Roller-furl the jib a few turns or change down to a smaller jib
- Reef the main
- Stow the jib and motorsail

In flat seas, flat sails or reduced sail area work well. In wavy conditions, the challenge is to keep enough power to punch through the waves without being overpowered.

Try to achieve proper power without compromising angle of attack. Focus on flat sails and additional twist before dumping the traveler (or moving the headsail leads outboard). An aft sheet lead position flattens the foot of the jib by pulling out on the clew. Think of it like the outhaul on the main. Moving the lead aft also increases twist, spilling power from the upper part of the sail. More twist widens the sailing groove and prevents being overpowered. In heavy air we want the top of the sail to luff before the lower section.

Steer to maintain a consistent heel angle. Head up slightly to feather through the puffs, and foot off a few degrees to maintain power in the lulls. This is much more critical than telltale activity. The jib telltales may stand up or even flutter on the inside.

A big backwind bubble in the main is preferable to the excessive heeling that further trimming would generate. When you must choose between a flogging main or excess heel and helm, it's time for less sail area. Try lots of twist, and perhaps an outboard jib lead, until you have a chance to change down your headsail or reef.

It is best to reduce headsail area before reefing the main. A small jib/big main setup gives quicker control over power, as we can dump the mainsail traveler in gusts. Further, a small jib is easier to handle, and a big jib/small main configuration creates pointing problems.

The one advantage of reefing is that it is often easier to accomplish than changing to a smaller headsail.

# Symptoms/Solutions

### The boat is slow.

Try deeper sails for more power. In light air or sloppy seas, add twist for easier flow and bear off a couple of degrees. In a moderate breeze over smooth water, try trimming the deep sails hard (to the point of nearly stalling the main).

In heavy air, reduce sail depth and power to reduce heel and restore helm balance.

### Poor pointing.

You may have too much twist. Trim the main to the verge of stalling the top leech telltale, and trim the jib until you get a hint of backwinding in the main.

When overpowered, it is common to lower the main traveler or ease the sheet, but it is better to keep the main trimmed and the main leech firm while feathering the boat or depowering the jib.

### The boat is slow and low.

Usually this is a sign of being overtrimmed or undercanvased. Ease the sheets to build speed. Add power all around. Change to a bigger genoa. Work on speed first, then pointing.

In a fresh breeze you may have too much sail shape and the jib leads may be too far forward, creating too much drag.

### Too much weather helm.

Reduce heel. Try flatter sails with more twist, and feather up in the puffs to reduce the angle of attack. If that doesn't work, try adding power to the jib and easing the main. Failing in that, shorten sail.

### Too little weather helm.

Add power—traveler up; backstay, outhaul, and halyards eased; jib leads forward. Bear off a couple of degrees. Move weight to leeward to increase heel.

In light air, you might be overtrimmed. Ease the main and jib sheets and bear off to add power and speed.

### Hypernarrow steering groove.

Tighten halyards to pull the draft forward and round the entry. Perhaps more effective, ease the genoa sheet a couple of inches. Sagging the headstay can also help.

### Overpowered one moment, upright and luffing the next.

The entire sail plan is filling and dumping at once. Adding twist will give a more gradual onset and release of power. Move the jib leads aft and ease the mainsheet while pulling the traveler to windward. This will also help an overworked autopilot.

### Excessive pitching.

You are sailing too high or your sails are too flat. Foot off for speed, add depth for power, and add twist to widen the sailing groove and control heel. Get weight out of the ends of your boat.

### Pounding in waves.

You need more power. Fall off slightly and add twist to keep from being overpowered.

# Sail Trim off the Wind

**Close Reaching.** As you bear away from close-hauled, ease the jib. Move the lead outboard and forward, chasing the clew of the sail. Otherwise the top of the sail will twist open, spilling power, and the bottom of the sail will hook in toward the boat, creating drag. In a fresh breeze, keep the halyard firm to hold the draft forward.

With the jib trimmed outboard and the vang tight, ease the mainsheet or lower the traveler. As the main goes out, the vang will prevent the boom from rising and the leech of the main from spilling. When overpowered on a reach, easing the vang will spill power, reduce heel, and balance the helm.

Trim to keep the leech telltales flowing. Ease the outhaul and backstay slightly to add power to the main.

**Beam to Broad Reaching.** As you bear off further, the boat stands upright. Ease sails. The top of the jib will spill open. Trim to keep the middle of the sail working.

The main should go way out—even against the rig if it doesn't luff first. Keep the vang firm enough to hold the top batten of the main parallel to the boom. If the jib jibes itself unexpectedly on a very broad reach, beware an uncontrolled jibe of the main. Turn immediately to windward, and straighten out once the jib returns to its normal position.

**Running.** Running dead before the wind under jib and main requires careful steering to avoid an accidental jibe. In light air, it often pays to reach up and sail with the jib in normal position, as the extra speed will make up for the extra distance.

When running wing and wing, especially in big following seas, a poled-out jib allows sailing above dead downwind, providing a wider steering lane and reducing the chances of an accidental jibe. Rig a whisker pole with topping lift, afterguy, and foreguy; trim it to position; then trim the genoa sheet through the end of the pole. Rig a preventer from the end of the mainboom to a block well forward on the rail, then back to the cockpit where it can be cast off easily. Anytime you ease the mainsheet, tighten the preventer just enough to prevent the boom from jumping around.

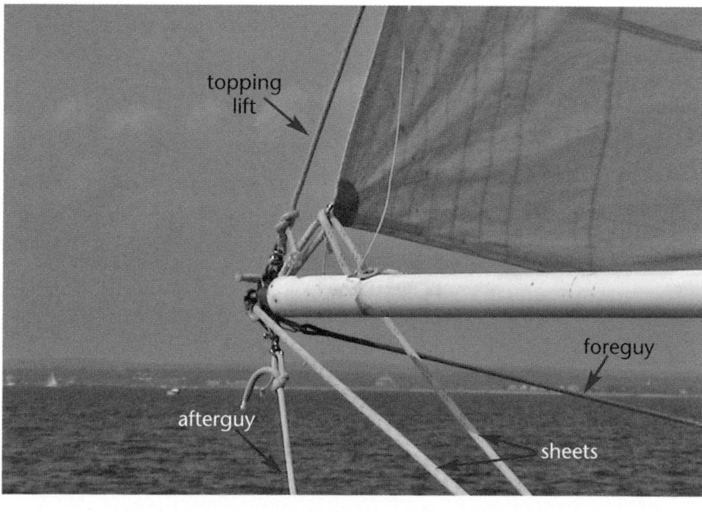

# Rig Tuning

An improperly tuned rig makes optimal trim and performance unattainable. Fortunately, rig tuning is straightforward. The goals are to:

- Eliminate mast side bend and lean.
- Set mast rake for proper helm balance.
- Tune pre-bend to match the mainsail design.
- Control mast bend and headstay sag.

## Masthead Rigs

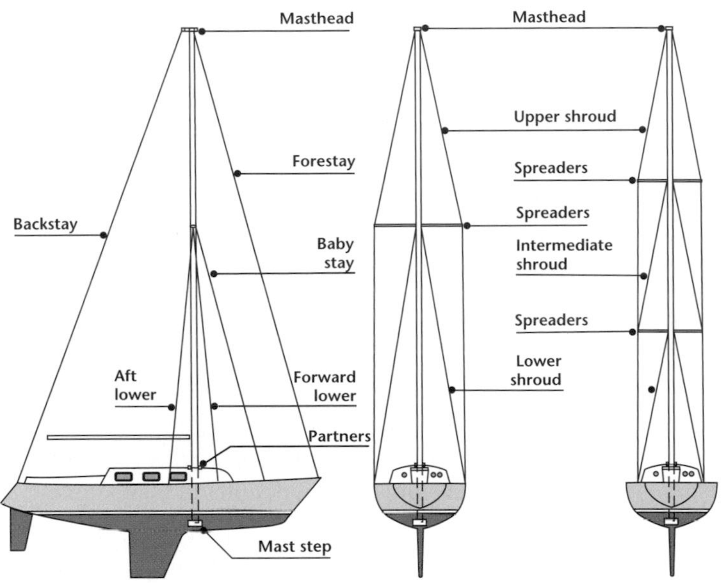


### Side Bend and Lean

1. Check that the mast step is centered and the mast butt is secured to it.

2. Center and block the mast at the partners. (Before stepping the mast, run a line from stem to midstern to check that the partners are centered in the deck.)

3. Tighten the upper shrouds evenly, counting turns and keeping the mast centered. Measure to chainplates and other points of symmetry with main halyard and shock cord to make sure the mast is centered. Do not overtighten. Back off if the mast goes out of column. Be careful not to strip the turnbuckle threads.

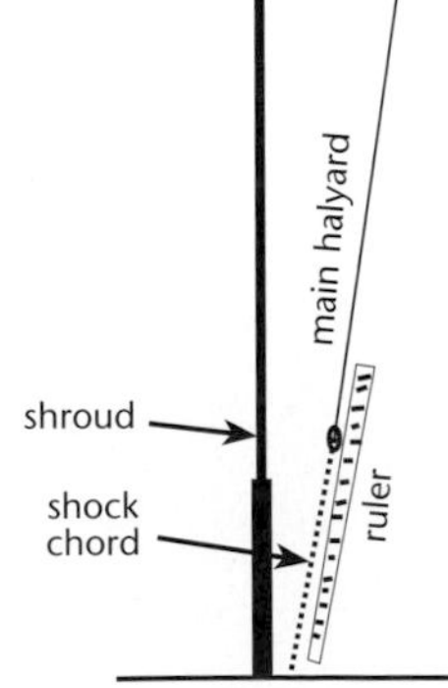


4. Proceed to the intermediates and lowers, tightening the shrouds evenly on each side and keeping the mast straight. This is the initial setting, with mast centered, straight side to side, and all shrouds firm.

5. Go sailing in a moderate breeze. Sail a series of tacks, counting turns to maintain symmetry as you tighten the leeward shrouds. Start with the uppers to eliminate lean; then tension the lowers to eliminate side bend.

6. Sight up the mast to check for side bend. If the middle bends to leeward, tighten the lowers. If the top appears to fall off to leeward, it may be the middle popping to windward. Either loosen the lowers or tighten the uppers. Overly tight lowers or loose uppers allow tip falloff and a narrow angle of intersection between the uppers and the mast. This can overload the shroud fittings and cause rig failure.

7. Proper tension will leave the leeward upper shrouds taut at 15 degrees of heel with a full crew on the rail. The uppers should be tighter than the lowers to allow for greater stretch over a longer distance.

8. Check the rig periodically, particularly after sailing in heavy air. Stretched uppers or overtensioned lowers can overload the upper spreaders.

9. From this base setting you may find it pays to fine-tune your rig to sailing conditions. Generally this would mean adding tension to the uppers in heavy air, and backing off a couple of turns in light air. Sometimes fine-tuning is best done with headstay adjustment.

## Rake

Rake is the fore-and-aft lean of the mast. Raking the mast aft creates weather helm. Changing the rake may simply require easing the forestay and tightening the backstay, or it may require moving the mast step.

You want a setting that provides some weather helm upwind in light air without becoming unbearable in a blow. Most boats are designed for some rake, but the amount depends on sail design, predominant conditions, and even crew size. Experiment with several settings in a variety of conditions. You want 3–4 degrees of weather-helm rudder angle in moderate conditions. You may find it pays to change rake to match conditions, adding headstay tension on heavy-air days.

## Pre-Bend

*Pre-bend* is tuned into your rig by a combination of compression (rig tension) and mast blocks at the deck partners. Your mast will need some pre-bend—from an inch to a few inches—depending on the luff curve of your main. If your main tends to be too deep, add more pre-bend. If you cannot get enough power from your main, straighten the mast by putting blocks in front of the mast at the partners. As your main ages you may find you need more pre-bend to remove depth from the stretched sail, but this will exacerbate the other problem of age—the draft creeping aft. Stiff, tapered, full-length battens can alleviate that problem.

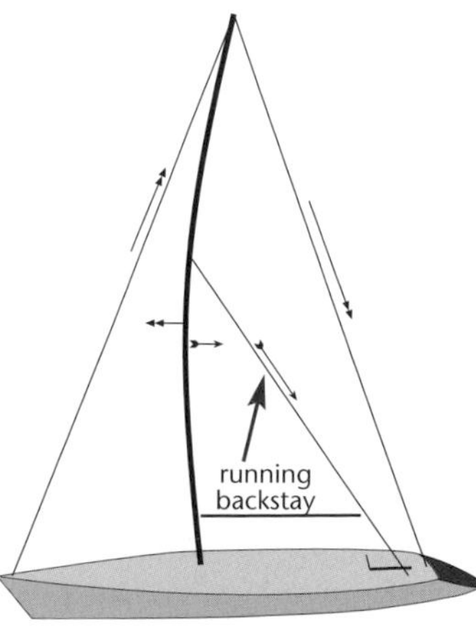


## Mast Bend and Headstay Sag

Working with the backstay and a combination of running backstay, baby stay, and/or vang, it is possible to control mast bend and headstay sag separately.

Backstay tension will bend the mast through compression as well as tighten the headstay. The mix depends on running backstay tension. If the runners are tight, they restrict mast bend, and the backstay impacts headstay sag. Looser runners allow more mast bend.

With a stiff mast, backstay tension translates primarily into headstay tension, controlling sag. A baby stay is then used to add bend. The backstay contributes to bend as well, particularly once bend has been initiated by the baby stay.

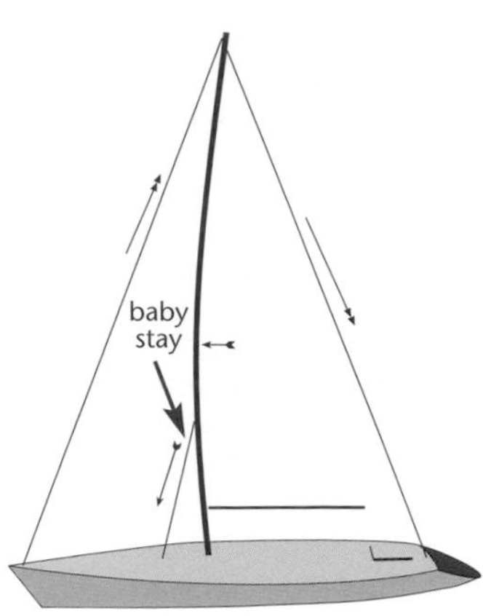


## Fractional Rigs

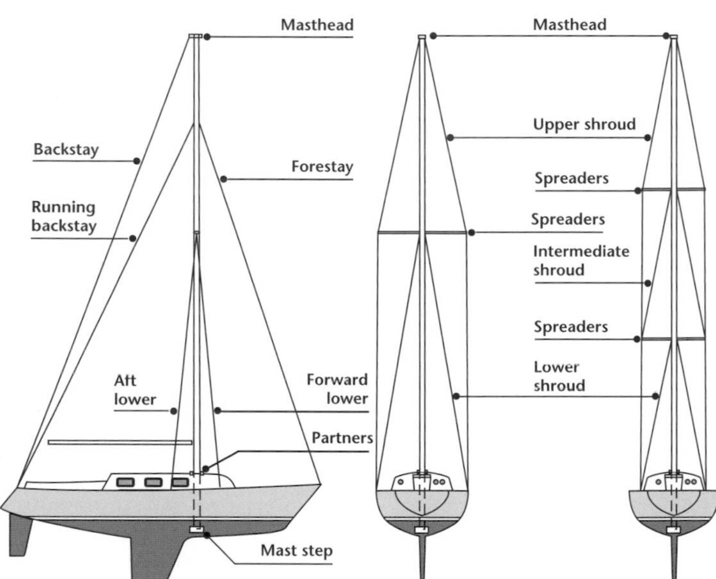


The varied configurations of fractional rigs (swept spreaders versus straight with runners, B&R rigs, etc.) make it difficult to generalize. The procedure described here is for swept spreaders. The straight-spreader procedure is a hybrid of this and the masthead procedure described above.

With swept-back spreaders, adjusting the shrouds affects lean, side bend, rake, sag, and mast bend.

1. Spreader sweep should be fixed. Use pins and/or epoxy to secure swinging spreaders.

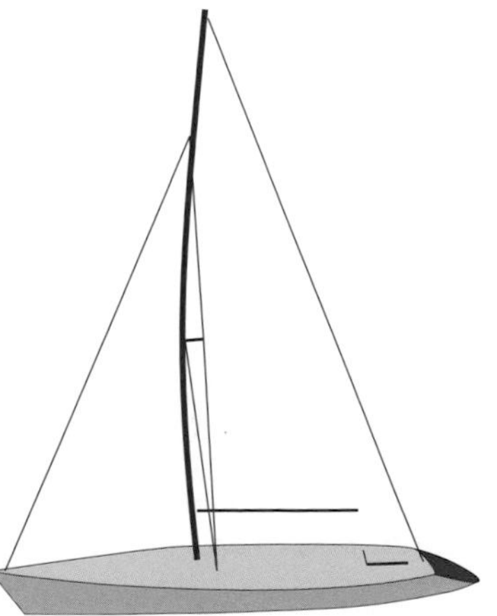

2. Center mast at step and partners.

3. With lowers loose, pull the backstay to max. Tighten the upper shrouds, keeping the rig centered and the mast straight side to side. If the mast tends to bend sideways, you may have to ease backstay slightly.

4. Release the backstay. The mast will still have bend. Tighten the lowers to remove bend as necessary to fit the main.

5. The rig is now tuned for headstay tension. Adding backstay tension will bend the mast and add more headstay tension.

6. To get bend more easily, ease the lowers. To translate backstay to headstay tension, tighten the lowers. There is a limit to the headstay tension you can achieve without running backstays. If your mast bends too much, try less spreader sweep. To encourage bend, add more sweep and ease the lowers.

7. Upwind in a breeze, the top of the mast will fall off to leeward and the middle will bow out to weather. This side bend depowers the rig to a greater degree than fore-and-aft bend. Easing the lowers may reduce side bend but will allow more headstay sag and fore-and-aft mast bend. The other solution is longer spreaders, which will push in harder on the middle of the mast. This can reduce but will not eliminate side bend, and may interfere with genoa trim.

8. Changing rake requires a complete retuning of the shrouds. Rake should be set for a balanced helm.

9. Shrouds may be adjusted to achieve proper mast bend and headstay sag for varied conditions. Upper and lower shrouds should be eased in light air for less bend and less headstay tension, and tightened a couple of turns for best performance in a big breeze. Keep track of base, light-air, and heavy-air settings.

10. Running backstays are required if sag is to be properly and independently controlled with a fractional rig.

Small changes in rig tune can have a surprising impact on your boat's performance. Carefully mark and note your current settings. That way, you can revert if you are unhappy with the changes you make.

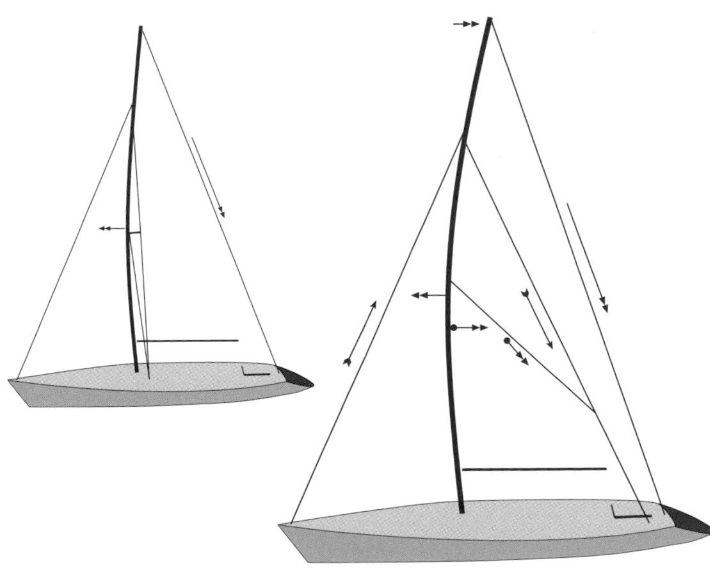

CHAPTER 3

# Using Nautical Charts

Bob Sweet

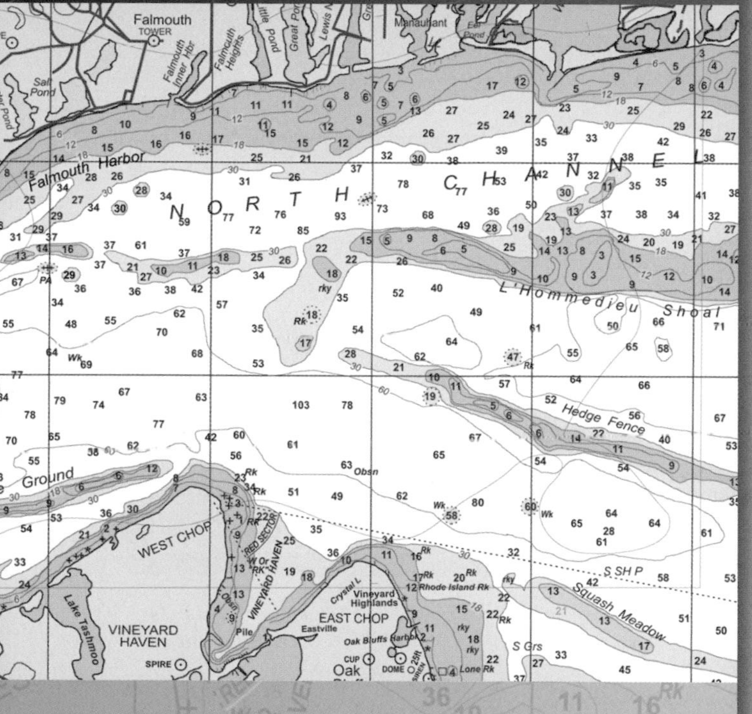

While GPS (Chapter 4) represents a quantum leap in navigation, it alone cannot provide safe navigation. Formal or informal, electronic or traditional, piloting always starts with a nautical chart. We offer this primer on chart reading and navigation for those who are new to the topic or seeking a refresher.

# Nautical Charts

Unlike highway maps—on which roads are already plotted—nautical charts require you to plot your own routes, or courses. Chart information typically comes from hydrographic organizations within each country of jurisdiction. In the United States, the National Oceanographic and Atmospheric Administration (NOAA) is the source. (Actually, charts are prepared by the National Ocean Service [NOS], which is part of NOAA.) In Canada, the Canadian Hydrographic Service provides charting information. In the United Kingdom, it's the British Admiralty. International standards are developed by the International Hydrographic Organization. Usually, commercial chart publishers will scan or copy charting information from these sources and perhaps annotate additional information to them. Updating charts is a constant task. Storms change features both above and below the water. Navigation aids are moved or replaced, depths change, and so on. The process of updating charts is expensive, so the responsible organizations only do it periodically. It's not uncommon to come across a chart that has not been updated for some time.

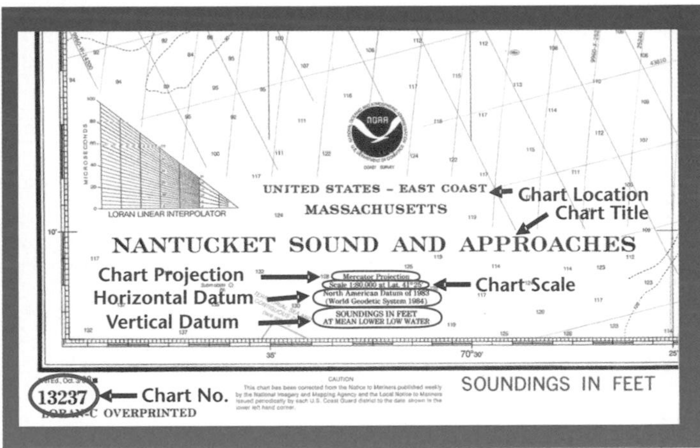


The title block provides important information like the vertical and horizontal datums used to make the chart. If your GPS is not set to the same datum, you will not be able to plot your position accurately.

GPS makes very accurate positional information available, and today it's common that your GPS is more accurate than the chart you are using. This poses a dilemma—which to believe? Prudent navigators treat charts as essential but not absolute. You must use your eyes and observations to refine what they tell you. Nonetheless, they are your primary source of information.

Over the centuries, cartographers have developed several ways of portraying a nearly spherical Earth on a flat chart. For the most part, nautical charts are prepared using one of two projections—*Mercator* and *polyconic*. Mercator projections maintain directional relationships better over long distances, making them the projection of choice for coastal and offshore navigation. Polyconic projections maintain proportions better and tend to be used for inland waterway and lake charts.

Virtually all coastal and offshore navigation charts are Mercator projections. Imagine a sheet of paper wrapped around a globe to make a cylinder that is in direct contact with the globe only at its equator. Now imagine that globe being lit from within so that its landmasses and other features are projected upon the paper cylinder. The result would be a Mercator chart of the world. In a Mercator projection, all parallels of latitude are horizontal and straight, and all meridians of longitude are vertical and straight. The parallels intersect the meridians at right angles. The result—and this is the great advantage of a Mercator projection—is that the navigator can measure and plot directions and distances directly on the chart and use them for navigation.

In the real world, of course, meridians aren't parallel. Thus, Mercator projections distort the shapes and relative sizes of landmasses and ocean basins. This distortion becomes exaggerated near the poles. Remember how huge Greenland and northern Canada looked in the Mercator maps in your school textbooks? However, this distortion is so small it's unnoticeable in Mercator charts covering local regions in low and middle latitudes.

The accompaning figure shows how a Mercator chart is made by projecting the surface of a globe onto a cylinder. Near the equator, the globe and the chart match closely, but the chart stretches as you approach the poles, and landmasses appear larger than they actually are.

The polyconic projection is used for charts of the Great Lakes and some major rivers. An example of this projection can be seen in the paper masters that are wrapped and glued on a sphere to form a globe. When flattened, the result is complex. Using a polyconic chart to travel over great distances would be

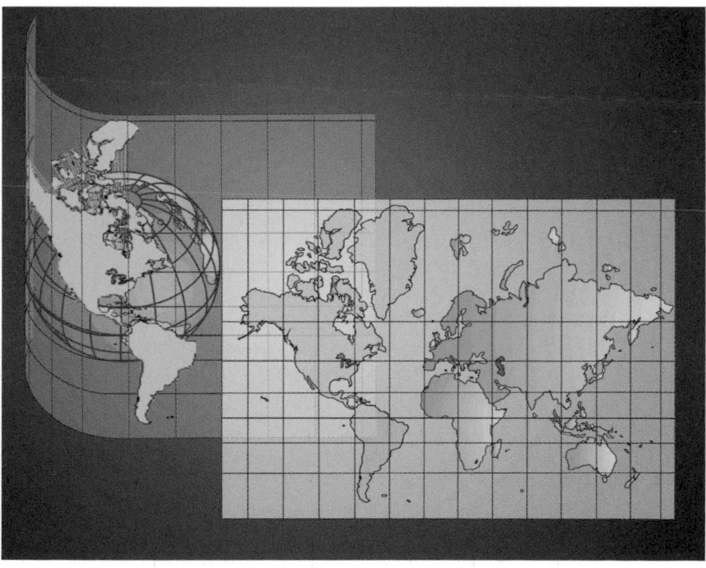

Coastal and offshore charts use a Mercator projection. Imagine a light at the center of the Earth projecting the Earth's surface features onto a cylinder that wraps around the equator. The resultant flat projection provides straight and perpendicular grid lines, making plotting easy. Feature shapes and relative positions are accurate, but there is an artificial enlargement of features toward the poles as compared with regions closer to the equator.

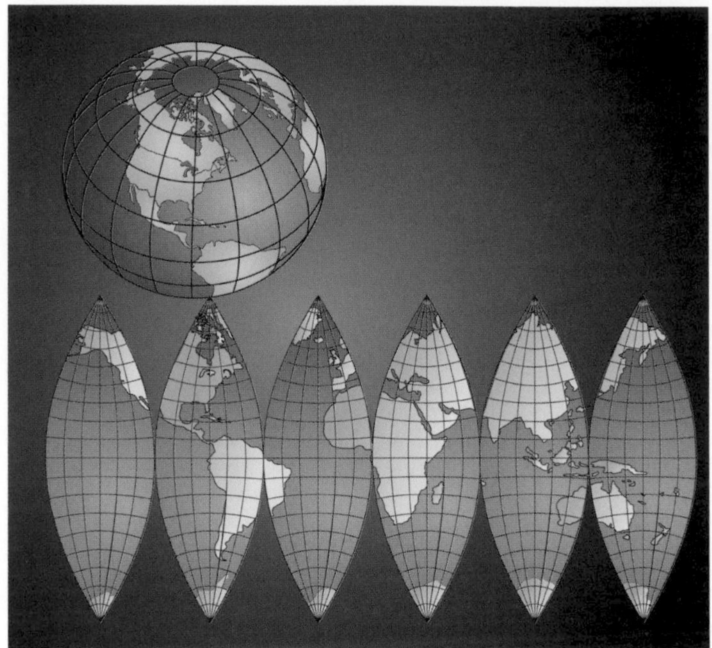

Rendering the Earth into a meaningful flat chart is a major challenge. If you simply unfold and flatten the Earth's surface, you will get something like this figure, which is similar to a polyconic projection. Notice that the grid lines are curved. This makes plotting difficult.

difficult. However, charts for local regions are made by peeling the globe so that the straight-line center meridian is directly on top of your local region of interest. Now, in this area, if you're traveling locally, the parallels appear straight and perpendicular, and it's possible to plot a course as you would on a Mercator chart.

Because charts for many interior rivers and lakes of the United States are scarce, some boaters use U.S. Geological Survey (USGS) topographic maps on these waters. In addition, local maps and guides may be available for popular boating areas. Unfortunately, these maps often do not show underwater features, and you may need to build your own chart using local and personal knowledge.

Nautical charts, unlike topographic and other maps, are rich in details about objects below the surface of the water. This is essential information for the navigator, so you need to understand the symbols the chart uses. The top illustration opposite shows a typical map including a body of water. Obviously, this kind of map wouldn't be of much help to a boater. But the addition of depth contours (similar to the elevation contours you find for land features on a topographic map—see middle illustration opposite) gives you some sense of the features under the water's surface.

On a road map, it's easy to see where you are. The map depicts clearly marked roads labeled with street signs. On nautical charts there are no roads. Nautical charts, therefore, need a scale and grid to provide a frame of reference that many maps do not have. A typical scale and grid are shown in the bottom illustration opposite.

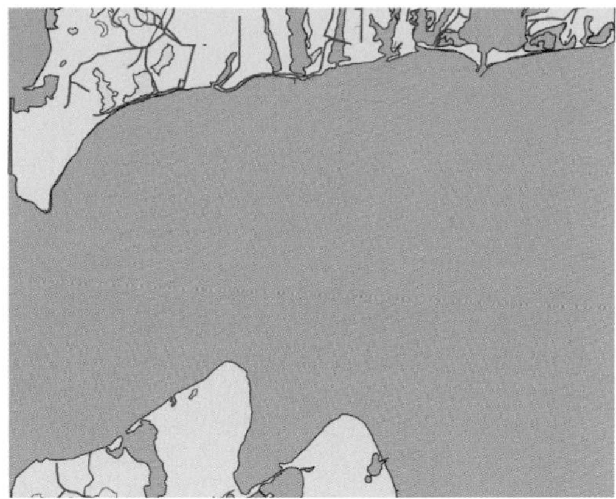

A map shows land features but tells little about the water other than the shorelines.

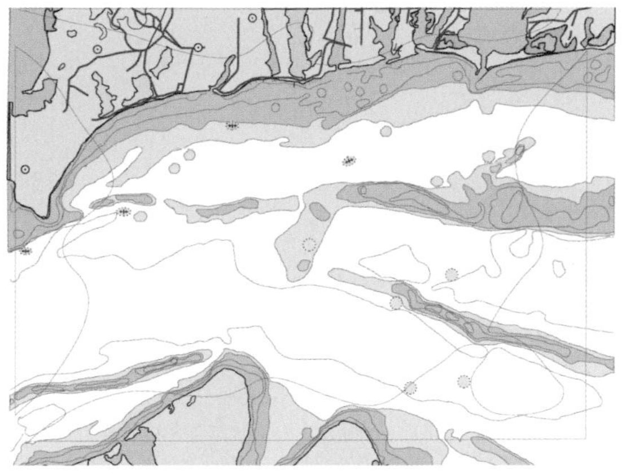

When underwater features such as depth contours are added, the map becomes a chart.

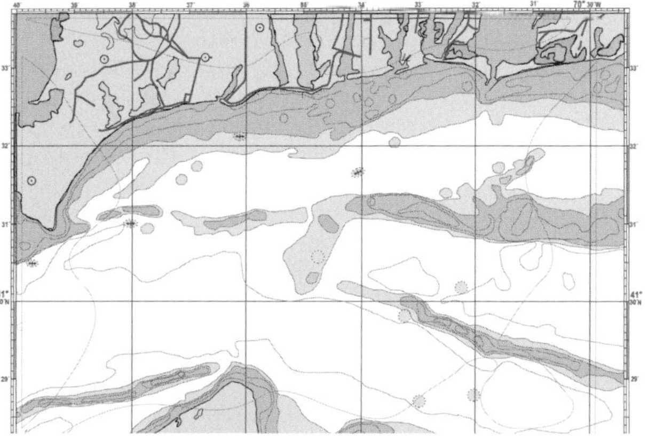

Maps of highways define paths and any marked features along the way. But there are no such features on the water. Therefore, a chart needs to provide a frame of reference. This is indicated by the grid. The grid comprises latitude and longitude lines, and a pair of latitude and longitude coordinates provide your location in numerical form.

## Depths

Nobody wants to run aground. Fortunately, nautical charts plot depth measurements, known as *soundings*, that help you avoid this unpleasant experience. The illustration shows how soundings appear on a chart. This might be the single most useful category of information a nautical chart offers.

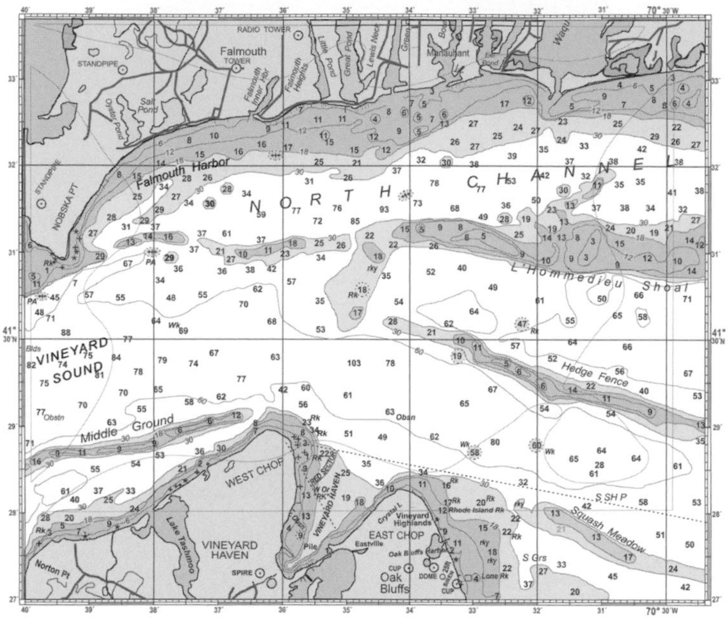


No nautical chart is complete without soundings. These specific measurements of depth are plotted on the chart to reflect the average least depth at each location. Today, most charts reference these soundings to a tidal datum called *mean lower low water.*

Because water levels fluctuate, particularly in tidal regions, soundings must be referenced to a vertical *datum*, or standard, that is identified on the chart. Depths on older charts were referenced to *mean low water* (MLW), which is the average local height of all low tides as recorded over a 19-year natural cycle. As a mariner, you could be reasonably sure that the depth you would encounter at a given time and location would be as deep or deeper than its charted sounding. Reasonably sure but not absolutely so. Why? Because in most regions low tides occur twice a day, and one tide is often lower than the other. When boating in such a region, the depths you encounter at the lower of the two daily low tides will be shallower than the average of *all* low tides. To minimize this potential hazard, most new charts use the more conservative vertical datum of *mean lower low water* (MLLW), which is the long-term average of the lower of the two daily low tides. With such a chart, you can traverse an area and count on having at least the sounding depth at almost any time except during the lower low tide when half the time the water level can be less than the sounding.

On U.S. charts, depths are generally expressed in feet. In Canada and much of the rest of the world, they are expressed in meters. Occasionally, you will see charts in which depths are expressed in *fathoms* (a fathom equals 6 feet). The units for depth are shown on the chart, usually in the title block.

To make charts easier to read, depth contour lines are drawn through points of selected constant depth. For historical reasons, in the United States these contours are generally plotted at some multiple of a fathom (6 feet), so you often see depth contours at 6, 12, 18, 30, and 60 feet. Elsewhere the contours are generally plotted in multiples of 6 meters, although other increments may be used. You need to look at the printed depths along the contours. You can tell a contour depth from a sounding because it is oriented with the contour, interrupts the contour line, and is printed in the opposite style of the soundings (italic vs. regular type). Cartographers also use color to help identify information. Shallow water is generally shaded blue; deep water is white. (The definition of what is shallow differs from chart to chart, so take a look at the chart's scale before making any assumptions.) Very shallow water that uncovers at low tide is usually shown in green; land is colored in tan. The type of bottom is often expressed by a combination of abbreviations and symbols, a few of which we'll touch on below.

## Scales

Charts come in a variety of scales, with the scale indicated as a ratio. For example, on a 1:40,000-scale chart, 1 inch or centimeter on the chart equals 40,000 inches (approximately half a nautical mile) or centimeters (400 meters) in the real world. A 1:20,000 chart is typical for local waters; a 1:10,000 chart may depict a specific harbor; and a 1:80,000 chart depicts a wider boating region. A 1:10,000 chart is considered "large scale"—ideal for navigation in narrow, rock-strewn waters. A 1:120,000 chart is considered "small scale"—excellent for "big picture" cruise planning but insufficiently detailed for picking your way among ledges, buoys, and islands. Large-scale charts show more detail but cover a smaller area. Think of it as "large scale = large detail." The accuracy of charted locations depends on scale. When the scale is larger, charted objects are placed more precisely.

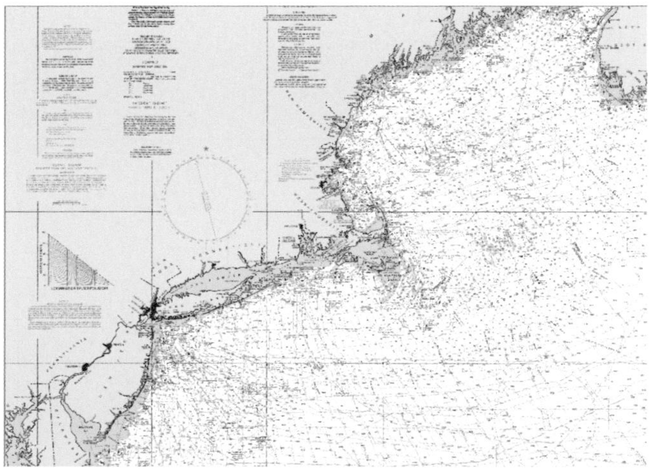

A chart's scale is a ratio of the distance between objects on the chart to the distances in the real world. This small-scale chart shows a large area, stretching from the mouth of Delaware Bay to the Gulf of Maine. This is a 1:1,200,000-scale chart; useful for passage planning.

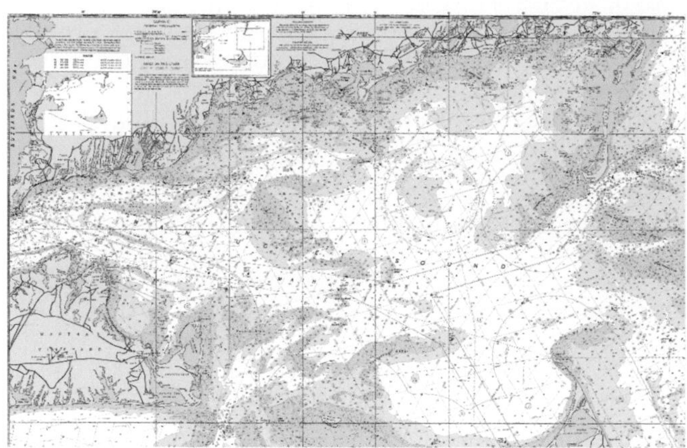

This coastal chart at 1:80,000 scale is good for coastal passages, but you'll need a larger scale to navigate narrow, complicated inshore waters.

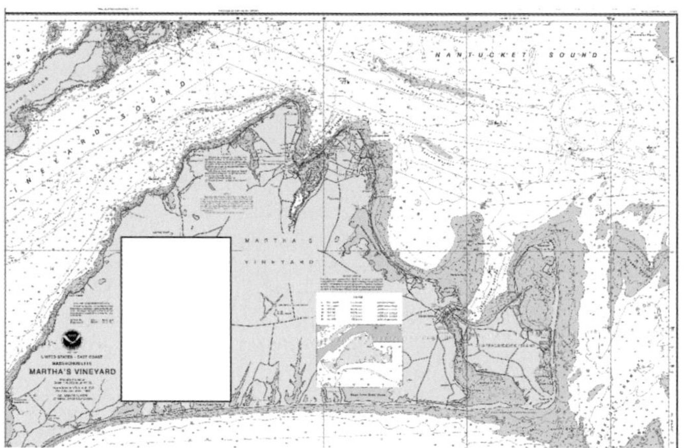


1:40,000-scale chart picks up inshore details you won't find on the 1:80,000-scale chart.

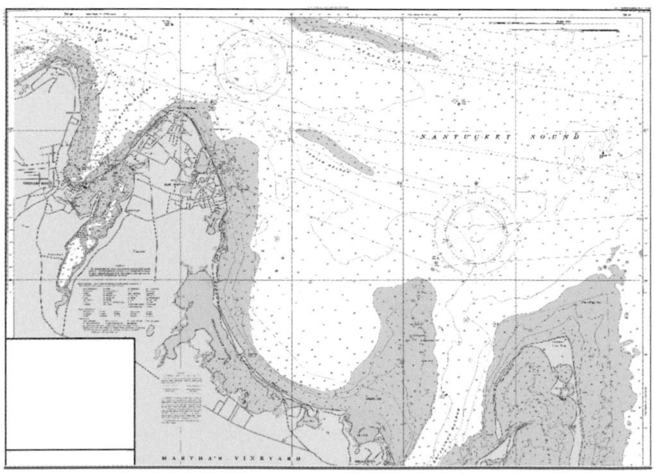


A more detailed harbor chart has a 1:20,000 scale.

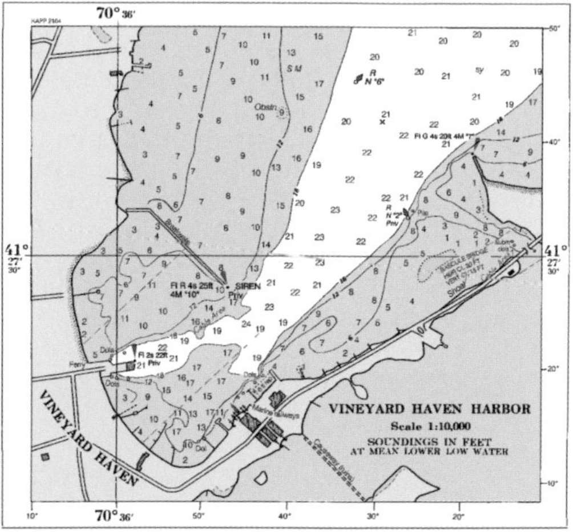


Some popular harbors have very detailed charts of 1:10,000 or even 1:5,000 scale. This is an example of a 1:10,000 chart.

## Updates

Although the information on charts is updated regularly, the charts themselves are updated only at intervals. Hydrographic organizations worldwide provide regular updates to charts known as *Notices to Mariners* (NTM). And the U.S. Coast Guard provides updated information in its weekly *Local Notices to Mariners* (LNM), a report that you can access on the Internet. To stay current, review these notices, locate a specific chart by its number (which is printed in the margin of a paper chart or the title block of a paper or digital one), and add the corrections to your copy. Today, commercial services can do this work, and you can purchase copies printed on demand that are updated to the date of printing. Revision dates are listed in the title block of the chart.

## Chart Grid and Horizontal Datum

To pinpoint our location on the surface of the Earth, we need a system of coordinates. Most nautical charts use *latitude* and *longitude* for this. Latitude and longitude have already been discussed and are explained further below, but it's important to note that there are other grid systems in use throughout the world. It's imperative that your GPS be set to the same grid system that is employed on your chart.

The Earth's shape is not uniform. Although globes depict a smooth, spherical Earth, our planet is oblong and uneven, and we need a mapping grid that takes this variability into account. This framework is called a *horizontal datum*. Today, most nautical charts reference World Geodetic System 1984 (WGS-84) as the horizontal datum. You need to set your GPS to the datum that was used to create your chart. For example, a few old charts in the United States may not have been updated from the older North American Datum 1927 (NAD-27). If you use the wrong datum in your GPS, you could inadvertently create mismatches of hundreds of yards or more, mistakes much like those that bedeviled the old cartographers.

## Coordinates

An object on a chart can be located using its nautical position address—its latitude and longitude. The chart provides a latitude scale, usually printed in the left and right margins. The longitude scale is usually printed in the top and bottom margins. Latitude is measured from 0° at the equator to 90° N at the North Pole or 90° S at the South Pole. Lines of equal latitude are called *parallels*. Parallels are horizontal slices through the Earth that are parallel to the equator. The parallel lines form the horizontal grid lines on your chart.

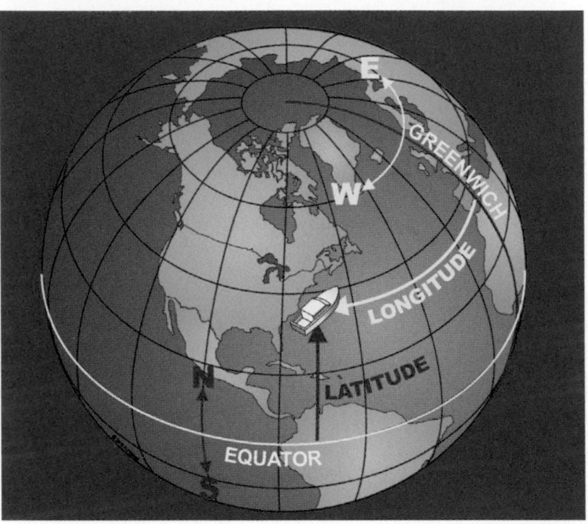


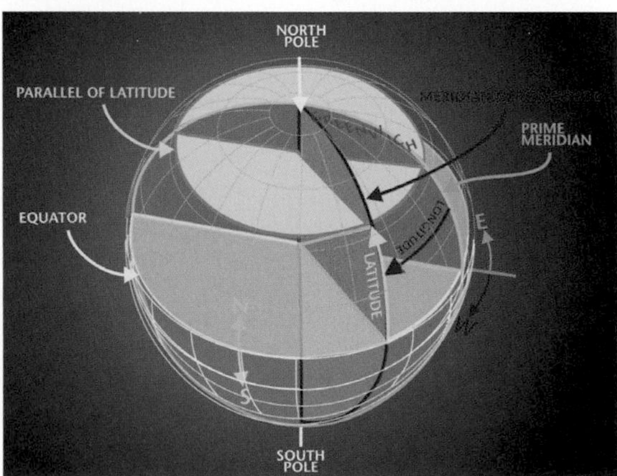


**Top:** *Latitude* and *longitude* provide a unique address for every location on the Earth. This grid system is based on a mathematical model for the shape of the Earth. Latitude is measured, either north or south, from 0° at the equator to 90° N or 90° S at the respective poles. Longitude is measured, either west or east, from 0° at the meridian (line between the poles) that goes through Greenwich, England, to 180° W or 180° E. **Bottom:** Lines of equal latitude are called parallels. The horizontal grid lines around the globe, which indicate equal latitudes, form horizontal circular planes that are parallel to the equator. Lines of equal longitude are vertical planes *(meridians)* that intersect an imaginary line through the Earth between the poles.

Lines of longitude, or *meridians*, are vertical slices that pass through both poles. Typically, meridian lines are printed at regular intervals on your chart and form the vertical axis of the chart grid. Meridians are numbered from 0° at the prime meridian (which, for historical reasons, passes through Greenwich, England), increasing by degrees both west and east until, on the opposite side of the world, they meet one another again at 180°. All meridians are *great circles*, a great circle being an imaginary line scribed on the Earth's surface by a plane passing through the exact center of the Earth. Except for the equator, however, no line of latitude is a great circle. Any two points on the Earth's surface can be joined by one and only one segment of a great circle, which always defines the shortest distance between those points. Unfortunately, great circles may not make practical courses to follow over great distances because your steering direction will constantly change, and your path will appear curved on a Mercator projection. But no matter. The *rhumb lines*—or courses on a single bearing—we follow in coastal navigation are only slightly longer than their great-circle equivalents. For local navigation, the differences aren't noticeable.

Each spot on the Earth is uniquely identified by its latitude and longitude. Scales on coastal nautical charts are generally divided into *degrees, minutes,* and *tenths of minutes* (a minute of angle being 1/60th of a degree). Great Lakes and river nautical charts often have scales divided into degrees, minutes, and *seconds.* (A second of angle is 1/60th of a minute.) One minute of latitude is always exactly equal to 1 nautical mile. This means that you can use the latitude scale for measuring distance on the chart. A minute of longitude, however, is equal to 1 nautical mile only at the equator, diminishing to nothing at the poles. Thus, the longitude scale cannot be used to measure distance.

## Chart Symbology

Charts use an array of symbols (see top illustration page 44) to depict rocks and other obstacles, depending on whether the obstacle is always visible, or is covered only at higher tides, or lies below the surface at all tides. If you run aground on soft bottom, often you need only wait for a higher tide to get off. If you encounter rocks or wrecks, however, you risk damaging your boat and possibly sinking—or at least ruining your afternoon! NOAA charts use a symbol that resembles an asterisk (*) to indicate rocks of unknown heights that are *awash* (breaking the surface at low tide). Underwater rocks often are indicated by a plus sign (+). Broader areas of potential danger are often shaded blue and bounded by a dotted line. For example, rocky regions bounded by a dotted line may be labeled with the term "Rk" or "Rks." Other dangerous zones may be labeled simply "Obstn," for obstruction. A sounding inside the blue area usually indicates the shallowest depth. If no sounding is shown, the depth generally is unknown. Regardless, you should avoid the shaded area altogether.

Wrecks, too, are shown by symbols. If any part of the wreck's superstructure is visible at low tide, it's usually indicated by a profile of a half-sunken boat. If only parts of the boat—such as masts or funnels—are visible, the wreck area is circled by a dotted line, the area within is shaded blue, and a solid line with three intersecting hatch marks is inserted into the middle of it all. (This symbol resembles a three-masted boat, with the long line representing the hull.) Usually, the chart also indicates which part of the wreck is visible at low tide—"Masts," for example.

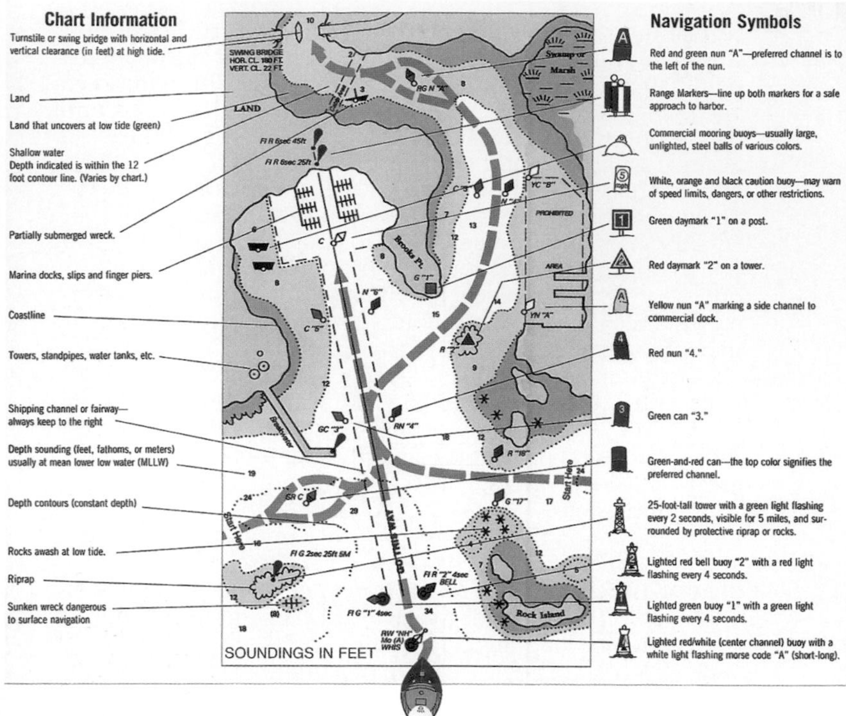


Charts use a symbol language to communicate features.

Restricted areas are generally bounded by a dotted line consisting of T-shaped symbols, often in magenta. Alternatively, dashed lines, either in magenta or black, may surround these and other defined areas. Given the heightened security surrounding bridges, naval ships, and other ships and facilities since 2001, you should consult the *Local Notices to Mariners* for updates and append your charts accordingly.

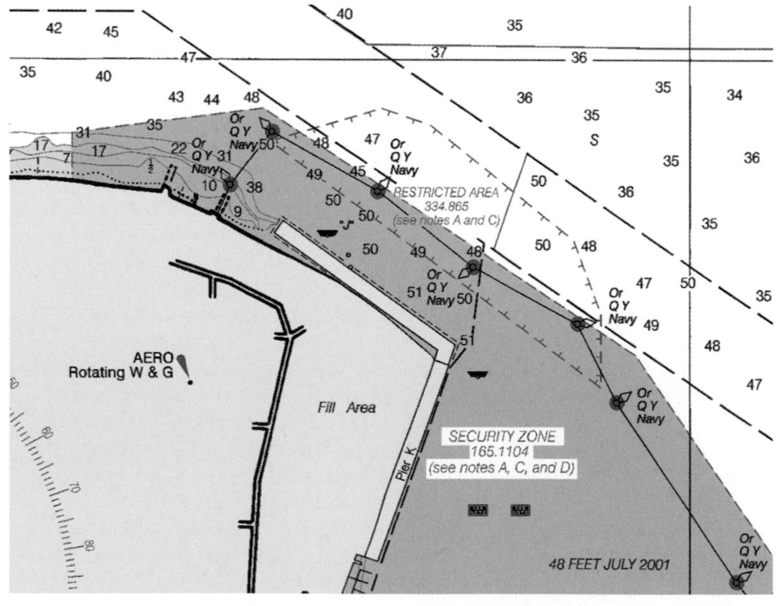


Charts also use symbols to define specific areas or restrictions.

## Navigation Aids

Buoys and beacons help define channels as well as mark a variety of underwater conditions or hazards. Navigation aids are either *lateral* or *informational* in North America. (Elsewhere a *cardinal* system for marking isolated offshore dangers is used in addition to the other systems.) Lateral marks indicate the sides of the channel. The United States and Canada use the "red-right-returning" rule of lateral marking: Keep the red buoys on your right when returning to a harbor, navigating up a river, or traversing the North American coast in a clockwise direction, and keep green buoys to your left. (Elsewhere in the world, the opposite applies.) In serpentine or complex waters, when it isn't absolutely clear which way is toward the nearest harbor or clockwise around the continent, consult your chart. Buoys with red-and-white vertical stripes indicate safe water or a center channel. Informational aids may mark danger or note local rules, such as no-wake zones. Some navigation aids are equipped with lights or audible devices. Charts generally show all significant navigation aids. Though a smaller-scale chart may not show all secondary buoys in inshore waters, it will be apparent from a lack of soundings and other details that larger-scale charts of these waters are needed for safe navigation. However, even a large-scale harbor chart may not show locally maintained, nongovernment navigation aids within a harbor or an approach channel. You'll need local knowledge for these. Government navigation aids are depicted with abbreviations or

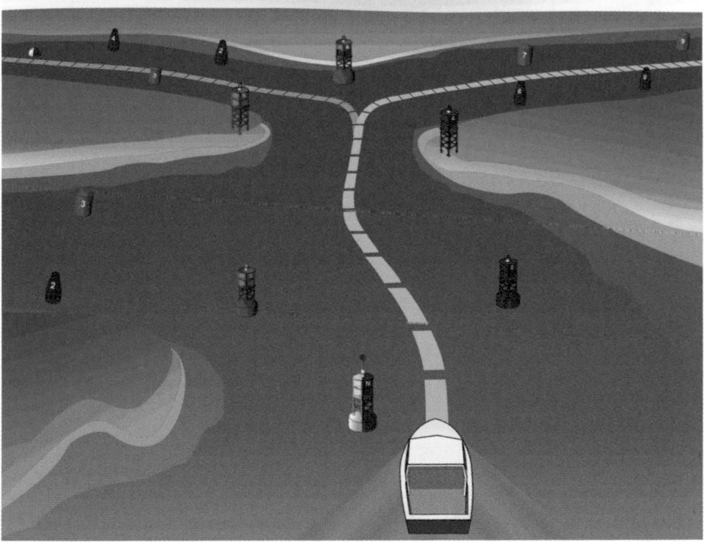

The United States uses the "red-right-returning" system. In other words, when you return from the sea, red navigation aids indicate the right-hand side of a navigable waterway; green navigation aids indicate the left side. Navigation aids with vertical red-and-white stripes indicate the center channel and can be passed on either side. Black-and-red aids indicate isolated hazards or danger. If you come to the junction of two channels, the preferred channel is indicated by the top color on a navigation aid. To use the preferred channel, imagine that the junction buoy is the color of the top band. In this figure it is green, indicating that you should keep it to your left. Therefore, the preferred channel is to your right. Buoys are floating navigation aids. Beacons are fixed to the bottom or the shore.

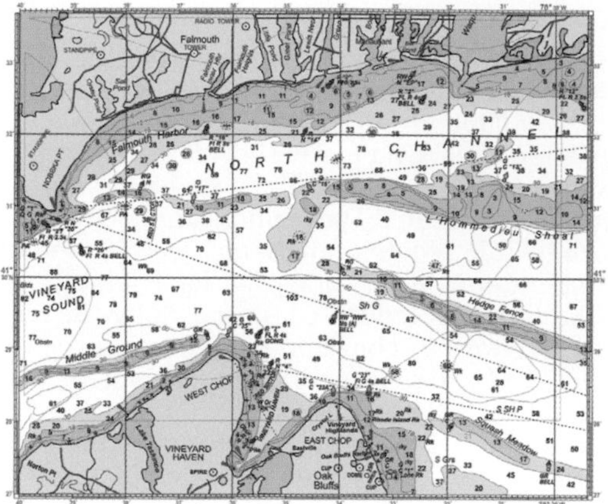


The chart section shown on page 38 is shown here with the symbols for navigation aids added.

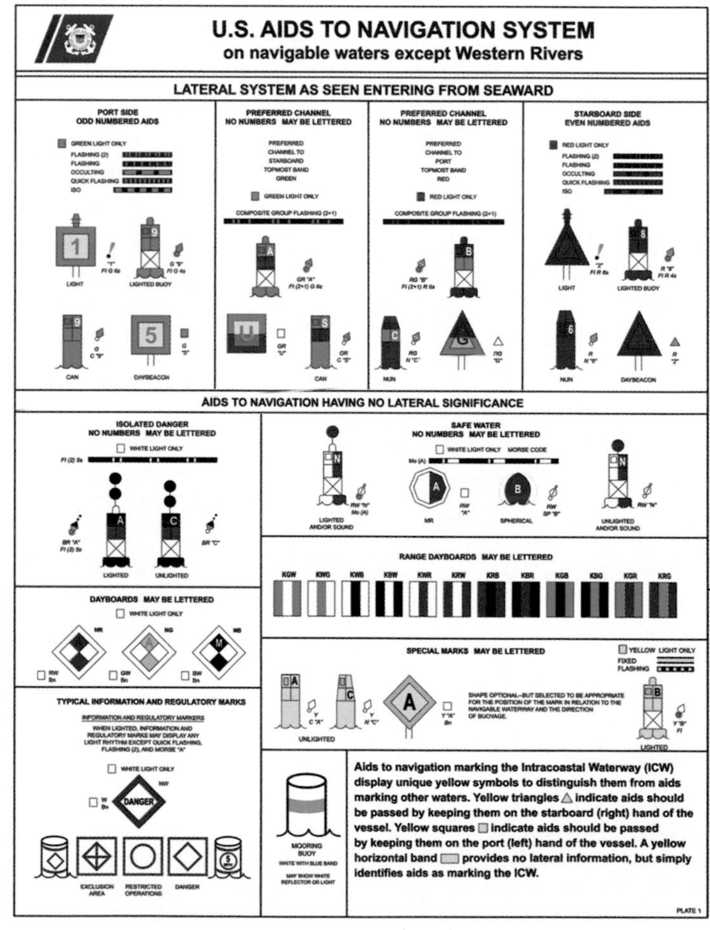


The U.S. Coast Guard standard symbols for navigation aids are shown on this and the next three pages. **Above:** The U.S. Aids to Navigation System follows the IALA (International Association of Lighthouse Authorities) -B system, which is also used in Canada, Mexico, South America, Japan, Korea, the Philippines, and the Caribbean. In the IALA-A system used elsewhere in the world, the colors of lateral buoys are reversed—i.e., green buoys mark the right side of the channel, red the left.

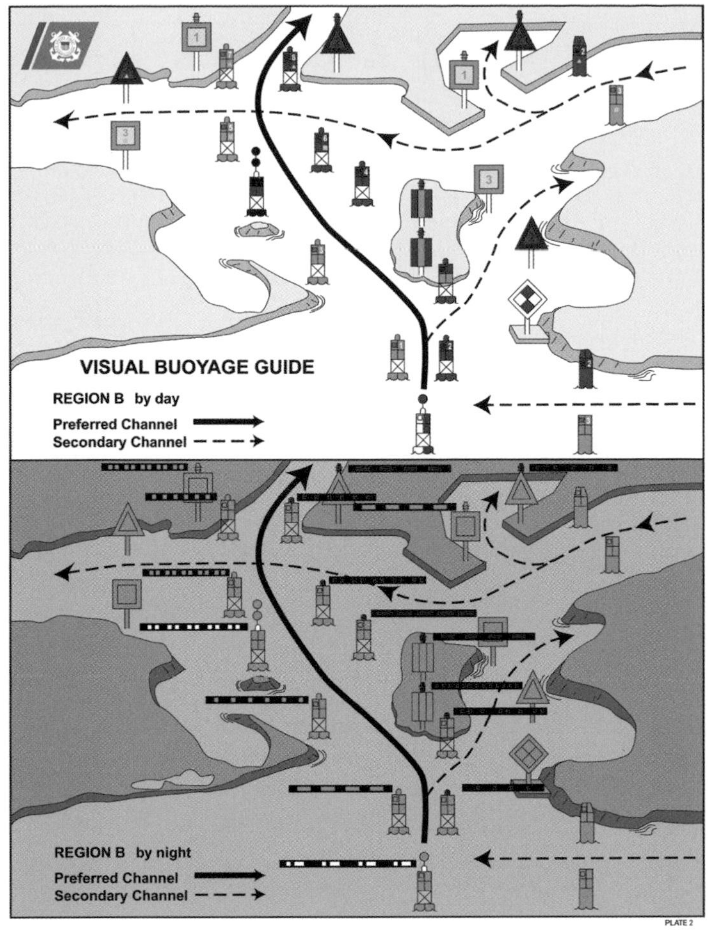


The lateral-system nav aids from the previous illustration are shown here in idealized fashion as they might appear by day and by night.

symbols that describe their appearance or characteristics. (Please note that charted buoy locations are approximate. Whereas beacons are fixed to the Earth, anchored buoys shift nominally with the tides and can be moved greater distances by powerful storm waves.)

Unlighted fixed nav aids, called *daybeacons*, are usually indicated by a green square or a red triangle. These objects may be on land or in shallow water on poles fixed to the bottom. (Most cartographers further distinguish between fixed and floating nav aids by using italics for the latter.)

*Lighted beacons* are indicated by symbols that resemble exclamation marks. The solid black dot of the exclamation mark charts the beacon's fixed location; the accompanying magenta teardrop flare helps distinguish the beacon from buoys or other navigation aids. The characteristics of the beacon are printed next to the symbol, indicating the light pattern, color, height, and usually the visible range. The light pattern is often flashing ("Fl"). The repetition interval of the flashes is identified by the number of seconds, such as "4s." If the light has a color, it is indicated by "R" for red, "G" for green, "Y" for yellow, and "W" for white, although most white lights are not labeled. Thus, "Fl R 4s" denotes a red light flashing at 4-second intervals.

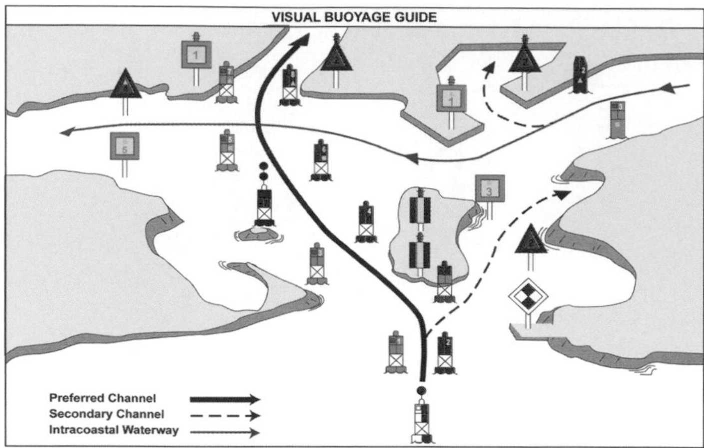


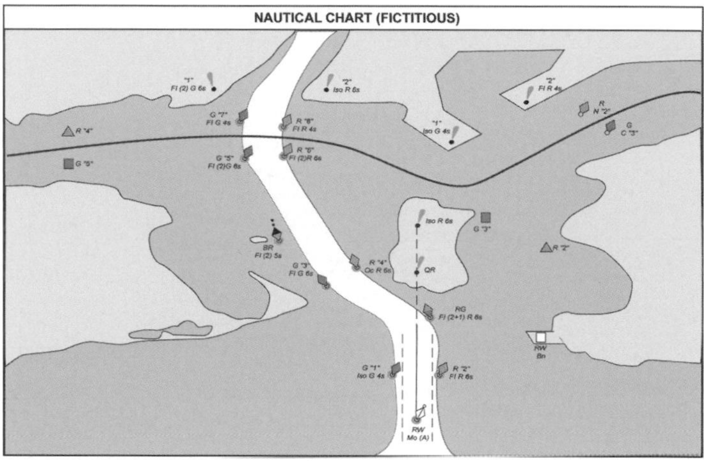


Here we see a visual buoyage guide as on page 47, this time with a corresponding idealized chart segment.

There are prescribed light patterns for certain navigation aids. For example, a lighted center channel (or safe water) buoy will flash a Morse code "A" (short-long) pattern with a white light. A junction buoy will flash a two short plus one short (2 + 1) pattern in the color of the top band (either red or green).

Buoys on NOAA charts are indicated by a small, open, black circle indicating the approximate position and a diamond flare (♦). The color of the diamond corresponds to the color of the buoy. If the buoy is lighted, the circle will be surrounded by a magenta-shaded circle. (Outside the United States, lighted buoys are denoted with a flare just as lighted beacons are, but the approximate buoy location is marked by a small hollow rather than the circle at the base of a diamond.) The color of the buoy is also given in the label, such as "R" for red, "G" for green, or "RW" for vertical red/white. On the water, the buoy's shape and color are significant. Unlighted conical red buoys are called *nuns* (shown as "N" on the chart). Unlighted cylindrical green buoys are called *cans* (shown as "C" on the chart). Lighted buoys are often conical or cylindrical as well, but they may also be a bell buoy, gong, or other *pillar* shape (generally a lattice tower on a flat base), and they have a wider range of colors. In addition to red and green, lighted buoys may be painted red/white, black, or yellow. Their lights are red, green, or white,

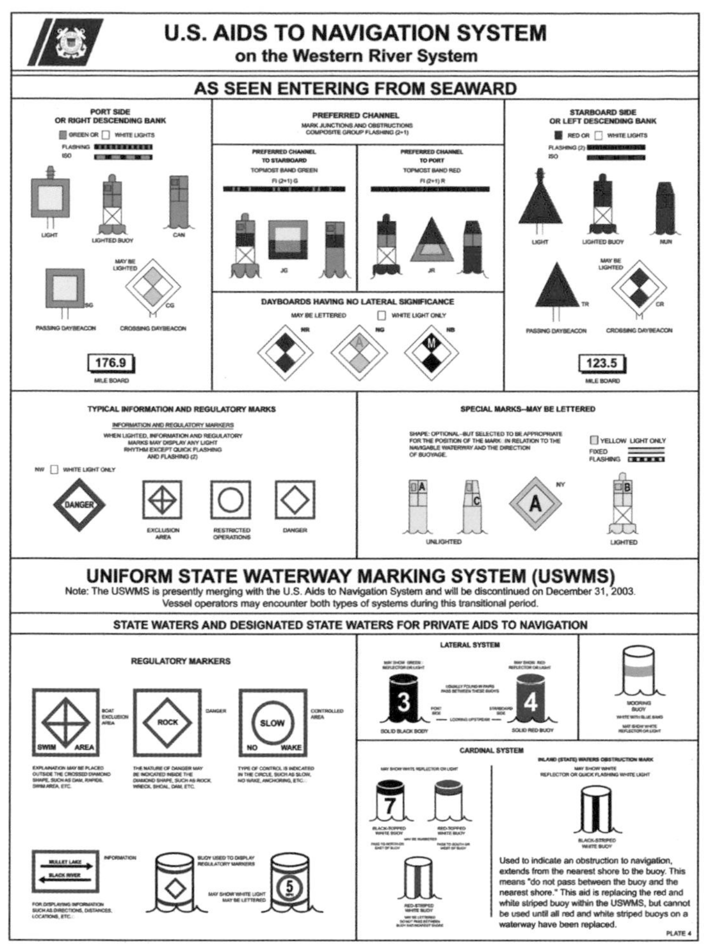


The Western Rivers System of nav aids used on the Mississippi River and its tributaries differs from the U.S. coastal IALA-B system in several respects, among which are that the nav aids are not numbered. The Uniform State Waterway Marking System used on lakes and inland waterways that are not covered by nautical charts, as well as some that are, has been discontinued in favor of the IALA-B system but may still be encountered here or there.

and the light color and pattern are shown on the chart. White lights are used on center channel buoys (red/white) as mentioned above. Buoy sounds are labeled as BELL, HORN, or SIREN if present.

# Plotting Tools

Now that you know something about charts, let's look at the tools that are used with them. You will need to get charted information into your GPS, and you should verify electronic positions by nonelectronic means from time to time. For both these reasons, you need the time-honored tools of piloting.

## Dividers

*Dividers* are used to measure distances and latitude and longitude coordinates on a chart. In its basic form, a pair of dividers comprises two arms ending in points, the distance between

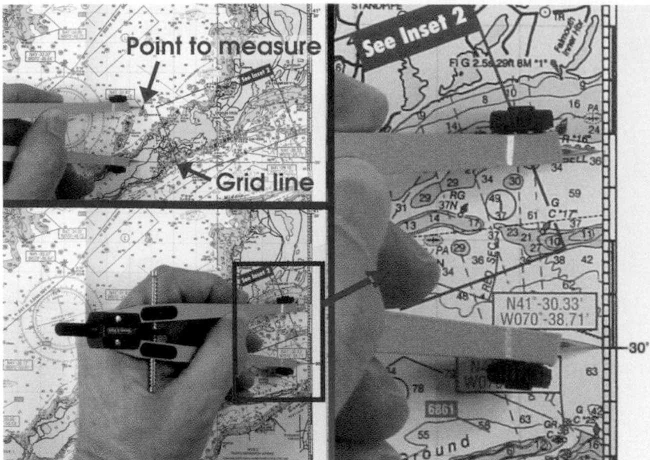


Dividers are used to make measurements on your chart. In this example, the latitude of an object or location is being measured. In the upper-left panel, one point of the dividers is placed on the object and the other point is opened to the closest grid line. Then that second point is traced along the grid line until it reaches the latitude scale on the side of the chart. Now you can read the corresponding value of latitude. In this example, the latitude of our object is 40° 31.84′ N.

which can be adjusted by means of a friction pivot. Friction pivots are quick and easy to adjust but can be inadvertently altered on a moving, bouncing boat. Other pivots use an adjustment screw to fine-tune the position, but setting these can be arduous. The best designs have quick-set capability in addition to an adjustment screw. With these dividers you can quickly open the arms to the approximate setting you want, then turn the screw to fine-tune and lock in the setting.

In addition to a pair of dividers, many mariners like to carry a *drawing compass*, in which a pencil replaces one of the points of a divider. A drawing compass, no doubt familiar to you from school days, is handy for plotting points at specified distances or tracing arcs of specified radii.

## Determining Coordinates

To determine the latitude of a spot on the chart, you simply place one point of the dividers on the spot of interest, then adjust the arms to place the other point on the nearest line of latitude. Once this gap is set, move the dividers along the line of latitude to the latitude scale in either margin. Now one point lies on the latitude line and the other marks the latitude measurement for your desired location. In the Northern Hemisphere, the value of latitude increases upward and is read as degrees, minutes, and tenths of minutes north (N).

Longitude is similarly measured by placing one point on the desired location and the other point on the nearest meridian line. You then transfer this setting to the scale in the top or bottom margin of the chart and read the longitude. In North America longitude is read as degrees, minutes, and tenths of minutes west (W), with values increasing to the left.

## Measuring Distance

Distance is measured using the two points of the dividers, one point placed on each end of the distance to be measured.

To measure the distance between two locations, place one point of the dividers on the first location and the second point on the other location.

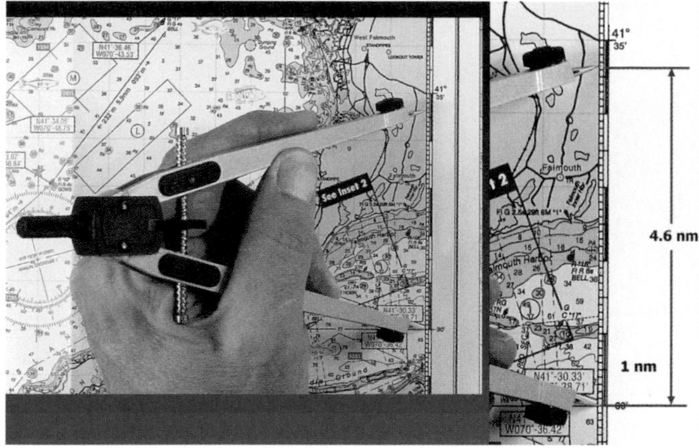


Without altering that setting, transfer the dividers to the distance scale on the chart or to the latitude scale on the side. One minute of latitude (not longitude) is exactly equal to 1 nautical mile, so you can use the latitude scale as a distance scale.

While maintaining that setting, move the dividers to the distance scale on the chart, put one point on zero, and read the distance to the second point. Alternatively, you can use the latitude scale and count the number of minutes (nautical miles) and tenths of minutes between the divider's points. *Note: Most charts have distance scales in nautical miles, statute miles, and kilometers. On the water it makes sense to use nautical miles due to the natural relationship with latitude.*

If the distance you wish to measure is greater than the dividers can span, you will need to draw a line between the two locations. Now you can use the distance scale or the latitude scale to preset the dividers to a convenient distance—for example, 5 nautical miles. Next, set one point of the dividers on one end of the line and *walk* the dividers along the line by advancing from point to point, counting the number of preset segments as you do so. Let's say that you've set the dividers to 5 miles and are measuring the distance between two buoys that are 12 miles apart. You count off two divider spans for 10 miles, then see that the remaining distance is less than the gap between the divider points. So you close the divider points until they precisely span the remaining distance, then read that distance on the chart scale: 2 miles. Add this distance to the sum of the fixed intervals you just counted, and you get the answer: 12.

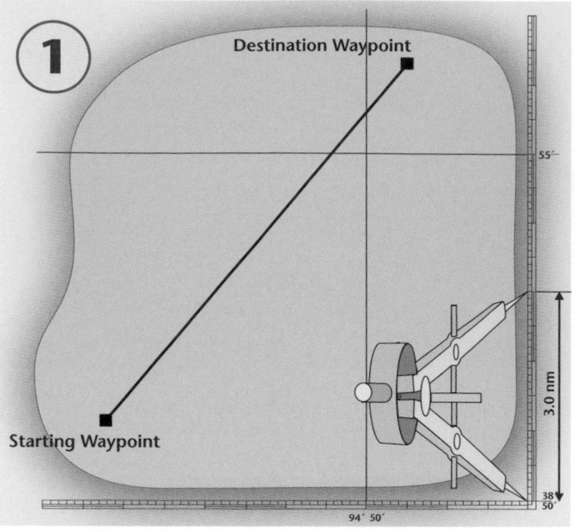
1
Destination Waypoint
Starting Waypoint
55′
3.0 nm
38°
50′
94° 50′

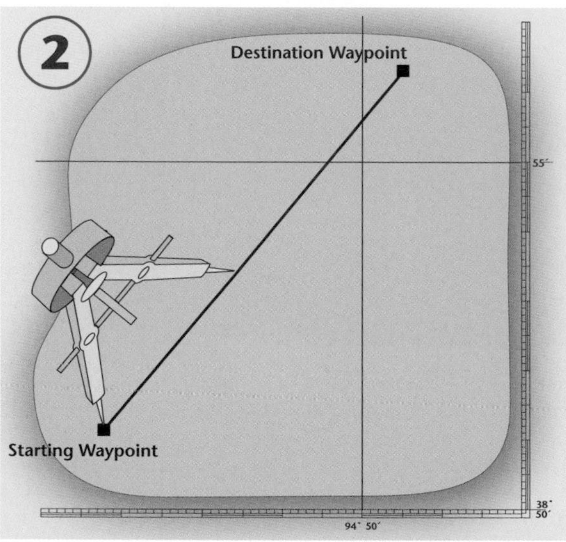
2
Destination Waypoint
Starting Waypoint
55′
38°
50′
94° 50′

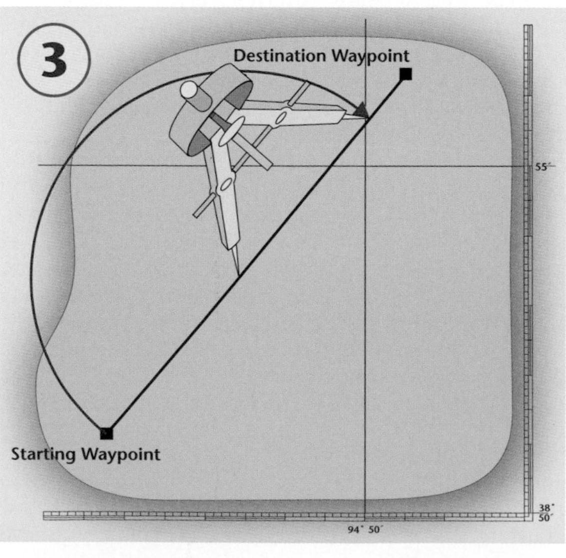
3
Destination Waypoint
Starting Waypoint
55′
38°
50′
94° 50′

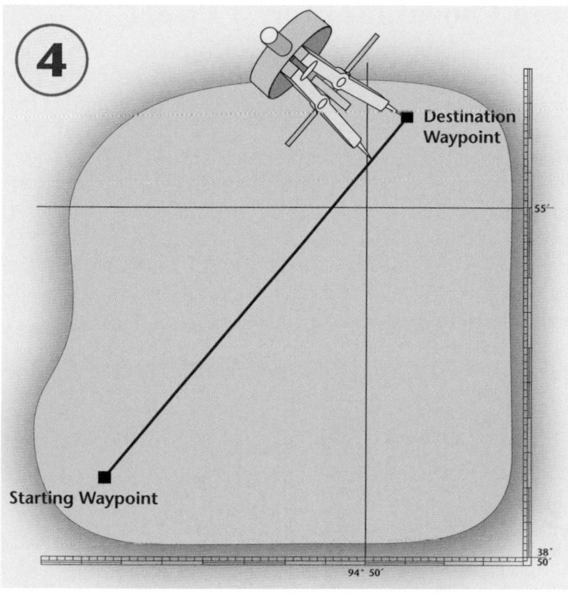


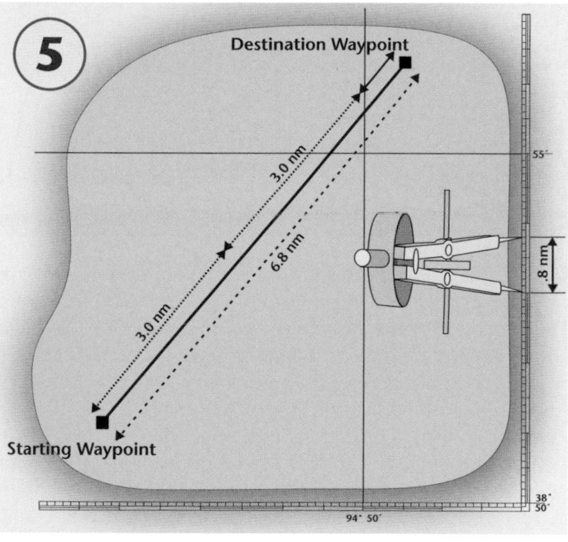


If the distance you want to measure is too large for your dividers to span, draw a line between the locations. Next, set the dividers to a convenient distance, such as 3 nm, using the latitude scale. Walk the dividers from one location toward the other, counting the number of 3 nm increments until the last increment is less than the dividers' preset distance. Now, set the dividers to measure that final increment, and go to the latitude scale to read that final distance. Add all the increments to get the total distance.

Some charts for locations such as the Great Lakes and major rivers use latitude and longitude scales calibrated in degrees, minutes, and seconds, whereas most nautical charts use degrees, minutes, and tenths of minutes. Because minutes and tenths of minutes correspond well with nautical miles and tenths, you may wish to convert any charts that use the more cumbersome seconds. To do so, simply divide the number of seconds by 60 to get tenths of minutes.

## Plotting Coordinates on a Chart

Your GPS continually provides the latitude and longitude coordinates for your position, but until you plot this position on a chart, it doesn't mean much. To do this, locate your GPS latitude on the appropriate chart's latitude scale and place one point of the dividers on that spot. Then adjust the dividers so that the second point rests on the nearest latitude line. Now move the dividers along the latitude line to your approximate location (by visually approximating the longitude) and make a small horizontal pencil mark. Then do the same for the longitude. Your current position is at the intersection of the pencil marks.

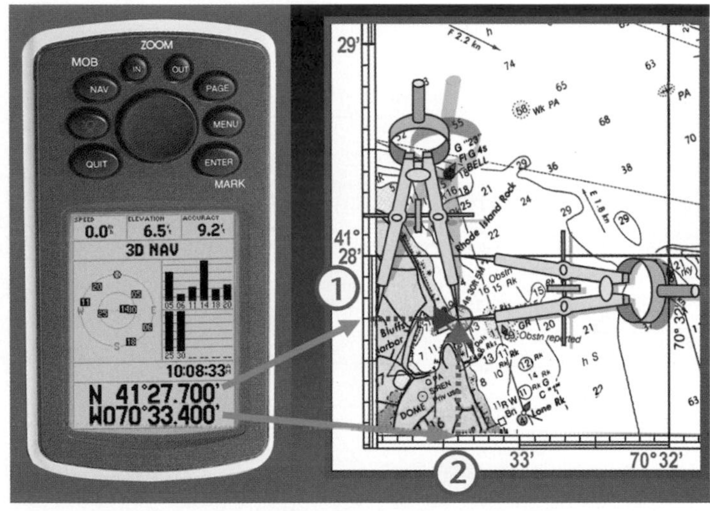


When you use a GPS, it will provide values for your current latitude and longitude. To determine where you are on the chart, you must plot these values. This process is similar to what was shown on page 50, only this time it's done in reverse. In the last example, we transferred chart information to the scales, but here we'll use the same basic techniques to transfer scale information onto the chart. First, place one of the divider points on the scale mark that corresponds with the GPS-derived latitude value. Then open the dividers so that the second point rests on the nearest grid line. Then drag the open dividers across the chart, stopping when you reach your approximate longitude. ("Eyeball" this location.) Draw a short pencil mark at this point. Then repeat this process to transfer the longitude value. Your location is where the two pencil marks meet.

## Parallel Rules

Perhaps the simplest tool for plotting is a set of *parallel rules*. This device comprises a pair of rules that are joined together by two or more swinging hinges. The rules serve as straightedges for plotting courses. The hinges allow you to expand or collapse the distance between the two rules while keeping the rules exactly parallel to each other. This is an easy and accurate way to transfer a plotted bearing line across a chart to the compass rose for measurement, or to transfer a measured bearing (say, the bearing to a nearby lighthouse measured on deck with a hand bearing compass, as described below) from the printed compass rose across the chart for plotting. The mechanics of the process are simple. You merely press down on one rule while swinging the other outward, then press down on the lead rule while you swing the trailing rule after it. Repeat as necessary, thus *walking* the rules across the chart without altering the bearing. This time-honored device is practical for working on charts at home or at sea. With a little experience, the parallel rules can be walked either across the chart or up or down on it to align with the region of interest. And because the compass roses printed on nautical charts allow you to measure directions relative either to true or magnetic north, using parallel rules obviates the necessity for converting from *true* to *magnetic bearings* and back, with its attendant risk of error.

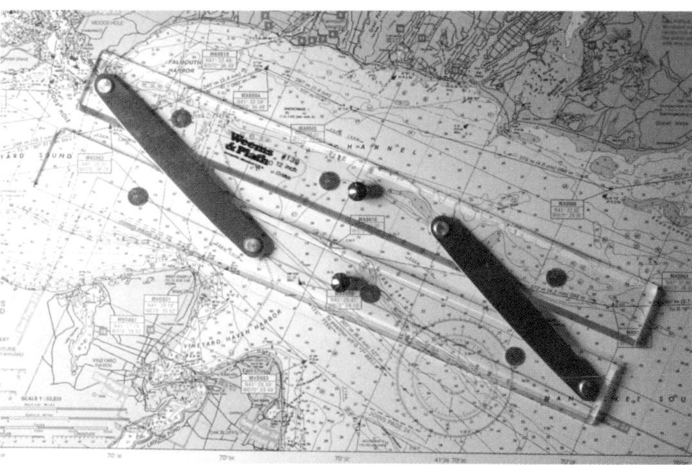

Plotting on a chart often involves transferring a course line to a compass rose, or vice versa. In doing so, it's crucial that the second line is drawn perfectly parallel to the first. Parallel rules are popular for this purpose.

A more modern variation of parallel rules is the *rolling parallel rule*. This device has only one straightedge and moves across the chart on a long roller, which preserves the proper orientation. What the device gains in simplicity, it loses in versatility. It can go only forward and backward, not side to side. A special variation called the *Bi-Rola* has rollers that are perpendicular to each other. By pressing on one or the other, you can move across or up and down to reach any spot on the chart and still maintain an accurate bearing. These devices work well on a chart table but may slip or shift on less uniform surfaces or in rough seas.

## USING THE COMPASS ROSE

The compass rose (which is printed in multiple locations on your chart) provides the chart's fundamental reference for magnetic directions. It is printed in a magenta ink that is distinctive when viewed with red light at night. (Navigators use a red light at night for illuminating charts and instruments, because this color has minimal effect on night vision, which is essential for keeping watch.)

The compass rose has two rings. The outer ring aligns with the chart grid of latitude and longitude lines—that is, with true north; the inner ring aligns with magnetic north. Within the inner ring is a legend that notes the local variation used for the chart. The variation describes both the magnitude of the difference in degrees and minutes between true and magnetic north for the charted location, and the direction of that offset, either east or west. (Magnetic north is moving, albeit slowly, so variation needs to be adjusted for this movement.) In addition, the legend identifies the date used for the variation and the amount by which it will change each year, east or west. You will need to adjust the variation accordingly if your chart is several years old and the annual change is significant.

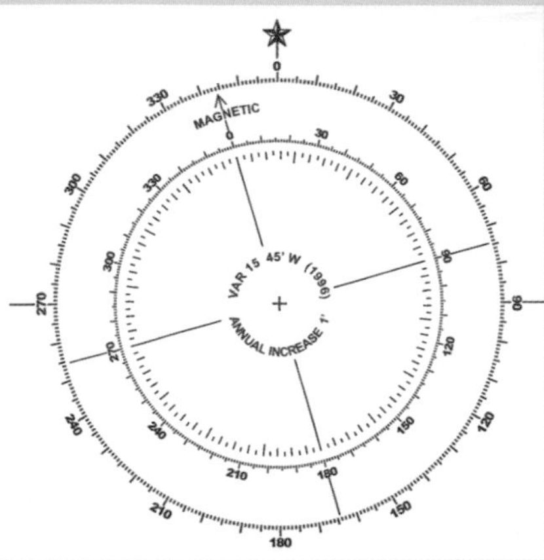


Charts are printed with one or more compass roses. The compass rose has two rings. The outer ring is aligned with the chart grid and true north. The inner ring is aligned with magnetic north. A legend at the center of the rose provides the local variation and its annual change. The compass rose simplifies the labeling of courses and bearings and provides instant reference between true and magnetic north.

Many mariners use the compass rose for laying out or measuring a course or bearing. Because the rose is rarely if ever located where you want to plot or measure a course, devices such as parallel rules are used to transfer the direction to or

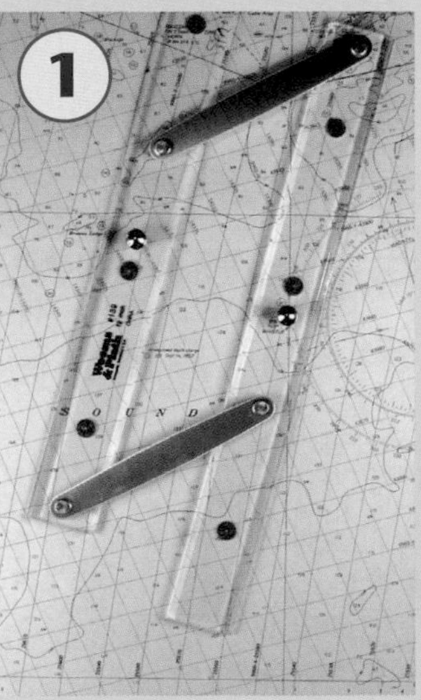


If you need to transfer that parallel line to a location beyond the reach of the parallel rules, simply walk them to the location by extending, contracting, and reextending the rules.

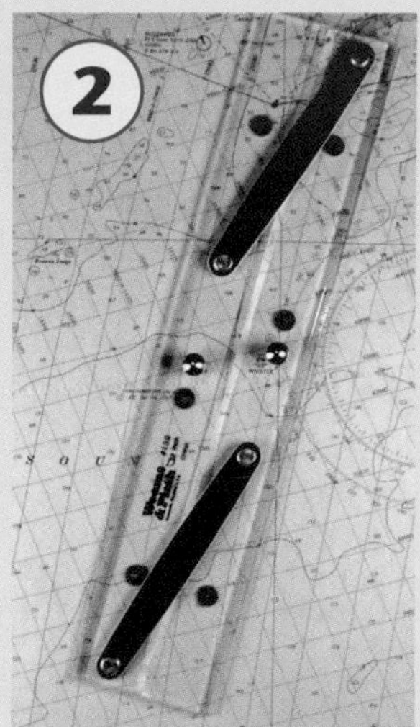

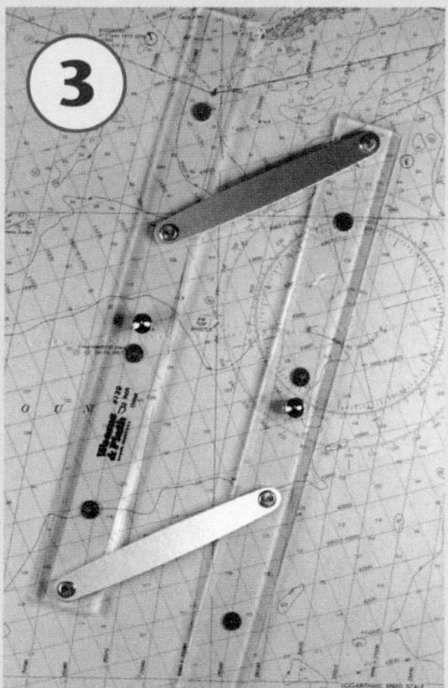

from the rose. Make sure you read your direction from the compass rose going the right way—that is, by imagining your boat at the center and reading toward the rose in the direction of the course or bearing.

To obtain the direction of a plotted course using parallel rules, align one rule with the plotted leg, then walk the rules across the chart to the nearest compass rose and read the course in degrees magnetic from the inner ring. The course is now ready to steer provided your steering compass doesn't exhibit significant deviation errors that you can't get rid of. See page 61 for more on deviation.

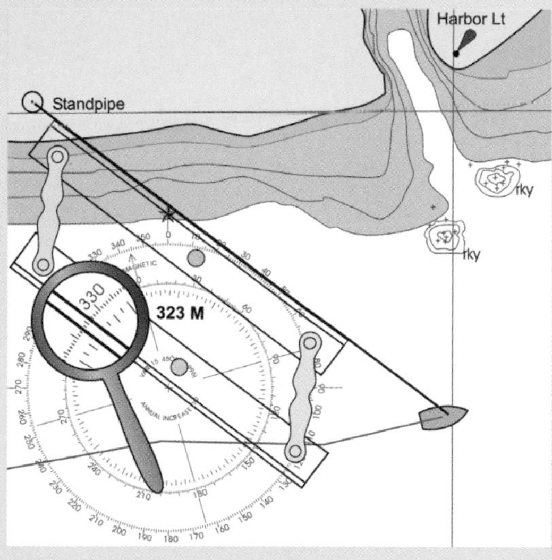


To plot a compass bearing on a chart, you place the parallel rules over the nearest compass rose. On the inner circle of the rose, find the bearing you measured on deck (either by sighting over your steering compass or using a hand bearing compass) and align one of the rules with this bearing and the center of the rose. Now open the rules and walk them as necessary until the leading rule intersects the charted object on which you took the bearing. This is a line of position, and you are located somewhere along this line.

## Protractor Plotting Tool

Alternatively, you can measure courses and bearings in degrees true using a *protractor plotting tool*. These tools are inexpensive

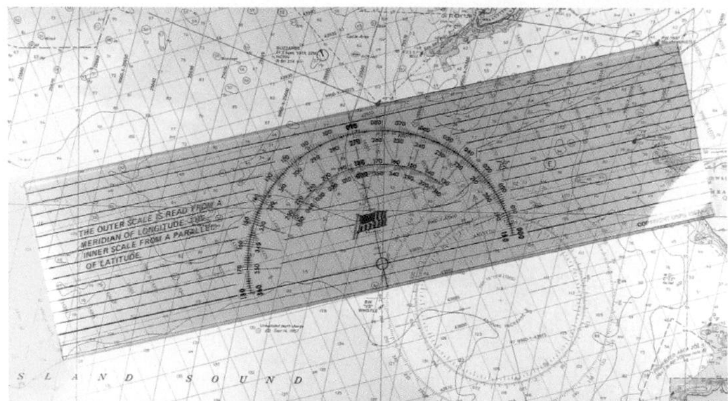


One of the simplest plotting tools has no moving parts. The *rectangular plotting tool* is imprinted with a series of parallel lines. You can move the tool across the chart by drawing intermediate lines, moving the plotter, and realigning one of the printed parallel lines with the plotted line on the chart.

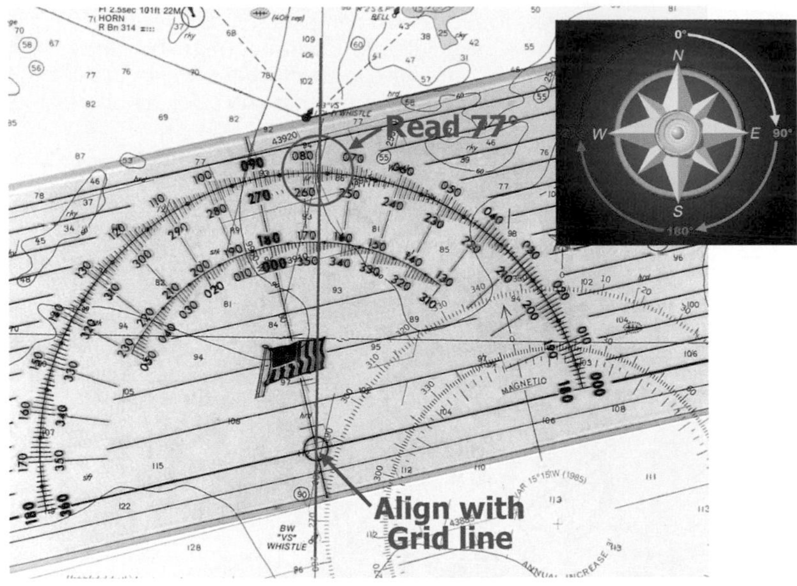


Course and bearing directions can be determined by using the scales on a protractor plotting tool. You need to align the bull's-eye with a grid line while you have the plotter aligned with the course line. You can align the top of the plotter or any of the printed parallel lines with the course line. Finally, you read the course direction from the appropriate protractor scale. Which scale to use? Use common sense. This simplistic compass rose (right) provides you with a sense of direction. Any course or bearing toward the top right of the chart will be between 0° and 90°. By the same token, any course or bearing toward the bottom right will be between 90° and 180°. Toward the lower left will be between 180° and 270°. Finally, toward the upper left will be between 270° and 360° (0°).

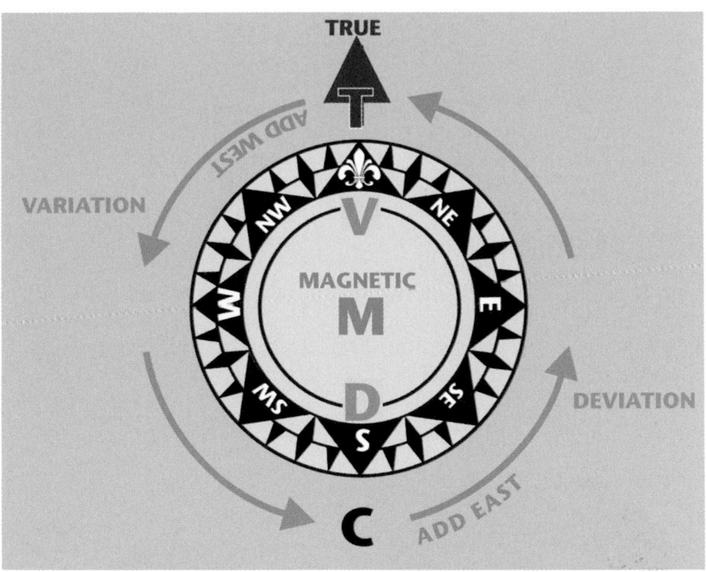


If you plot your bearings and courses in degrees true but steer them in degrees as read on a compass, you'll have to convert from one to the other. This is why so many small-boat navigators prefer to do their plotting in degrees magnetic. When you convert from true to magnetic, you need to add westerly variation—remember, "West is best." By the same token, if your compass has residual deviation (see page 61), to go from magnetic direction to what you would read on the compass, you will add westerly deviation. In other words, going down (T to M to C), you add west. Conversely, going up (C to M to T), you add east. This diagram provides an easy way to remember this—you always add counterclockwise. On the "west" side of the diagram, you add west (either V or D). On the "east" side you add east. If your compass has negligible deviation and you plot courses and bearings in degrees magnetic, no conversions will be necessary.

and reliable. If you're in cramped quarters or on a small charting table, protractors can be less cumbersome than parallel rules. Plus, because a protractor scale is printed directly on the plotting tool, you won't need to access the compass rose for angles. This added flexibility is especially helpful when lack of space forces you to do your plotting on a folded chart. Murphy's Law being what it is, the nearest compass rose is always folded underneath and therefore inaccessible. The simple *rectangular plotting tool* shown opposite was designed by the United States Power Squadrons. Two protractor scales and parallel lines are printed on the template, with one for use with latitude lines and the other (printed in reverse order) for use with longitude lines.

To plot a course, align the course's starting point (whether a navigation buoy or simply a waypoint) on the plotter edge, orient the plotter's bull's-eye on a latitude or longitude line as appropriate, and read a direction in degrees true from one of the protractor's scales. This device takes some practice in order to avoid reading or using the wrong scale, and it requires those pesky conversions between true and magnetic bearings and courses that you can avoid by using parallel rules. Most navigators prefer to use parallel rules.

# Compasses

Now that you have the tools to plot your bearings and courses, you'll need tools to measure and steer them. The most fundamental of these is the ship's magnetic steering compass, and no boat should be without one.

## Ship's Compass

Even if you use GPS to set and monitor your courses, you will find it easier to steer and hold a course using the steering compass, and it serves as an essential backup when all else fails. It is a wise investment to get the best compass you can afford. Generally, larger is better. The best have a spherical chamber containing a flat or dished card.

The magnetic compass is the most fundamental and important navigation instrument on your boat. Shown here are two powerboat compasses. The compass card is suspended in a liquid-filled bowl of oil and pivots on a fine point. This allows the card to stay level as the boat pitches and rolls. On the left is a front-reading compass. The card is read on its front surface against a lubber line etched in the glass. This style is a little more difficult to use. A top-reading compass card (right) is more intuitive, because its orientation matches directions around you and those of a chart's compass rose. The top-reading card also gains an advantage of some magnification from the fluid-filled bowl. The cards in powerboat compasses are dampened (intentionally slowed) to counteract the dynamic motions of fast boating and thus improve readabilty.

Sailboat compasses are a bit different from powerboat compasses in that they are dampened less and are designed to perform under greater angles of heel. The version on the right is designed for a bulkhead mount and provides a scale of heel as well as compass heading.

All steering compasses are dampened to counteract the quick motions of a boat, but compasses designed for sailboats are dampened differently from those used on powerboats. In addition, many sailboat compasses provide an additional scale indicating the degree of heel for the boat.

To be useful, your compass probably needs to be compensated. Nearby metallic objects on a boat influence the way the Earth's magnetic field affects a compass. These effects are different for each heading, because a change in heading alters the relative alignment of the metallic objects between the compass and the Earth's magnetic field. Most compasses incorporate built-in magnets that can be rotated to compensate for onboard influences. Usually, there is one magnet for north-south compensation and another for east-west. By running known courses, it is possible to adjust these magnets iteratively until the compass readings are quite accurate. Although compensation can counteract most effects, there is always some residual error. Usually, however, you can reduce this error to 2 degrees or less, depending on the heading, at which point you may choose simply to ignore it. If the residual errors are larger, you can construct a deviation table that provides the difference between the compass reading and the actual magnetic course for each direction of the boat. Then you can apply these corrections whenever you steer a compass course by adding or subtracting the deviation as appropriate (see page 59). Compensation to within a degree or two is obviously the more practical solution. Although you can adjust your compass yourself with careful measurements and a lot of patience, this is a challenging task best left to a professional.

Typically, magnetic compass cards are marked in 5-degree increments. This seemingly wide margin between hash marks is okay, because the boat's natural motion makes it difficult to hold a reading to better than a degree or two. The longer hash marks—marking 10-degree increments—are painted to a width of 1 degree, making an "eyeball" estimate of your heading easier. In most marine compasses, the card sits suspended in a thick liquid such as mineral oil, the viscosity of which helps dampen the motion of the boat so that the reading appears relatively steady.

Most compasses present a heading in one of two ways. You can read your heading either against the *lubber line* on the front edge of the compass card (front reading), or across the top of the card against a pointer on the far side (top reading). The latter is preferable because the numbers will increase clockwise, just as the numbers on a compass rose do. The front- or direct-reading card displays numbers in a counterclockwise progression, which can lead to confusion.

## Hand Bearing Compass

From time to time you'll want to take visual bearings in order to fix your location, determine your speed, or measure the relative course of a nearby vessel. At such times it pays to have a *hand bearing compass*, which is nothing more than a handheld magnetic compass with a built-in sight. Simply aim the sight at the other boat or charted object and read its bearing off the compass. Hand bearing compasses come in a variety of configurations and cost as little as $25. Some marine binoculars contain an integral compass, which is displayed as you view a distant object; most such units have crosshairs for accurate sighting.

Hand bearing compasses are subject to onboard magnetic disturbances, just as your ship's compass is. These influences

A hand bearing compass is essential equipment on your boat. Taking bearings on landmarks and navigation aids with this device is quick and easy. Shown here is a Ritchie small-boat "hockey puck" hand bearing compass.

may be different at different locations on the boat. Therefore, you should always use the hand bearing compass from a single spot near the helm. (Also, be sure not to brace the compass against any wire shrouds or metal fittings.) To quickly check the deviation of a hand bearing compass, point it at the bow and compare its reading with that of the ship's compass. If they are close, you are in good shape. If they differ (and you know that your steering compass is accurate), apply that difference to any reading you take with the hand bearing compass while on that heading. If the ship's compass reads 5° lower, for example, you need to subtract 5° from each reading of the hand bearing compass. Keep in mind that this deviation will change for every new boat heading. Although the deviation is usually not significant and can probably be ignored, you should check it on all headings to be sure.

CHAPTER 4

# Using GPS

Bob Sweet

# Meet Your GPS

All GPS receivers offer similar functions. The generic layout shown here is typical. Use your GPS manual to identify any differences in detail.

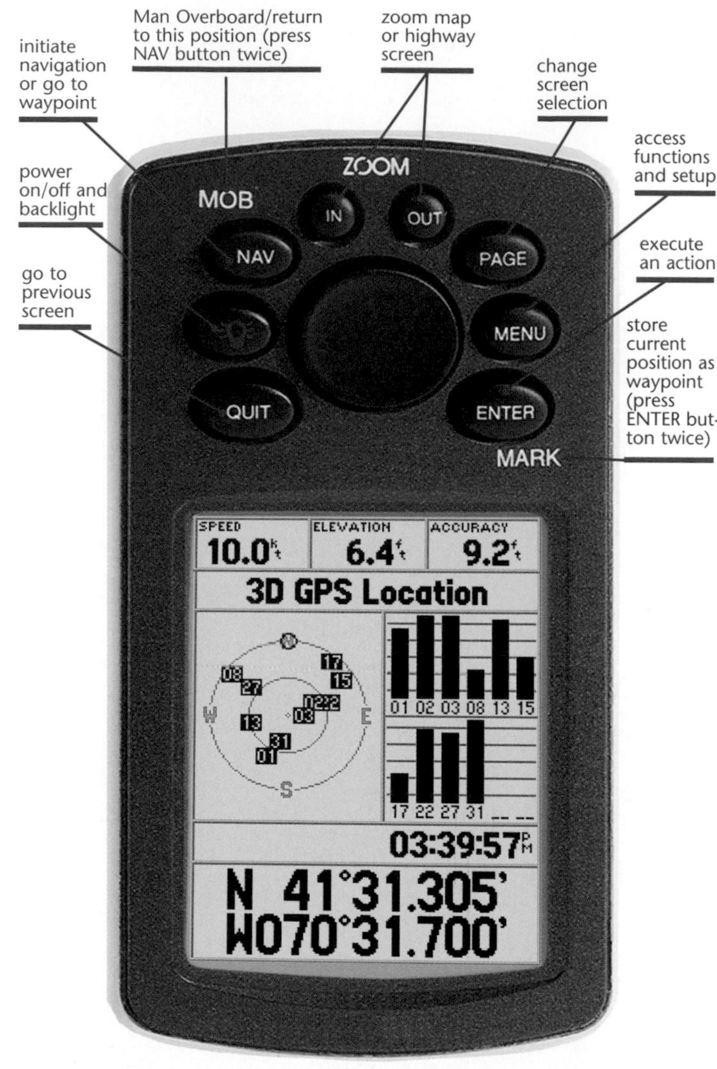


## Buttons

The many GPS functions are controlled by a set of buttons, restricted in number by the space available. Most of the buttons control how the GPS processes and displays information. The button labeled NAV or GoTo controls navigation functions. Press the ENTER button to execute actions. Press the QUIT or ESC button to revert to a prior screen instead of executing an action. The labels may vary slightly by model, but the general approach is always the same.

## Screens

You can select screens as needed. The **Satellite Screen** indicates the quality of the GPS position and tells you if part of the sky is blocked to the GPS antenna. The **Position Screen** indicates the latitude and longitude of your current position and the precise time. (In this example, Satellite and Position appear on one screen; other models present them separately.) The **Map Screen** shows your current position with respect to other objects (waypoints) stored in your GPS, and the active course line. The **Highway Screen** shows a 3-D representation of your active course with your current position in the foreground and your next waypoint in the background. This is likely to be the most valuable screen to keep you on course.

**Satellite/Position Screen**

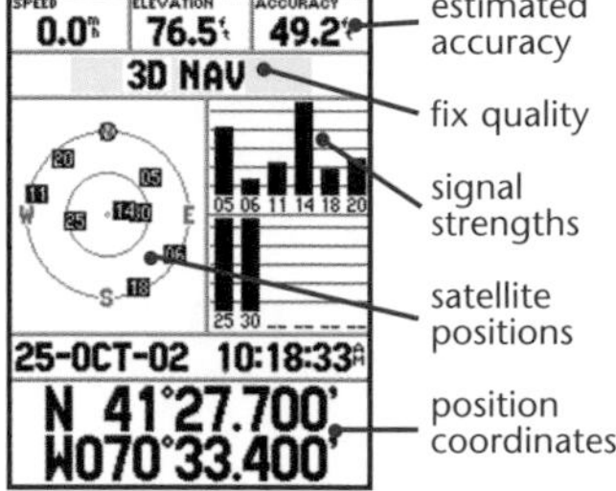


**Map Screen**

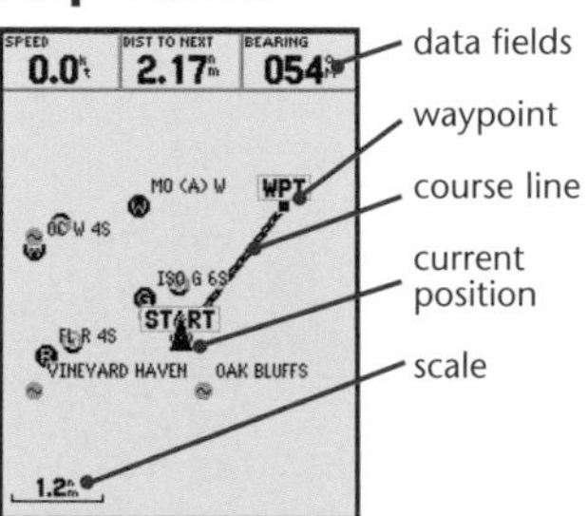


**Highway Screen**

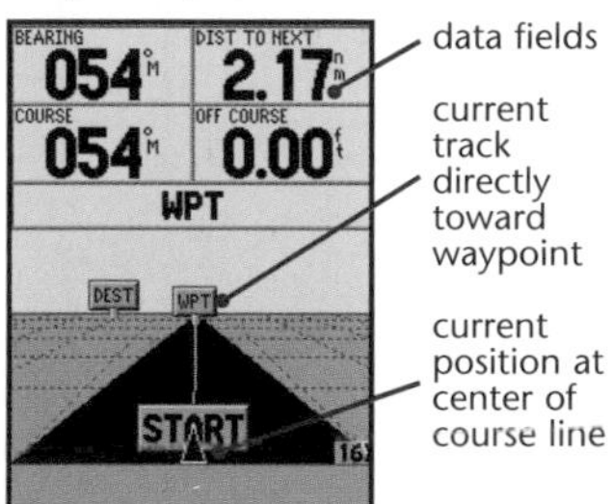


**Map Screen with Map***

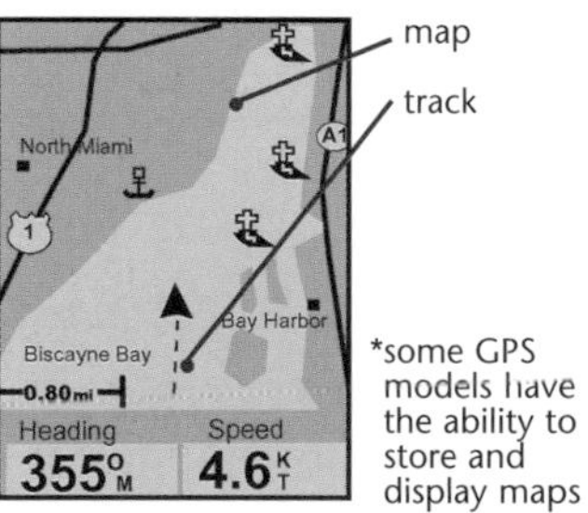


*some GPS models have the ability to store and display maps

## Menus

Use menus to program the GPS, to initiate and control navigation, and to select display format. Most menus are accessed via the **Main Menu** using the MENU (or ENTER) button, or by paging to find the Main Menu screen. In addition, most GPS sets offer screen-dependent menus that control how data are displayed on an individual screen. Access these from the current screen by pressing the MENU (or ENTER) button.

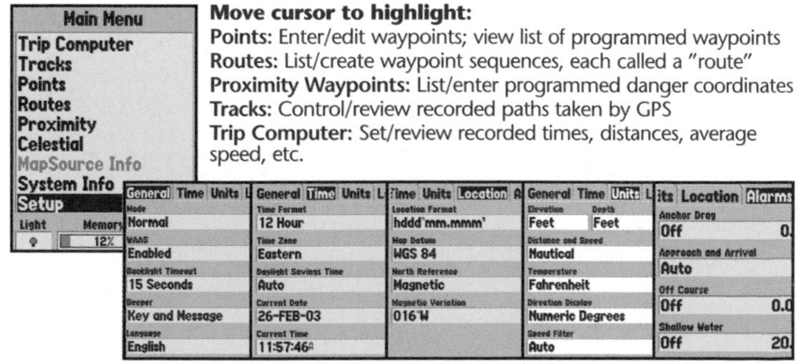


**Move cursor to highlight:**

**Points:** Enter/edit waypoints; view list of programmed waypoints

**Routes:** List/create waypoint sequences, each called a "route"

**Proximity Waypoints:** List/enter programmed danger coordinates

**Tracks:** Control/review recorded paths taken by GPS

**Trip Computer:** Set/review recorded times, distances, average speed, etc.

# Where Are You?

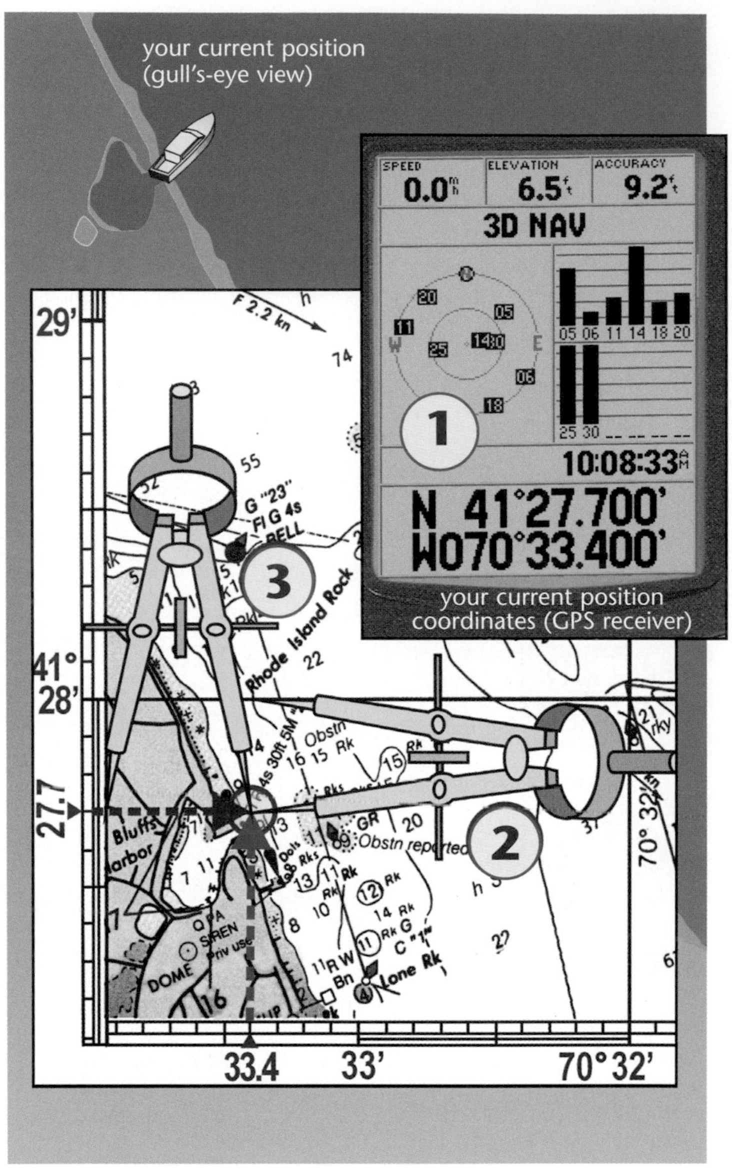


Navigation begins with knowing where you are, particularly as you begin your cruise. The GPS receiver provides that information with great precision in the form of a latitude and a longitude ①, but these coordinates are meaningless until you transcribe them onto a chart. Using dividers, first locate the latitude on the latitude scale with one point of the dividers and then set the second point on the nearest grid line. Transfer this distance across the chart to the region of the GPS longitude ②. Next, mark the longitude similarly and transfer it up along the grid line to refine the position ③. You now know where you are.

# Where Are You Going?

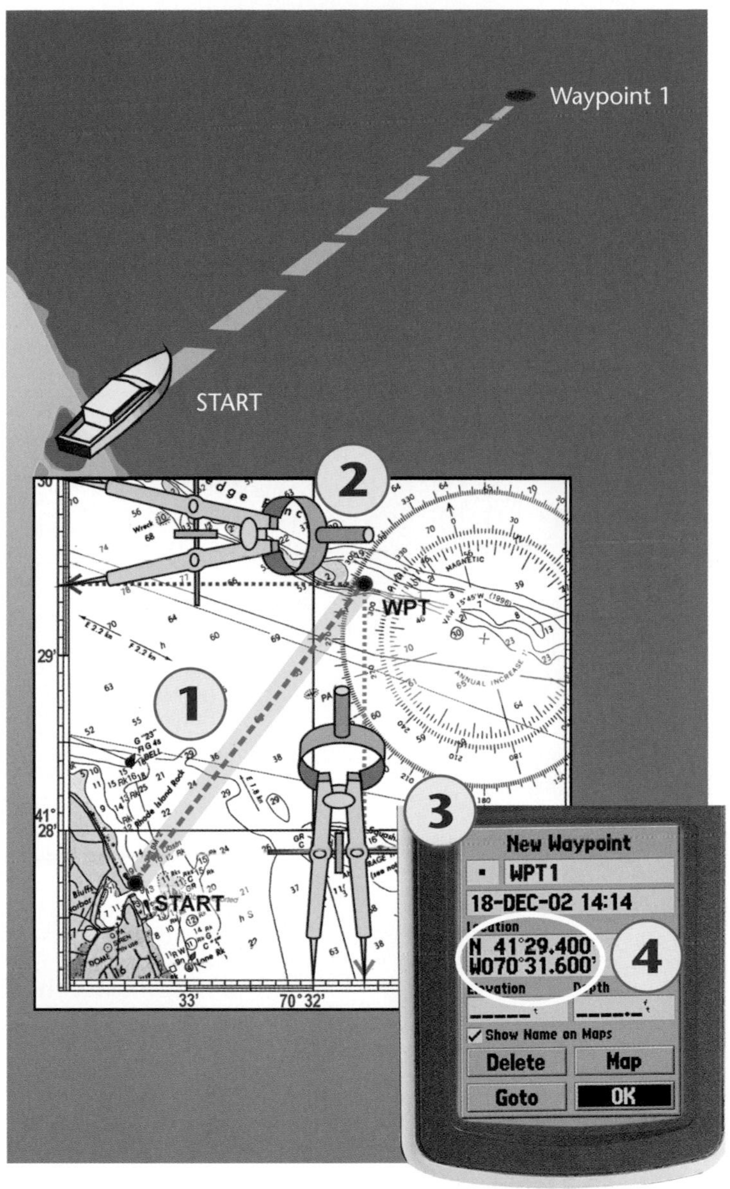


The next step is to determine where it is you plan to go. In this example, you have decided to go to WPT1 (waypoint 1). First, plot this course ① and ensure the path is safe. Second, determine the coordinates of WPT1. Use dividers to pick off its latitude ② and longitude ③. Now, access the New Waypoints Screen ④ and enter the measured latitude and longitude into your GPS (see page 74). Your GPS will now give you the course and distance to WPT1 (see page 68).

# Navigating Using GPS

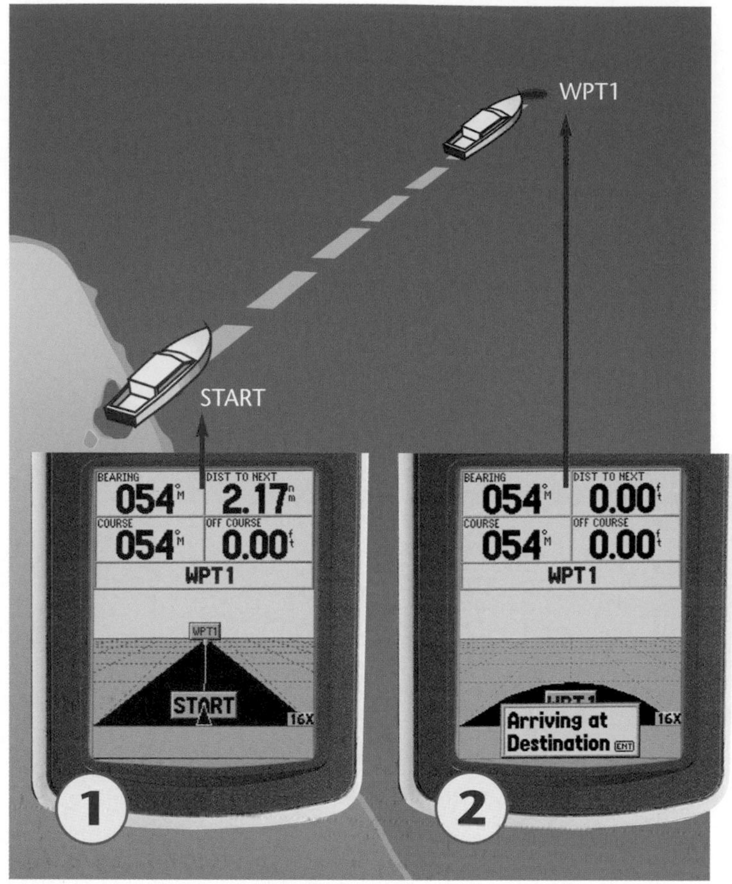


Using the GoTo command (see page 75), enter WPT1. You can select the Highway Screen to display your course ①. It tells you that the bearing to WPT1 is 54° and the distance is 2.17 nm. Steer your boat to 54° and stay in the center of the highway. Alternatively, you can choose to use a different screen, such as the Map Screen, for navigation. Most GPS models alert you with a text message and an audio alarm as you approach WPT1 ②. Your GPS displays the remaining distance as 0.00 nm—you have arrived.

## Along the Way

Your GPS continuously updates your position on the Position Screen (latitude and longitude). You can select a number of data fields to present information about your course, speed, estimated time of arrival, and many other choices. It is important for you to prequalify the path from START to WPT1 to ensure that this path is free of charted hazards. As long as you stay on course, you should encounter no charted obstacles.

# Marking a Spot

While on the water, you may have occasion to mark specific spots. This is easy using your GPS: just press the MARK key while you are on the spot.

In this example, you have spotted a partially exposed wreck near (not on!) your chosen path. To mark the spot on your course near the wreck for future reference, press the MARK (ENTER) key once. (On many GPS models, MARK is not a key but a second function on one of the buttons—you may need to press the button twice to save the mark.) The New Waypoint Screen comes up with the coordinates already entered and the OK field highlighted. To save this waypoint with the name 002, just press ENTER. Edit the names later, when you're no longer at the helm (see page 74).

# Planning an Extended Cruise

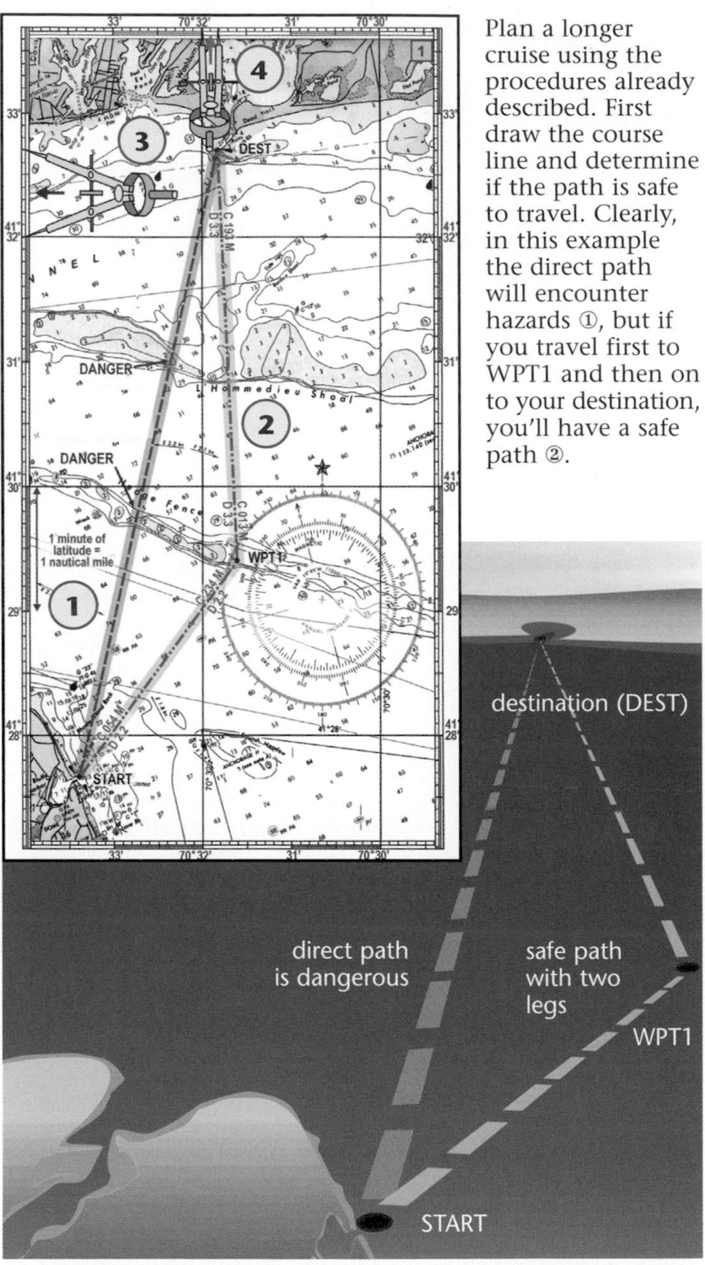


Plan a longer cruise using the procedures already described. First draw the course line and determine if the path is safe to travel. Clearly, in this example the direct path will encounter hazards ①, but if you travel first to WPT1 and then on to your destination, you'll have a safe path ②.

Measure the coordinates of your destination ③ and ④ and enter them into your GPS as another waypoint (DEST). As long as you stay on the two-legged route from START to WPT1 to DEST you should be safe from underwater hazards.

Alternatively, you can store this sequence as a Route that, once selected, will automate the selection of the DEST waypoint as soon as you reach WPT1.

Repeat this process to plan a cruise of any length and any number of legs within the limits of your GPS model.

# Traveling the Second Leg

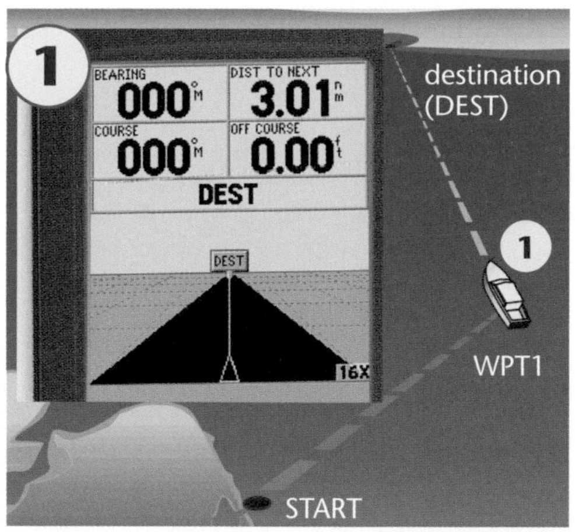


Now let's look more closely at the second leg. In our example, when you reach WPT1 ①, you need to tell the GPS where you want to go next (unless you're following a programmed route). Use the GoTo command (accessed via the NAV button on the model shown, see page 75) to select DEST as your next waypoint. Now, the Highway Screen displays the new bearing you steer to reach your destination.

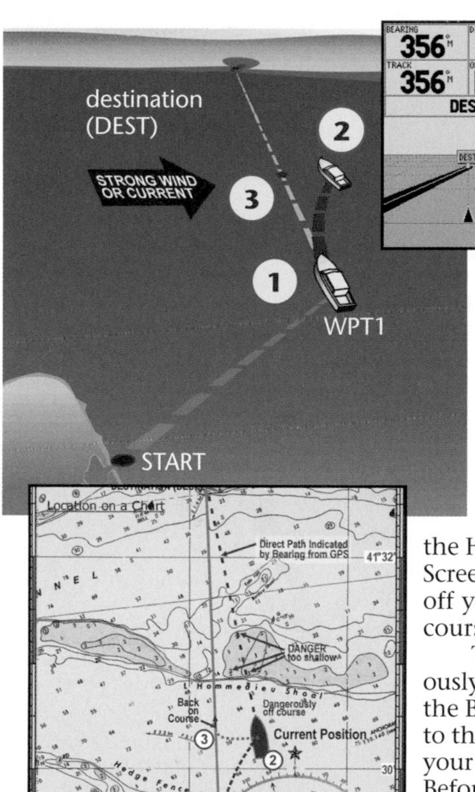


Unfortunately, steering this new course doesn't ensure you'll stay on the course line. If there is a cross-wind or current as shown, you may be pushed off your course line ②. Both the Highway and Map Screens show you to be off your prequalified course line.

The GPS continuously updates and shows the Bearing and Distance to the waypoint from your current position. Before taking the direct path to DEST, check it on a chart by plotting your current position and drawing the new course line to ensure there are no new obstacles. In this example, you must return to your original course line for the second leg at ③ before you can proceed safely.

# Staying On Course

Let's "rewind" back to WPT1 to find out how to prevent getting off course in the first place. Intuitively, you want to head toward your destination, but clearly that won't work in this example.

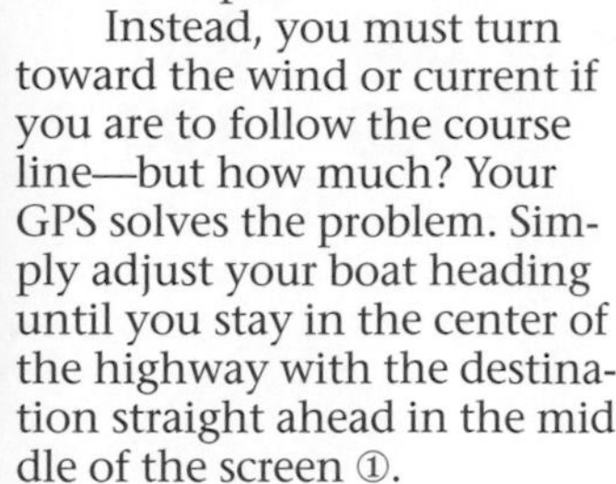

Instead, you must turn toward the wind or current if you are to follow the course line—but how much? Your GPS solves the problem. Simply adjust your boat heading until you stay in the center of the highway with the destination straight ahead in the middle of the screen ①.

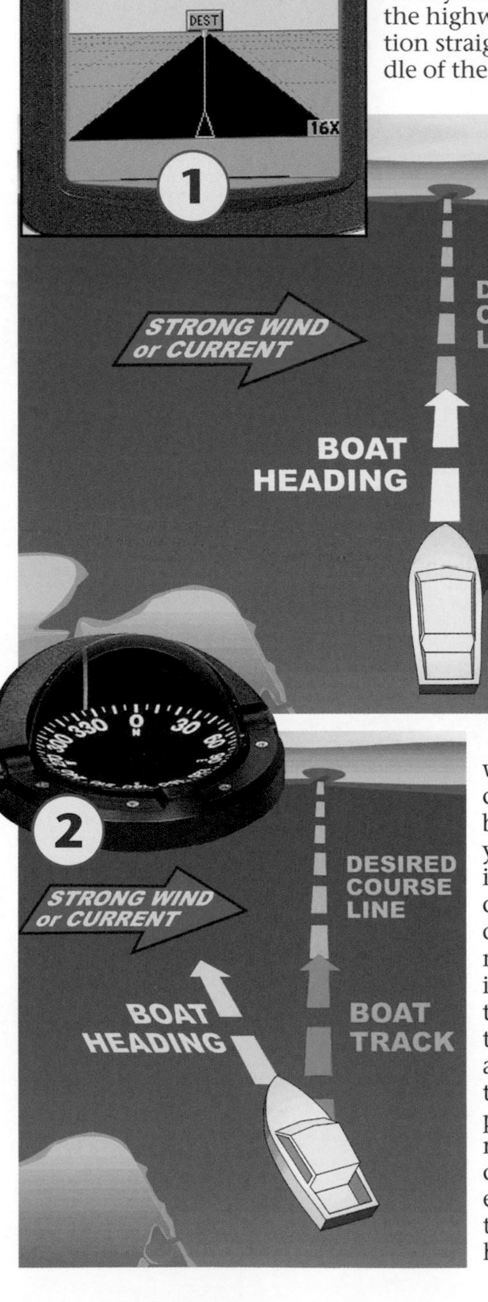


Now, your boat will stay on the course line. Your boat heading and your compass ② indicate a different direction, because due to wind or current you are proceeding "crabwise" along the course line. Note the compass heading and stay on it even though it doesn't point to your destination. Periodically check your GPS to ensure you stay in the center of the highway.

# Double-Checking Your Position

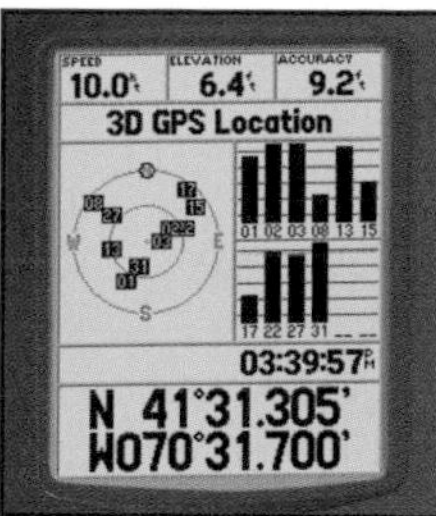


Your latitude and longitude as displayed on your GPS look OK, but how do you know for sure? This simple technique will confirm your position rather quickly and without charts.

In advance of your trip, store the coordinates of visible objects into your GPS. Then, on the water, sight on at least one of these objects using a hand-

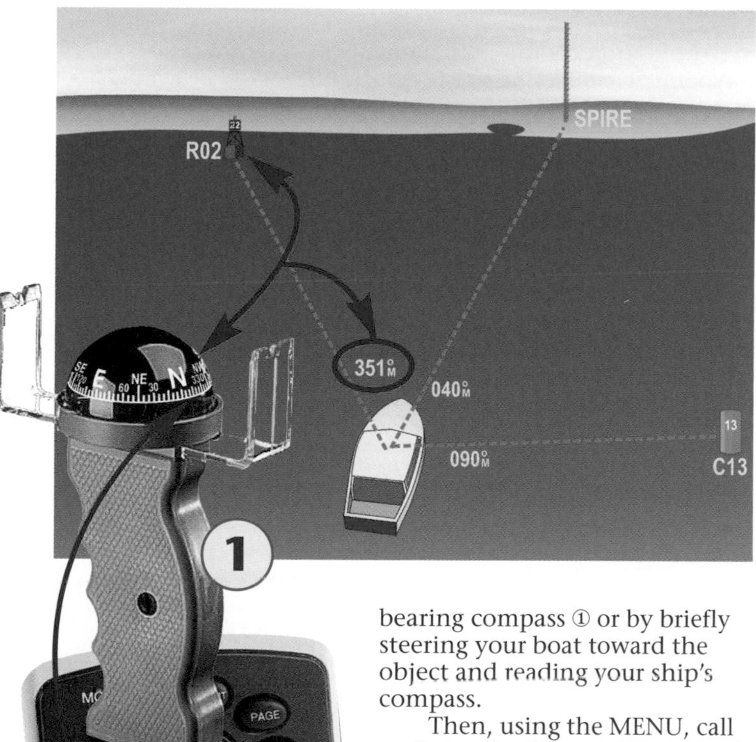


bearing compass ① or by briefly steering your boat toward the object and reading your ship's compass.

Then, using the MENU, call up Points (or Nearest Waypoints) and look for the sighted object. This screen will display the bearing and distance to that object ②. Compare your compass reading with the GPS reading. If they match, your GPS is likely to be accurate. If they don't match, plot your position on charts using the visual bearing(s).

The GPS also displays your elevation; but GPS accuracy in elevation is only 100 feet or so. An elevation error does not mean your horizontal coordinates are wrong.

# More on Waypoints

GPS provides your position with high precision, but to use it for navigation you need to enter waypoints. Waypoint navigation involves sailing a sequence of straight-line segments called "legs." The endpoints for each leg are stored in the GPS as waypoints.

## Entering Waypoints

Obtain the coordinates of waypoints you plan to use for navigation as shown on page 67. There are four ways to store those waypoints in your GPS. If your model doesn't permit Manual entry use the Scroll method.

**Manual:** Enter coordinates manually by accessing the New Waypoint Screen. Using the cursor button, scroll down until the coordinates field is highlighted, and press ENTER. You will be presented with a single highlighted character. Use the cursor to scroll up or down to change the character (number) until it corresponds to your desired entry. Then use the cursor to scroll right or left to change the values of other characters. When you're satisfied with the entered values for latitude and longitude, press ENTER to accept. Scroll to "OK" or "Save" and press ENTER to accept. Your GPS will assign a number in the name field. You can change the name (or the symbol displayed with the waypoint) in the same manner as entering values into the coordinates field.

**Scroll:** An easier way to store coordinates in your GPS is to scroll the cursor on the Map Screen. The cursor's coordinates are shown on the screen. Press MARK to access and edit the New Waypoint Screen, and then Save. For some GPS models, this is the method by which you access the New Waypoints Screen. Usually, it is quicker and easier to scroll to the general area of the desired waypoint, press MARK, edit the details of the coordinates until you're satisfied, and then Save.

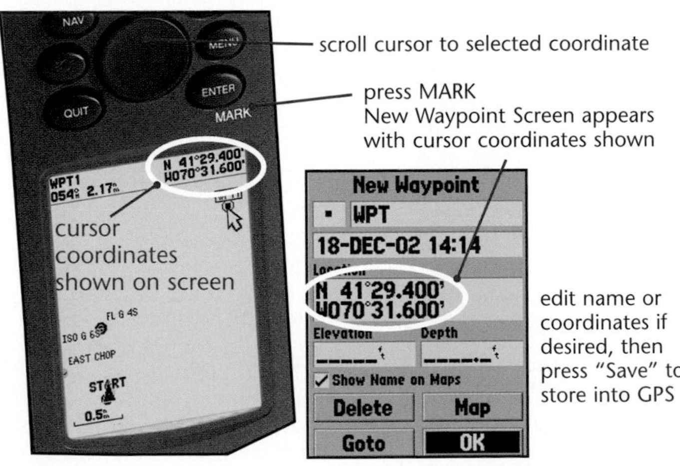


**MARK:** On the water, mark your current location by simply pressing the MARK key. See page 69.

**Computer:** Using digital chart software, you can plan routes on a computer and then load the corresponding waypoints and routes via cable into your GPS for navigation. See page 77.

## Navigating with Stored Waypoints

**GoTo:** Use the GoTo button (accessed through the NAV button on some models) to see a list of stored waypoints. Select the desired waypoint and press ENTER. The GPS now computes Bearing and Distance to that waypoint from your current location. However, you must use charts to determine if that path is safe.

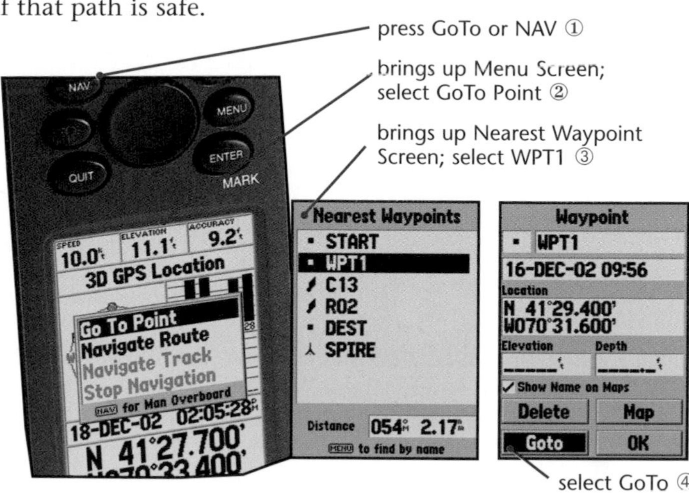


**Scroll:** Using the cursor on the Map Screen, scroll to a waypoint until it is highlighted and then activate it by selecting GoTo and ENTER. You also can scroll to particular coordinates and use GoTo to create a temporary waypoint. While scrolling, you will be presented with the cursor coordinates and the Distance and Bearing from your current position to the cursor.

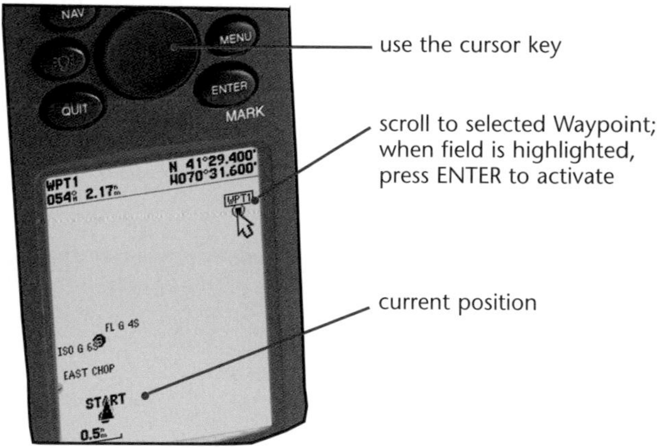


**Route:** The Route function automates the selection of sequential waypoints along your cruise. To create a route, select Route from the Main Menu. Then, in the order you wish to navigate them, select waypoints already stored in your GPS. Once this sequence is stored, you can select and activate a Route using the Menu or the NAV button (if your GPS has one). The GPS then will present your entire route on the Map and Highway Screens, and provide Bearing and Distance to each waypoint in the selected sequence. For your return trip, reverse the order of waypoints in a route by selecting Invert Route with the Menu function.

# WAAS and GPS Accuracy

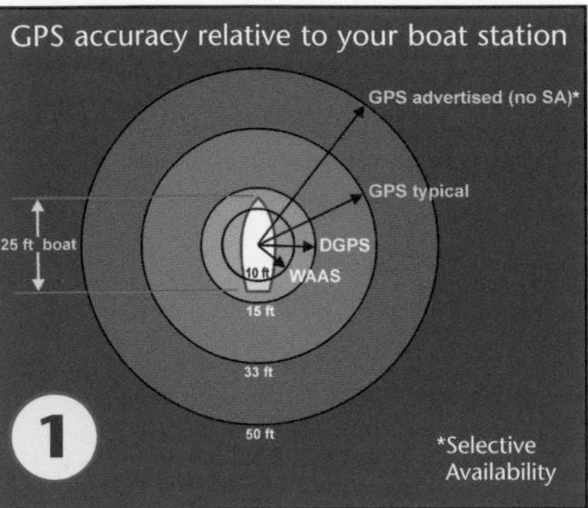


GPS fixes are quite accurate. In open water, knowing your position to within 30 to 50 feet ① is extraordinary compared with the accuracy of traditional navigation tools.

However, when you attempt to navigate within a harbor or channel, you may prefer somewhat higher accuracy. You have a choice of two systems to do that—DGPS or WAAS. Differential GPS (DGPS) is a U.S. Coast Guard system designed for mariners. Designed for aircraft by the Federal Aviation Administration, Wide Area Augmentation System (WAAS) also provides excellent service for boaters.

In both systems, fixed receivers at precisely known locations listen to the GPS satellites in view. Atmospheric and other factors cause the signals to produce a fix with some error. By adjusting the signals from each satellite until the right answer is obtained, these stations derive a set of corrections. Each system then transmits these corrections to your GPS.

WAAS transmits corrections at the same frequency as the GPS signals ② via geostationary satellites over each ocean. Once you enable WAAS in your system setup, your GPS receives these corrections and applies them to yield accuracies of 10 feet or better. But beware, your chart is likely to be less accurate than the GPS. Only newer GPS models have the software needed to receive WAAS corrections.

To receive DGPS corrections, you must have a DGPS antenna and receiver on your boat.

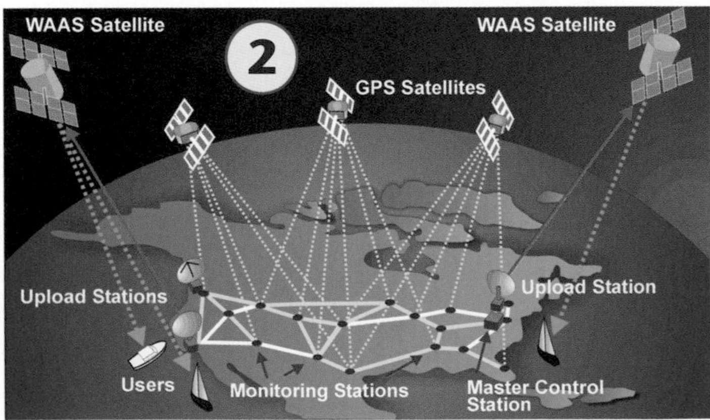

# Connecting Your GPS

Your GPS receiver is designed to share its data with other equipment both on and off your boat. Connecting the GPS to a computer is quite easy ①. The manufacturer of your GPS model can provide you with a cable designed to connect your GPS to the serial port on your computer ②.

The navigation software you select will then tell you how to set up the GPS. Now you can plan and monitor your cruise on a digital chart displayed on your PC.

GPS also can provide data for display on a radar screen or to control the autopilot in an integrated system ③.

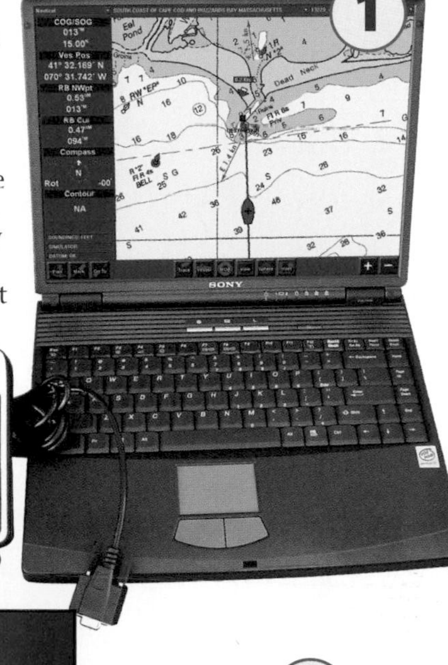

connecting cable for a Garmin handheld GPS

3

GPS communicates with other electronics using a protocol called NMEA 0183. There are only three wires involved: Data In, Data Out, and Ground. The Data Out from the GPS goes to the Data In port on the radar, autopilot, computer, etc. You can supply up to about three devices from a single GPS; however, the Data In port on any device can listen to only one source. You may need to solder wires onto special connectors, available from the GPS manufacturer.

CHAPTER 5

# Using VHF and SSB Radios

Bob Sweet

# Keeping in Touch on the Water

A number of options exist for communicating between boats or with the shore. Here's an overview:

## Near Shore

**Cellular phones** are especially convenient for conversations with those on land. However, the coast guard and other search-and-rescue agencies cannot direction-find an emergency cell phone call, and coverage is limited by the locations of relay towers on land.

**VHF (very high frequency) radio** (see pages 82–86) is the first choice for emergency calls as well as for routine communications. The VHF emergency channels are constantly monitored by national coast guards. VHF range is slightly greater than line-of-sight, since very high frequency radiowaves bend slightly over the horizon, but boat-to-boat transmissions are generally limited to about 20 nautical miles and may be shorter between powerboats with low antenna heights. Ship-to-shore calls may be possible at up to 30 miles due to the greater height of shore-based antennas.

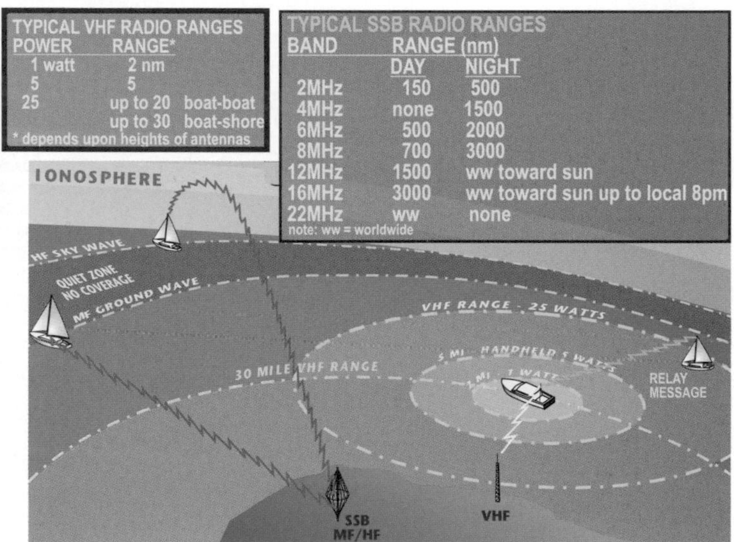

TYPICAL VHF RADIO RANGES

| POWER | RANGE* | |
|---|---|---|
| 1 watt | 2 nm | |
| 5 | 5 | |
| 25 | up to 20 | boat-boat |
| | up to 30 | boat-shore |

* depends upon heights of antennas

TYPICAL SSB RADIO RANGES

| BAND | RANGE (nm) DAY | NIGHT |
|---|---|---|
| 2MHz | 150 | 500 |
| 4MHz | none | 1500 |
| 6MHz | 500 | 2000 |
| 8MHz | 700 | 3000 |
| 12MHz | 1500 | ww toward sun |
| 16MHz | 3000 | ww toward sun up to local 8pm |
| 22MHz | ww | none |

note: ww = worldwide



## Offshore

**SSB (single sideband) radio** (see pages 88–90) is the popular choice for ship-to-ship and ship-to-shore communications beyond VHF range. Radiowaves at SSB high frequencies (HF) reflect from the ionosphere and thus can reach other transceivers thousands of miles away under the right propagation conditions. You must match your transmission frequency to the distance and atmospheric conditions. At shorter ranges out to 150 to 200 miles during the day (or as much as 500 miles at night), medium-frequency (MF) SSB signals (called groundwaves) wrap around the surface of the Earth. Worldwide weather broadcasts and e-mail services can be received as well.

**Satellite phones** offer reliable voice, fax, e-mail, and data communications throughout the world but are expensive. One company, Inmarsat, supports regular and emergency distress calls (except in polar regions) using satellites in geostationary orbit. Iridium and Globalstar provide satellite coverage using low orbiting satellite networks.

**Ham radio** (amateur radio) remains popular among cruisers, since licensed ham operators can speak with other licensed hams on land or sea, often in scheduled group gatherings or "nets," and can ask a shore-based ham to patch them through a telephone line without paying the stiff fees charged by SSB High Seas marine operators.

The General Class License required for voice communications over ham frequencies requires some knowledge of radio theory and ham operating protocol and the ability to receive Morse code at five words per minute. Passing the exam is not difficult, and ham radio equipment is less expensive than SSB while operating at similar frequencies and over similarly impressive distances.

NOTE: Neither ham radio nor a satellite phone is a proper substitute for an SSB marine radio, because the coast guard does not continuously monitor ham frequencies or satellite phone communications. This chapter will therefore concentrate on VHF and SSB radio communications.

**EPIRBs** (Emergency Position-Indicating Radio Beacons, see page 93) are stand-alone portable units that can be activated in a distressed boat, a lifeboat, or in the water to summon help offshore. EPIRB signals are relayed via overhead satellites to coast guard and other search-and-rescue centers. Modern EPIRBs identify the boat from which they came and even provide GPS coordinates to rescuers, but a beacon does not allow two-way communications.

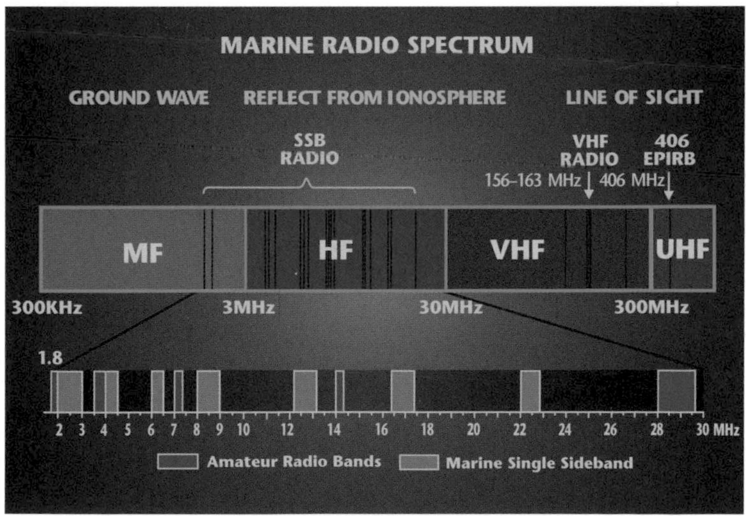

# Meet Your VHF Radio

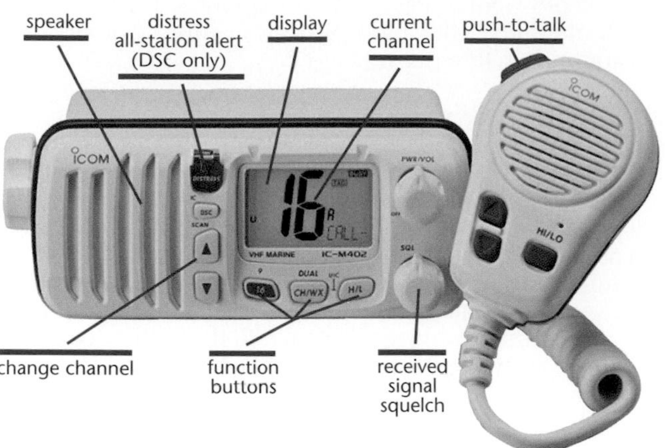


VHF marine radios are available as either fixed or handheld. Virtually all fixed units offer the legal maximum transmitting power of 25 watts, whereas most handheld transceivers (like the one shown in page 84) are limited by battery capacity to no more than 5 or 6 watts. The great advantages of handheld radios are their portability and their self-contained antennas, but their dependable boat-to-boat transmission ranges are limited to 3 to 5 miles or so by power level and antenna height. Fixed radios like the one shown above require a separate antenna, but a good antenna installed high on a sailboat's masthead or a powerboat's flybridge provides much greater communication ranges.

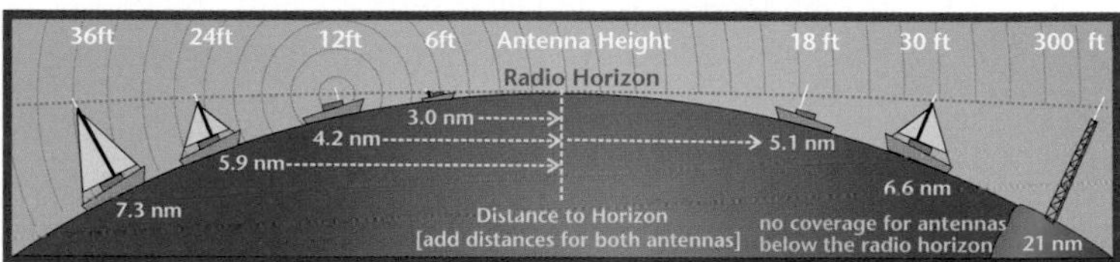


VHF antennas transmit equally in all horizontal directions, but longer antennas provide extra "gain" by focusing the available energy to lower elevations as illustrated below. Gain is described in decibels (dB). Since sailboats heel, a lower-gain antenna avoids missed coverage. Powerboats don't have tall masts that extend range, so they sometimes benefit from a higher gain—say, 6 dB. A 6 dB antenna might be 8 feet long and weigh 5 pounds, whereas a 9 dB antenna might be 24 feet long and weigh as much as 12 pounds.

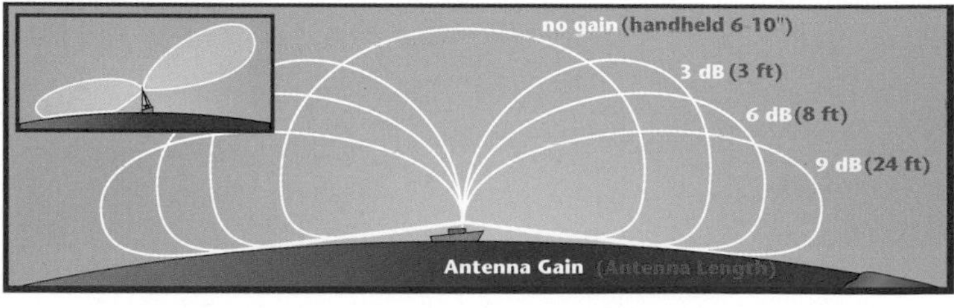

All VHF radios must have a 1-watt power setting for short-range communications to minimize stepping on other users over a wide area. All radios manufactured since 1987 switch automatically to the 1-watt setting when transmitting on channels 13, 17, 67, and 77 but permit a manual override to maximum power for emergency bridge-to-bridge communications on channel 13.

## VHF Radio Controls

A typical VHF radio includes the following features and controls:

**Microphone:** You must press the transmit button (on side) to talk. Many microphones have remote controls for channel selection, volume, and power level.

**Channel Select:** Up-down buttons (or rotary dial) to change the active channels for transmission and reception.

**Volume:** Controls the speaker sound level.

**Squelch:** Represses all signals below the threshold set by the control, thus eliminating annoying static. Reduce the squelch until static can just be heard, then advance it slightly to eliminate static.

**Emergency:** This protected switch is found only on radios equipped for digital selective calling (DSC, see page 92). Press only in an emergency. It sends a digital signal on the DSC emergency channel (70) providing your identity and (if interfaced with GPS or loran) your location, and sounds an alarm on all DSC-equipped radios.

**HI/LO:** Switches a fixed VHF radio between the 1-watt transmit level mandated for short-range communications and the optional high-power level (25 watts for fixed units) required for longer-range communications.

**WX:** Switches the VHF radio from the communication channels to the NOAA weather receive-only channels. Some models also provide an automated alarm in response to a NOAA weather alert.

**DSC:** Since 1999, new VHF radio models must be equipped with digital selective calling, or DSC (see page 92). Pressing the DSC button permits you to call another DSC radio whose number is stored in your radio, much as if you were dialing a phone number. The digital signaling alerts the other radio that you have called and automatically switches that unit to the working channel you have selected.

**Note:** Pre-DSC VHF marine radio models were still recently being manufactured and will remain in use for years to come.

## Other VHF Functions

A good VHF marine radio may also offer the following functions:

**16/9:** Pressing this button immediately sets the channel to 16 (the distress, safety, and calling channel). A second press sets the channel to 9 (the standard alternate calling channel).
**Scan:** Pressing this button (and on this example, holding the button down for a second) causes the radio to continuously scan through the channels that you have "tagged" until a signal is heard. It will continue scanning after the signal ends until you press the channel select button or the 16/9 button.
**Priority Scan:** Ensures that channel 16 is scanned between each of the other frequencies on your scan list.
**Intercom:** Some VHF models can be operated from a remote microphone, which might be placed at the helm while the radio itself is below decks. The intercom function permits direct conversations between someone at the radio and someone at the remote microphone. Such conversations are not transmitted.
**Dual/Tri-Mode Watch:** Scans the radio between distress/signaling and intership channels.
**Panel Lighting:** Illuminates the display and buttons for nighttime use.
**Hailer:** Interfaces the microphone through external loudspeakers for hailing nearby boats. These hails are not transmitted.
**Scrambler:** Some VHF radios will accommodate add-on devices to scramble communications on all channels except the emergency channels 16 and 70, so that confidential conversations cannot be overheard.

## VHF Use

Recreational boats, in addition to hired vessels with no more than six passengers, are considered "voluntary vessels" and are not required to carry a VHF radio or to maintain a license to operate one domestically (so long as you do not visit or communicate with a foreign port). If you do have a VHF radio, however, you must monitor channel 16, the international distress channel, at all times. Having all radios tuned to 16 increases the probability that a distress call will be heard, and relayed if necessary.

If you carry both a VHF radio and an SSB MF/HF transceiver, you must use the VHF rather than the SSB whenever possible. The reason is simple: VHF communications, unlike SSB, are incapable of hogging a channel over ranges of hundreds or even thousands of miles.

Handheld VHF radios like the one shown at right are not permitted for use on shore. However, you may use yours to communicate with your ship at 1 watt using the ship's name followed by "unit 1." Most handheld radios do not have DSC capability and therefore cannot provide coded distress alerts or position information.

# VHF Channels

The marine VHF band falls between 156 and 163 megahertz (MHz). Within this narrow band are many channels, only a few of which concern the recreational boater. But with these few channels you can contact the coast guard and other rescue services, communicate with other vessels, and call marinas, restaurants, bridge tenders, harbormasters, and other shoreside stations. You can receive marine weather reports and navigational notices, and you can contact shore-based marine operators who, for a fee, will connect you with the land-based telephone grid or with other boats that are beyond your direct VHF range.

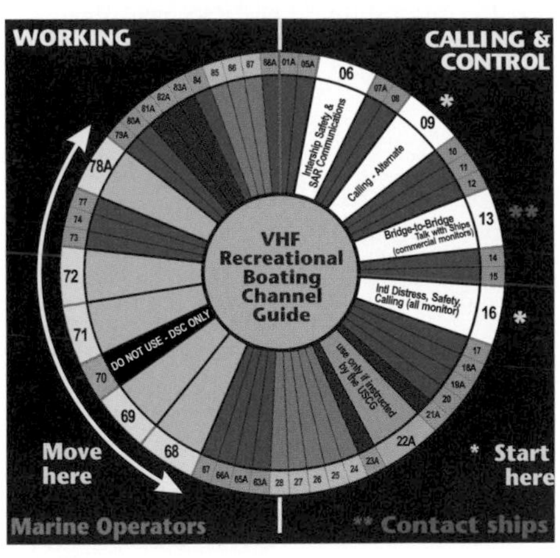


**VHF CHANNEL USAGE** has been established by international treaty and is enforced in the U.S. by the FCC. Recreational boaters should confine their communications to the channels that are drawn wider in the graphic above. You will initiate most calls on channel 16 (or 9 if you are in certain areas, know that it is monitored, or have prearranged this channel). When the other party answers, immediately arrange to switch to a working channel so as to keep CH16 open (see page 86).

**CHANNEL 16** is the International Distress frequency and is also used for safety messages and calling (initiating a contact). Anyone hearing a distress call must monitor this channel and await a response from the coast guard. If none is heard, relay the distress call and attempt contact—you may be able to relay communications between rescue personnel and the vessel in distress. When you contact the coast guard on CH16, you will usually be directed to switch to CH22A for further communications.

**WORKING CHANNELS** are intended for messages about the needs of the ship, including fishing reports, rendezvous, scheduling repairs, and berthing information. General conversation is prohibited, so as to keep the channels as free as possible. Use channel 72 for ship-to-ship messages only.

**COMMERCIAL SHIPS** are required to monitor channel 13 in addition to channel 16. When crossing paths with commercial ships, you are well advised to contact them via channel 13. Describe your vessel, your location relative to the ship (e.g., "I'm a 30-foot white sloop one-half mile off your port bow"), and what you are planning.

**WEATHER CHANNELS** are designated for receive-only. Meteorological services (NOAA in the U.S.) broadcast continuous weather reports on these channels. Scan to find the strongest signal for your area. Channels are labeled as WX1, WX2, . . . etc.

**MARINE OPERATORS** can link you to land lines for a fee. Make advance arrangements or place collect calls.

# VHF Radio Call Procedures

Marine frequencies are crowded. Take the time to pre-plan your call and message and write your station ID information in the blanks below so you have it handy:

Your Boat Name phonetically ______________________
Your MMSI (if DSC equipped)* ______________________
Your Call Sign (if you have a license)** ______________

*Note: The Maritime Mobile Service Identity, or MMSI, is the nine-digit number that is assigned to a DSC marine radio and identifies its operator just as your telephone number identifies you at home. Only the new, digital radios have MMSIs. If your radio and the one you're calling are both DSC-capable, you can direct your call selectively to the station you want. And in case you're wondering, digital and analog radios can talk to each other just fine.

**Note: If you have an FCC radio license, use the call sign after the name of the boat at the beginning and end of the session.

## When You Make a Call

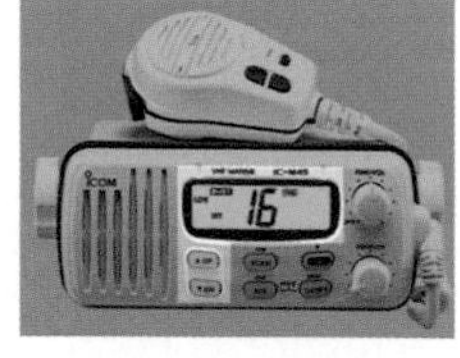

**Select:** Usually you will initiate a call on CH16 (or CH9 when CH16 is crowded). Set the POWER to LO unless the call is urgent or must reach some distance. If another channel has been prearranged, use it or the listed channel of a shore station.

**Listen:** You may not interrupt or "step on" other communications. Wait for a brief period of silence. (Set the volume and squelch, then listen.)

**Press:** After pressing the MIC PTT (push-to-talk) button, wait a second before speaking to ensure that your transmitter is operating and will not cut off the first part of your message.

**Speak:** Hold the MIC a few inches from your mouth and slightly to the side. Speak normally, but clearly and distinctly. In less than 30 seconds, say " 'Boat A' (up to three times, followed by MMSI or call sign if applicable) calling 'Boat B' (three times), Over."

**Listen:** Release MIC PTT button. If no answer, repeat in 2 minutes, then again in another 2 minutes. If still no answer, try again after no less than 15 minutes.

**Exchange Messages:** If you get an answer, listen for " 'Boat B' calling 'Boat A.' " Assuming you and your caller are not using DSC-capable radios, your caller should direct you to a working channel such as "six-ate" (not sixty-eight), then say, "Over." (DSC radios automatically retune from CH70 [the DSC digital call channel] to an analog working channel for the follow-on voice communications.) Tune to the working channel within 1 minute, press MIC, and say, " 'Boat A' calling 'Boat B,' " then provide your message, followed by "Over."

**End:** After the last message, either party says, " 'Boat Name,' Out."

# Radio Speak for VHF and SSB Radios

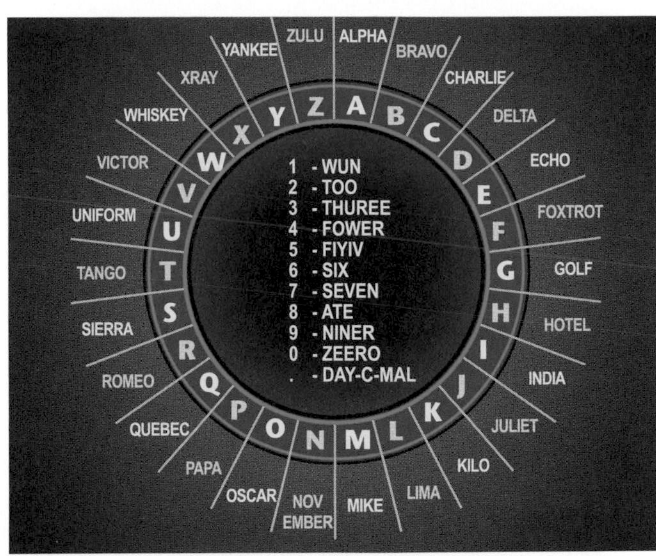


**PHONETIC ALPHABET** use is recommended when speaking on VHF or SSB radio, because words, letters, and numbers can be distorted over the air, leading to mistakes. The phonetic terms above are internationally recognized. Speak slowly and clearly, emphasizing syllables when spelling out words or numbers.

**PROCEDURE WORDS** are used as shorthand, as follows:

**Over:** Signifies that you have ended your transmission but expect a reply.

**Out:** Indicates that you have completed your communication.

**Roger:** Acknowledges that a message was received and understood.

**Affirmative:** Indicates agreement. Alternatively, say "Yes."

**Negative:** Indicates disagreement. Alternatively, say "No."

**Say Again:** Requests the sender to repeat the last transmission.

**This is "name of boat":** Used to identify you.

**Wait:** Indicates that you must pause, but want the other station to continue to listen, followed by "Wait Out" to resume.

**I Spell:** Precedes phonetic spelling.

**Break:** Marks a change in message.

**Word after (or before):** Points to a specific word.

**Silence (see-lonce):** spoken by Coast Guard three times to keep routine traffic off an emergency frequency during a Mayday situation, and maintained until lifted with "Silence Fini" (see-lonce fee-nee).

# Meet Your SSB Marine Radio

Most SSB marine radios are digitally tuned and provide about 100–150 watts of transmitting power. They can tune in the frequency range from 0.5 to 30 MHz (500 to 30,000 kilohertz), which includes shortwave and ham bands, and they transmit on allocated marine bands.

A typical SSB marine radio is shown below. Models (there are fewer to choose from than is the case for VHF radios) vary by signal quality, power, and the functions offered. SSB radios with DSC capability are available but still very expensive and thus found mainly on commercial ships, where they are required.

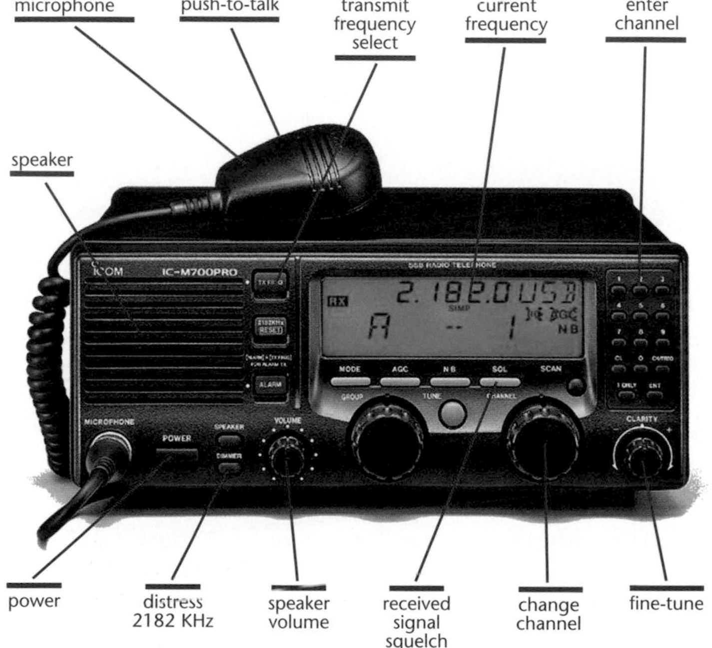


**Microphone:** You must select a frequency band and then press the transmit button (on side of microphone) to talk.

**Channel Select:** Internationally allocated marine frequencies usually are pre-programmed. They can be selected using a digital keypad or (in this model) with two rotary knobs, one to select a frequency band and the other to tune a frequency within the selected band.

**Clarity:** Fine-tunes the received frequency to compensate for any minor differences between the transmitter and the receiver.

**Volume:** Controls the speaker sound level.

**Squelch:** Cuts off reception of all signals below the level set by the control. Adjust to the level at which static can just be heard, then advance slightly to eliminate static. Stronger signals still will be received.

# Using SSB Radios

SSB marine radios require a station license to operate. A VHF radio must be installed and used in preference over SSB. Beyond VHF range, SSB provides generally reliable communications, but SSB radios are somewhat more complex to operate. They offer channels in seven frequency bands ranging from 2 MHz (2000 KHz) to 22 MHz (22,000 KHz). The selection of a particular band and channel depends upon the application (voice, digital, or telex), the locations of the two stations, the time of day, the season, and other propagation factors.

The international SSB distress frequency is 2182 KHz, which has a range of up to about 200 miles via groundwave propagation by day, or 500 miles by night. You may need to transmit distress signals on other frequencies in order to reach assistance.

**Antenna:** The frequencies employed with SSB radios require a much longer antenna than those used with VHF. On a sailboat, the backstay can be converted into an antenna by electrically isolating the top and bottom of the wire. The antenna is connected to an antenna tuner, which matches the characteristics of the antenna to the transceiver for each frequency used. On a powerboat, a whip antenna, typically 23 to 30 feet long, is used. Generally, these antennas must be supported at an intermediate height as well as at the bottom.

**Grounding:** Effective radiation of MF/HF energy requires a good ground plane (the ocean) and the system must have good coupling between the boat and the sea. This can be accomplished using metallic plates within the hull below the waterline. These plates couple effectively to the ocean at SSB frequencies, even through the hull.

**Licenses:** To operate an SSB radio, you must have a Station License for your boat and a Restricted Marine Operators Permit (RP) for each user. In the U.S., the Station License is obtained by filing FCC Form 605 and Form 159 (fee processing form). The RP is obtained by filing Forms 753 and 159. These forms can be obtained at www.fcc.gov. These licenses are not required for VHF, radar, or EPIRB used on recreational boats not communicating with or entering foreign ports.

**Channels:** By international treaties, marine radios are restricted in the frequencies that can be transmitted. The International Telecommunications Union (ITU) has designated frequencies for safety and working channels across the MF and HF bands. Most modern SSB radios come preprogrammed with those frequencies. You can listen to any frequency but must transmit only on allocated frequencies unless you also are licensed as a ham radio operator. The channels are numbered with the first one or two digits reflecting the band; channel 401 is in the 4 MHz band, and channel 2236 is in the 22 MHz band. Separate frequencies are used for receiving and transmitting for each channel. For example, channel 241 transmits on 2.06 MHz but receives on 1.635 MHz; channel 401 transmits on 4.065 MHz and receives on 4.375 MHz; etc.

**Calling:** You must give your call sign each time you call another vessel or coast station, at the end of each transmission that lasts more than 3 minutes, and every 15 minutes during ship-to-shore calls. In addition, you must maintain a log of all distress, emergency, and safety calls, and a log of all adjustments or maintenance signed by a licensed technician.

# SSB Frequencies

The major consideration in using SSB communications is selection of a frequency band. You must transmit on only those frequencies allocated for your purpose within the band you select.

MF/HF radio waves travel beyond line-of-sight, either hugging the Earth (medium frequencies) or reflecting from the ionosphere (high frequencies). The characteristics of the ionosphere change dramatically from day to night, with seasons, and through an 11-year sunspot cycle.

**SSB Coverage**

```
Range    |---|---|---|---|---|---|----|----|------|------|------|------|-------|
         0  200 400 600 700 800 1000 1500 2000  3000   4000   5000   6000   7000 mi
Night    Range (mi)
 2 MHz   |--------500 (groundwave)
 4 MHz   |xx200------------------------2000
 6 MHz   |xxxxxx500-------------------2000
 8 MHz   |xxxxxx500--------------------------3000
12 MHz   |xxxxxxxxxxxxxxxxxxxxxxxxxxxxxxxxxxxx
Day
 2 MHz   |--200 (groundwave)
 4 MHz   |xxxxxxxx
 6 MHz   |---------500
 8 MHz   |--------------700
12 MHz   |xxxxxx500*-----------------2000
16 MHz   |xxxxxxxxxxxx750*-----------------------4000..........6000
22 MHz   |xxxxxxxxxxxxxxxxxxxx1500*----------------------------------7000
xxx Skip zone, no coverage          Min Range-------Max Range
* no coverage until late morning, minimum range for local noon
```

**Nighttime:** The ionosphere is lower and less reflective at night, so frequencies above the 8 MHz band may pass right through out to space. Consequently, you will need to use lower frequencies than during the day. Frequencies near 2 MHz can be used out to about 500 miles, propagating as groundwaves, but these medium frequencies may be absorbed and not reflected by the ionosphere to greater distances. Using higher frequencies, you might get reflection and much greater distances via one or more "hops," but these signals may be absorbed and not reflected at shorter ranges, creating a "skip zone." For example, using the 6 MHz band, you may be able to communicate as close as 500 miles or as far as 2,000 miles via multiple reflections, or hops. As soon as these signals reach a time zone experiencing daylight, however, conditions will change, causing the signals to be absorbed and go no farther.

**Daytime:** The ionosphere is much higher, thicker, and more reflective. Many of the nighttime frequencies will be absorbed. Groundwave propagation still works near 2 MHz and can be used out to about 200 miles during the day, but it is susceptible to interference. Begin with the nominal frequencies shown in the table, and adjust upward or downward to increase or decrease the distance to be reached. Listen to other transmissions at various frequencies and attempt to correlate distance with frequency. Usually, the strongest signal will be received at the highest frequency that just reaches the desired range. PC software is available to help with frequency selection.

# Emergency Calls

There are three types of calls (DISTRESS, URGENCY, and SAFETY). These are transmitted on VHF CH16 or SSB 2182 KHz. The procedures are slightly different for each, as follows:

**DISTRESS:** is reserved for situations involving risk of life and/or grave and immediate danger. It calls for immediate assistance. It has priority over all other forms of traffic. (If you are using a DSC-equipped radio, initiate your Mayday call by pressing the Distress button as outlined on page 92.)

**Distress Signal:** MAYDAY
Provide the following message:

MAYDAY, MAYDAY, MAYDAY...
This is:
Boat Name ____________________(repeat three times)
Call Sign (if you have a license)_____________(once)
MAYDAY, Boat Name____________________
Position is: Lat_______________Lon_______________, or
______nm_______(N,S,E,W) of______________________
Nature of Distress ________________
Assistance Required ________________________________
Boat description ______________________________
No. of persons on board ________Other_______________
OVER

**URGENCY:** is reserved for situations involving the safety of the ship or some person on board that is serious but has not yet reached the level of immediate peril (loss of steering, medical difficulty, etc.). It calls for assistance.

**Urgency Signal**: PAN-PAN (pronounced PAHN-PAHN)
Provide the following message:

PAN-PAN, PAN-PAN, PAN-PAN...
ALL STATIONS (or particular coast guard station) (once)
This is:
Boat Name____________________(once)
Call Sign (if you have a license)_____________(once)
Urgency message (assistance required): _________________
Position is: Lat_________Lon___________, or
______nm_______(N,S,E,W) of______________________
This is: Boat Name_______________(once)
OVER

**SAFETY:** is reserved for information regarding navigation safety. The coast guard encourages all mariners to transmit safety messages when they spot a hazard to navigation (buoy off-station, floating log, etc.).

**Safety Signal:** SECURITE (pronounced SAY-CUR-I-TAY)
Provide the following message:

SECURITE, SECURITE, SECURITE...
ALL STATIONS (once)
This is:
Boat Name____________________(once)
Channel # for message: ____________________________
OUT (go to channel, repeat above, and provide message)

# Using DSC-Equipped VHF Radios

DSC (Digital Selective Calling) helps to free up crowded channels and vastly speeds rescue operations. On VHF, channel 70 is dedicated to DSC. (On SSB, the DSC frequency is 2187.5 KHz to call the U.S. Coast Guard.)

DSC transmits a digital signal that includes the MMSI (Maritime Mobile Service Identity) number unique to your boat, as well as your position (if your VHF transceiver is connected to a GPS receiver). It also transmits data about the type of call and the intended recipients. DSC calls can be placed to all users for distress or selectively to a single ship or group for routine message traffic. When not transmitting, your DSC-equipped VHF transceiver monitors channel 70 (SSB monitors 2187.5 KHz), sounds a tone corresponding to the type of incoming call, and automatically tunes to the appropriate frequency for the subsequent incoming message.

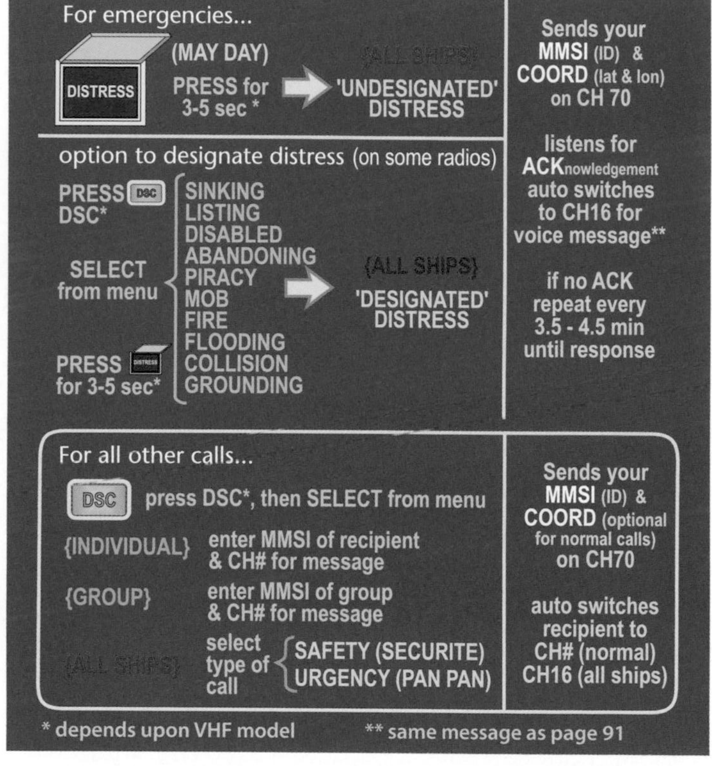


**MMSI:** You must register your DSC radio. You will provide key information about your identity and boat that will be essential in the event of a distress. To make individual or group calls, you will need the MMSIs of the radios you wish to call. The U.S. Coast Guard group MMSI is 003669999. In addition, local USCG and Canadian Coast Guard stations have individual MMSIs. Contact local authorities for these numbers.

(Note: SSB DSC frequencies include 2187.5, 4207.5, 6312, 8414.5, 12577, and 16804.5 KHz. Ships equipped for GMDSS [Global Maritime Distress and Safety System] will monitor these frequencies in addition to VHF CH70.)

# EPIRBs and GMDSS

The Global Maritime Distress and Safety System (GMDSS) provides a worldwide method for monitoring and providing assistance at sea. One of the key components of this system, particularly for offshore operations, is the EPIRB (Emergency Position-Indicating Radio Beacon). Radio reports are preferred, but in some situations the radio may not be available, such as after abandoning ship. For these applications the EPIRB is essential.

An EPIRB is a self-contained radio beacon. Several types and categories are available, but the most current system uses a 406 MHz transmitter to send coded messages to satellites. Two types of satellites receive these messages. Low orbiting satellites receive the message when over the EPIRB and relay it when near a local ground terminal (Local User Terminal). Geostationary satellites are higher and can relay messages immediately.

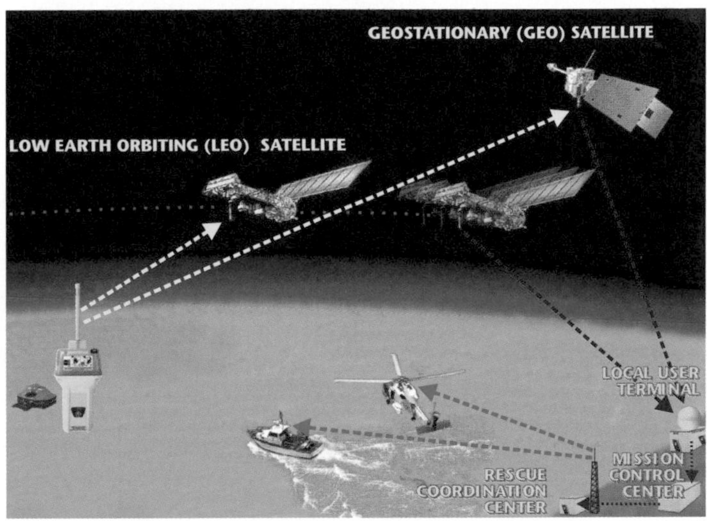


Each EPIRB is registered, so the ground station knows the identity of the sender and the location, which is ascertained by the satellites. Position location accuracy can be enhanced by EPIRBs that incorporate a GPS unit.

Once an alert is received and verified, the rescue operators attempt land contact at the address and number in the registration. Then a message is sent to the local rescue coordination center that directs the rescue.

The EPIRB is only a signaling device, so the nature of the distress is unknown to rescuers. It is the communication mode of last resort but effective in quick response. The EPIRB can be used only under life-threatening conditions.

Some EPIRBs contain a 121.5 MHz aircraft frequency as well. This frequency originally was intended to be monitored by commercial aircraft, but its use by recreational boaters is prohibited by the U.S. Coast Guard as of 2007.

If choosing an EPIRB, insist on a 406 MHz model. The 406 MHz channel is digital and can pass information quickly. You have a choice of manual or automatic (the latter being activated by immersion), and the option of an internal GPS unit for precise position information that will be transmitted along with the distress signal.

CHAPTER 6

# Rules of the Road and Running Light Patterns

**Charlie Wing**

# Why the Rules Matter

We are all familiar with the rules governing vehicular traffic: stay to the right; pass on the left; give way at an intersection to a vehicle on your right; don't exceed the speed limit. These rules are easily remembered because streets and highways are marked with reminders: solid and dashed lines marking traffic lanes, stop signs, traffic lights and speed limit signs.

Piloting a boat is more like driving in an open field—there are no streets, no traffic lights, and no signs. Despite the differences, however, there are remarkable similarities between the rules for vehicular and boating traffic.

The International Regulations for the Prevention of Collision at Sea (COLREGs) are the "Rules of the Road" for the ocean. The United States Inland Rules govern U.S. Great Lakes, bays, inlets, rivers, and waterways that connect to the sea. The boundary between the two jurisdictions is shown as a dashed magenta (red) Demarcation Line on nautical charts. The two sets of Rules are, fortunately, identical in most respects. In this chapter we clearly indicate where they differ.

This chapter does not include the entire text of the 225-page Rules. What it does contain is visual explanations of the rules you are likely to encounter as a recreational boater. In all cases we've provided the corresponding rule number from the official rules.

**Purpose of the Rules.** The purpose of the Rules is NOT to grant one boat the "right-of-way" over another. Avoiding a collision between two boats requires the participation of both. Rather, the purpose of the Rules is to present, in any situation where two boats encounter one another, guidelines for the action required of each. Under the Rules, one boat is designated the **stand-on vessel**; the other the **give-way vessel**. These designations carry obligations for each vessel to act in a specified way to avoid collision. Note that the Rules do not address situations involving more than two boats. In such instances common sense must be the principal guide.

**Application (Rule 1).** The Rules apply to ALL VESSELS on the high seas and navigable waters connected with the high seas.

**Responsibility (Rule 2).** Nothing in the Rules exonerates any vessel or its owner, master, or crew from the consequences of neglect to comply with the Rules or neglect of precaution which may be required by the ordinary practice of seamen or by the special circumstances of the situation.

**Key Definitions (Rule 3).**

*Underway:* not anchored, grounded, or otherwise attached to shore. A boat does not have to be moving either through the water or over the ground to be underway.

*Restricted visibility:* any condition other than night that reduces visibility, including fog and heavy rain.

*Vessel:* anything that carries people or cargo on or in the water, including kayaks, personal watercraft, seaplanes, and supertankers.

*Give-way vessel:* the vessel obligated to keep out of the way of the other.

*Stand-on vessel:* the vessel obligated to maintain its course and speed unless an alteration is necessary to avoid collision.

*Power-driven vessel:* any vessel underway with an engine that does not fall into any of the other categories defined below.

*Sailing vessel:* a sailboat underway with sails only, not using an engine.

*Vessel engaged in fishing:* any boat fishing with equipment that limits its ability to maneuver (nets, trawls, etc.).

*Vessel not under command:* a vessel unable to maneuver as required by the Rules, due to mechanical breakdown or any other reason.

*Vessel restricted in her ability to maneuver:* a vessel that, due to the nature of her work, cannot maneuver easily. Examples include buoy tenders, dredges, dive boats, mine sweepers, and tugs with difficult tows.

*Vessel constrained by her draft:* a vessel that may go aground if it deviates from its course. (The *Inland Rules* do not contain this definition.)

**Lookout (Rule 5).** Every vessel must at all times maintain a proper lookout by all means available in the prevailing circumstances and conditions (including radar even under conditions of unlimited visibility) so as to make a full appraisal of the situation and of the risk of collision.

**Safe Speed (Rule 6).** Every vessel must at all times proceed at a *safe speed* so that she can take proper and effective action to avoid collision and be stopped within a distance appropriate to the prevailing circumstances and conditions.

**Risk of Collision (Rule 7).** Every vessel must use all available means appropriate to the prevailing circumstances and conditions to determine if risk of collision exists. When there is *any doubt,* risk must be assumed to exist. Risk exists if the compass bearing (or relative bearing, if you are on a steady course) to an approaching vessel does not appreciably change as the vessel draws nearer.

**Action to Avoid Collision (Rule 8).** Action to avoid collision must, if circumstances permit, be positive, made in ample time, and with due regard to good seamanship.

Alteration of course and/or speed to avoid collision must, if circumstances allow, be large enough to be readily apparent to the other vessel; a succession of small alterations of course and/or speed should be avoided.

If necessary to avoid collision or to allow more time to assess the situation, a vessel must reduce speed or take all way off by stopping or reversing engines.

**Remaining Rules (Rules 9–37).** Rules 9–18 (see *At-a-Glance Guide*) spell out the actions to be taken to avoid collision. Rule 19 (see *What to Do in Fog*) specifies conduct in restricted visibility. Rules 20–31 (see pages 98–103 and 105) describe lights and shapes to display, and Rules 32–37 (see *Sound Signals*) specify sound signals.

# Power-Driven Vessels Underway *(Rule 23)*

| RULE/VESSEL | GROUPS | SHAPES | BOW | STERN |
|---|---|---|---|---|
| **BOTH INTERNATIONAL AND INLAND**<br>**Rule 23(a)**<br>Power-driven<br>≥50 m | 2 Mastheads<br>Sidelights<br>Sternlight | None | 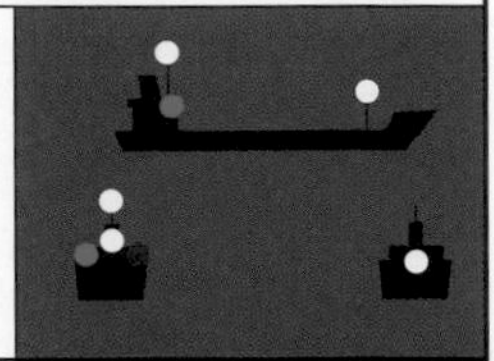 | |
| **INLAND (GREAT LAKES ONLY)**<br>**Rule 23(a)**<br>Power-driven<br>≥50 m | Masthead<br>Sidelights<br>All-around for 2nd masthead + stern | None | 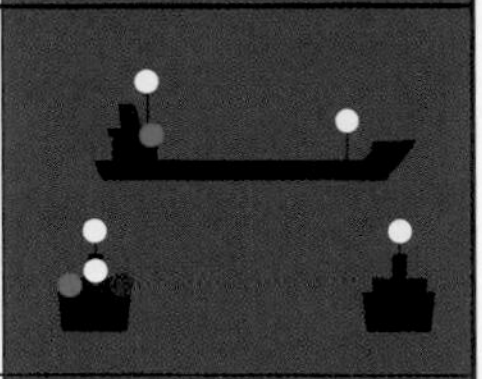 | |
| **BOTH INTERNATIONAL AND INLAND**<br>**Rule 23(a)**<br>Power-driven<br><50 m | Masthead<br>Sidelights<br>Sternlight | None | 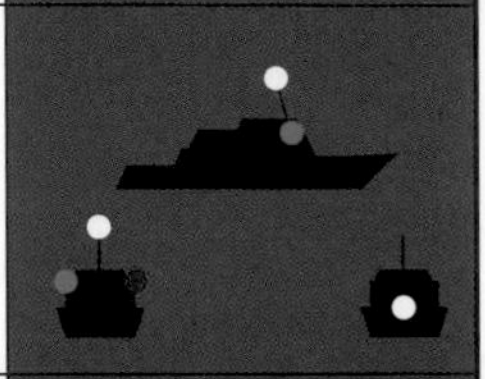 | |
| **Rule 23(c)**<br>Power-driven<br>optional <12 m | Sidelights<br>All-around in lieu of masthead and stern | None | 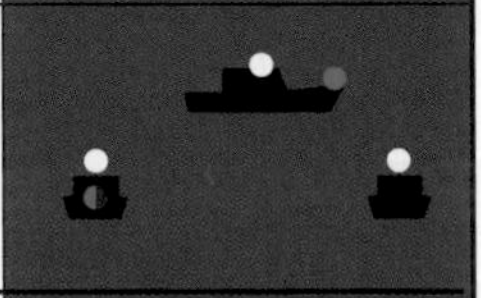 | |
| **INTERNATIONAL ONLY**<br>**Rule 23(c)(ii)**<br>Power-driven<br><7 m & <7 kn max. | Sidelights if practical<br>All-around | None | 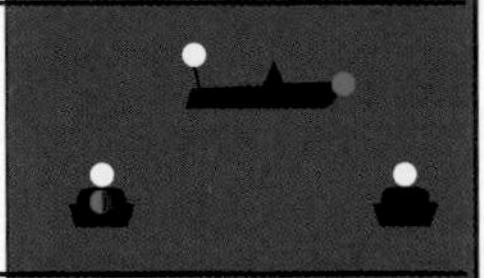 | |
| **BOTH INTERNATIONAL AND INLAND**<br>**Rule 23(b)**<br>Submarine | 2 Mastheads<br>Sidelights<br>Sternlight<br>Flashing Yellow, 1/sec. for 3 sec., followed by 3 sec. off | None |  | |
| **Rule 23(b)**<br>Hovercraft in displacement mode<br><50 m | Masthead<br>Sidelights<br>Sternlight | None | 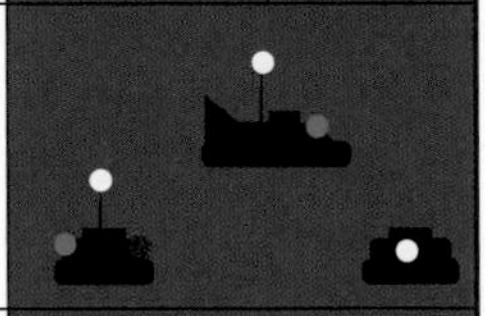 | |
| **Rule 23(b)**<br>Hovercraft non-displacement mode<br><50 m | Masthead<br>Sidelights<br>Sternlight<br>Flashing Yellow | None | 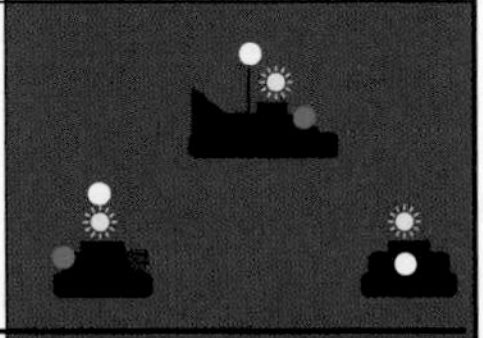 | |
| **INLAND ONLY**<br>**Rule 23(a)**<br>Law Enforcement<br><50 m | Masthead<br>Sidelights<br>Sternlight<br>Flashing Blue | None |  | |

# Vessels Towing and Pushing *(Rule 24)*

| RULE/VESSEL | GROUPS | SHAPES | BOW | STERN |
|---|---|---|---|---|
| **BOTH INTERNATIONAL AND INLAND** | | | | |
| **24(a)**/Towing astern (Tow 200 m) | 2 vert. Mastheads<br>Sidelights<br>Sternlight<br>Towlight | None | | |
| If vessel 50 m, add | Masthead aft | | | |
| **24(a)**/Towing astern (Tow > 200 m) | 3 vert. Mastheads<br>Sidelights<br>Sternlight<br>Towlight | ◆ | | |
| If vessel 50 m, add | Masthead aft | | | |
| **24(b)**/Composite (treated as single power vessel) | Masthead<br>Sidelights<br>Sternlight | None | | |
| If composite 50 m, add | Masthead aft | | | |
| **24(c)**/Pushing ahead or towing alongside (not composite) | 2 vert. Mastheads<br>Sidelights<br>Sternlight | None | | |
| If vessel 50 m, add | Masthead aft | | | |
| **24(e)**/Vessel/object being towed astern (other than 24(g)) (Tow 200 m) | Sidelights fwd<br>Sternlight | None | | |
| **24(e)**/Vessel/object being towed astern (other than 24(g)) (Tow >200 m) | Sidelights fwd<br>Sternlight | ◆ | | |
| **24(g)**/Partly submerged 100 m long (<25 m wide) | All-arounds forward & aft | ◆ | | |
| (25 m wide) | Add all-arounds on beams | | | |
| Partly submerged >100 m long (<25 m wide) | All-arounds forward & aft and every 100 m | ◆ ◆<br>aft fwd | | |
| (25 m wide) | All-arounds forward & aft<br>Add beam all-arounds every 100 m | If tow >200 m | | |
| **INTERNATIONAL ONLY** | | | | |
| **24(f)**/Multiple vessels/objects being pushed ahead | Sidelights fwd | None | | |
| **24(f)**/Multiple vessels/objects being towed alongside | Sidelights<br>Sternlight | None | | |
| **INLAND ONLY** | | | | |
| **24(f)**/Multiple vessels/objects being pushed ahead | Sidelights fwd<br>Special flashing | None | | |
| **24(f)**/Multiple vessels/objects being towed alongside | Sidelights<br>Sternlight<br>Special flashing | None | | |
| **24(f)**/Multiple vessels/objects being towed alongside BOTH sides | Sidelights<br>2 Sternlights<br>Special flashing | None | | |
| **INLAND Western Rivers except below Huey Long Bridge** | | | | |
| **24(i)**/Pushing ahead or towing alongside (not composite) | Sidelights<br>2 Towing lights<br>NO mastheads<br>NO sternlight | None | | |

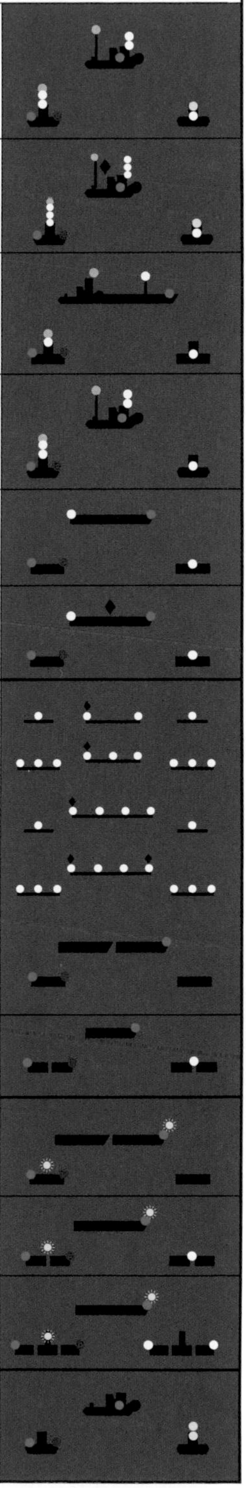

# Sailing & Rowing Vessels Underway *(Rule 25)*

| RULE/VESSEL | GROUPS | SHAPES | BOW | STERN |
|---|---|---|---|---|
| **BOTH INTERNATIONAL AND INLAND** | | | | |
| **Rule 25(a)**<br>Sailing only<br>any length | Sidelights<br>Sternlight | None | 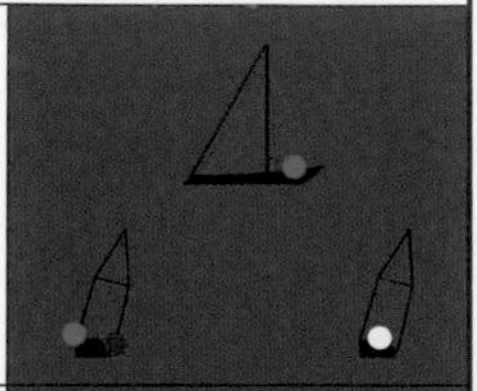 | |
| **Rule 25(b)**<br>Sailing only<br><20 m option | Tri-color | None | 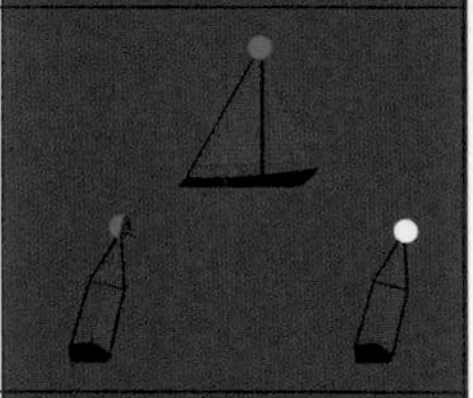 | |
| **Rule 25(c)**<br>Sailing only<br>optional any length | Sidelights<br>Sternlight<br>R/G all-around | None | 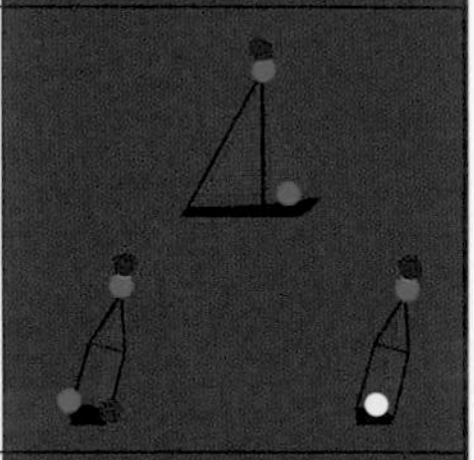 | |
| **Rule 25(d)(i)**<br>Sailing or Rowing<br><7 m | Sidelights<br>Sternlight | None |  | |
| **Rule 25(d)(ii)**<br>Sailing or Rowing<br><7 m option | All-around<br>or show only<br>to prevent<br>collision | None |  | |
| **Rule 25(e)**<br>Motorsailing<br>≥50 m | 2 Mastheads<br>Sidelights<br>Sternlight | ▼ |  | |
| **Rule 25(e)**<br>Motorsailing<br><50 m | Masthead<br>Sidelights<br>Sternlight | ▼ |  | |
| **Rule 25(e)**<br>Motorsailing<br><12 m | Masthead<br>Sidelights<br>Sternlight | ▼<br>Optional<br>under<br>Inland<br>Rules | 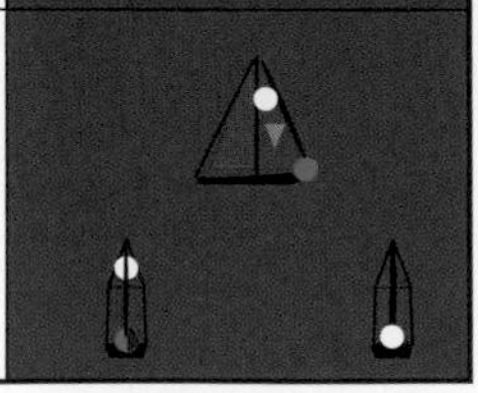 | |

# Fishing Vessels
## *(Rule 26)*

| RULE/VESSEL | GROUPS | SHAPES | BOW / STERN |
|---|---|---|---|
| **BOTH INTERNATIONAL AND INLAND** | | | |
| **Rule 26(b)**<br>Trawling,<br>making way<br>≥50 m | Masthead<br>Sidelights<br>Sternlight<br>G/W all-around |  | 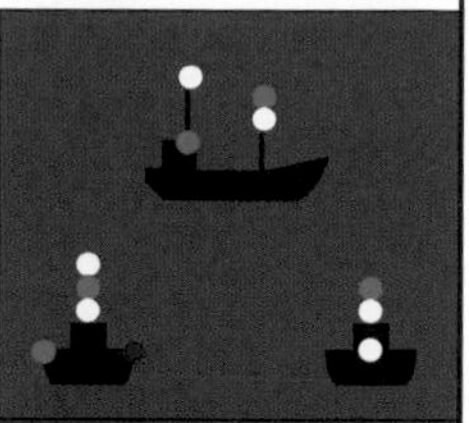 |
| **Rule 26(b)**<br>Trawling,<br>making way<br><50 m | Sidelights<br>Sternlight<br>G/W all-around |  | 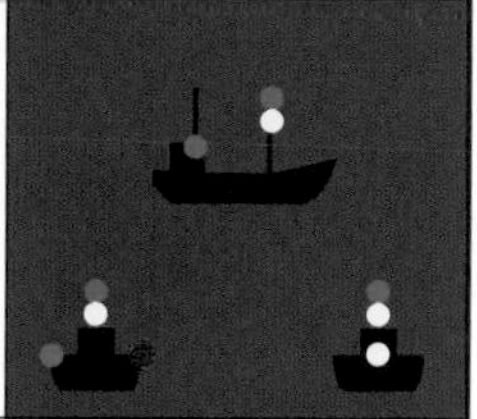 |
| **Rule 26(b)**<br>Trawling,<br>not making way | G/W all-around |  | 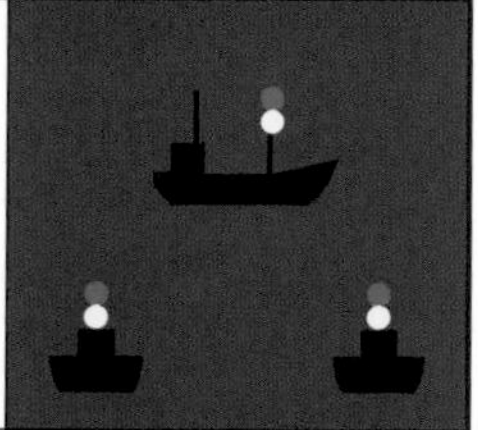 |
| **Rule 26(c)**<br>Fishing other<br>than trawling,<br>making way<br>Any length | Sidelights<br>Sternlight<br>R/W all-around |  | 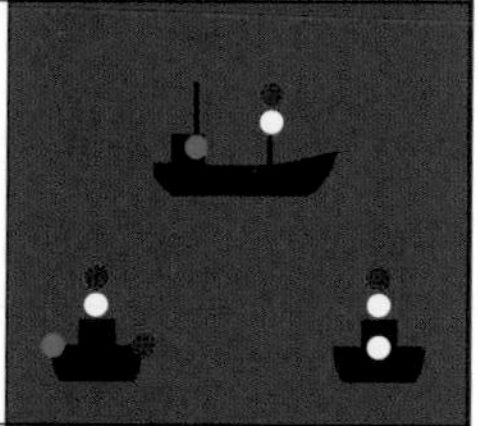 |
| **Rule 26(c)**<br>Fishing other<br>than trawling,<br>not making way<br>Any length | R/W all-around |  |  |
| **Rule 26(c)**<br>Fishing other<br>than trawling,<br>making way<br>Gear out >150 m | Sidelights<br>Sternlight<br>R/W all-around<br>All-around | <br>gear<br>side | 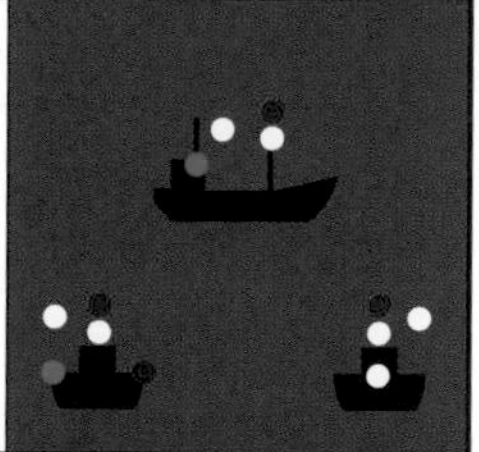 |
| **Rule 26(c)**<br>Fishing other<br>than trawling,<br>not making way<br>Gear out >150 m | R/W all-around<br>All-around | <br>gear<br>side | 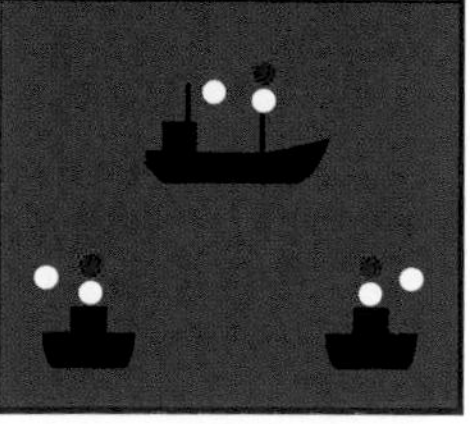 |

# Vessels Not Under Command or Restricted in Ability to Maneuver *(Rule 27)*

| RULE/VESSEL | GROUPS | SHAPES | BOW | STERN |
|---|---|---|---|---|
| **BOTH INTERNATIONAL AND INLAND** | | | | |
| **Rule 27(a)**<br>Not Under Command<br>Making way | Sidelights<br>Sternlight<br>R/R all-around | | | |
| **Rule 27(a)**<br>Not Under Command<br>Not making way | R/R all-around | | | |
| **Rule 27(b)**<br>Restricted in Ability to Maneuver<br>Making way<br><50 m | Masthead<br>Sidelights<br>Sternlight<br>R/W/R all-around | | | |
| **Rule 27(b)**<br>Restricted in Ability to Maneuver<br>Making way<br>≥50 m | 2 Mastheads<br>Sidelights<br>Sternlight<br>R/W/R all-around | | | |
| **Rule 27(b)**<br>Restricted in Ability to Maneuver<br>Not making way | R/W/R all-around | | | |
| **Rule 27(b)**<br>Restricted in Ability to Maneuver<br>Anchored<br><50 m | R/W/R all-around<br>W all-around | | | |
| **Rule 27(b)**<br>Restricted in Ability to Maneuver<br>Anchored<br>≥50 m | R/W/R all-around<br>2 W all-around | | | |
| **Rule 27(d)**<br>Dredging or Underwater Operations<br>Not making way | R/W/R all-around<br>R/R all-arnd obstr. side<br>G/G all-arnd clear side | obstr. side<br>clear side | | |
| **Rule 27(e)**<br>Diving, but unable to display Underwater Operations lights | R/W/R all-around | Int'l Code Flag "A" | | |
| **Rule 27(f)**<br>Mine-clearing<br>Making way<br>≥50 m | 2 Mastheads<br>Sidelights<br>Sternlight<br>G Δ all-around | | | |
| **Rule 27(f)**<br>Mine-clearing<br>Making way<br><50 m | Masthead<br>Sidelights<br>Sternlight<br>G Δ all-around | | | |

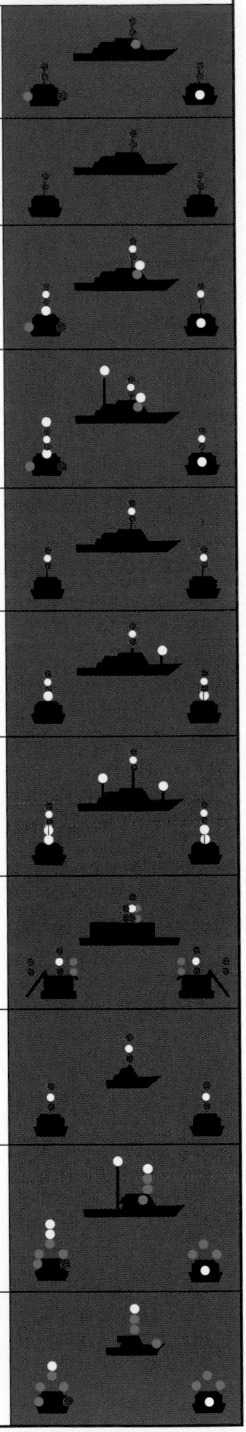

# All Other Vessels
## *(Rules 28–31)*

| RULE/VESSEL | GROUPS | SHAPES | BOW | STERN |
|---|---|---|---|---|
| **INTERNATIONAL ONLY**<br>**Rule 28**<br>Constrained by Draft<br>Making way<br>If 50 m, add | Masthead<br>Sidelights<br>Sternlight<br>R/R/R all-around<br>2nd Masthead | cylinder | | |
| **BOTH INTERNATIONAL AND INLAND**<br>**Rule 29(a)**<br>Pilot Vessel on Duty<br>Underway | Sidelights<br>Sternlight<br>W/R all-around | Int'l Code Flag "H" | | |
| **Rule 29(a)**<br>Pilot Vessel on Duty<br>Anchored | W/R all-around<br>Anchor Light | Int'l Code Flag "H" | | |
| **Rule 29(b)**<br>Pilot Vessel off Duty<br>Making way<br><50 m | Masthead<br>Sidelights<br>Sternlight | None | | |
| **Rule 30(a)**<br>Anchored<br>50–100 m | 2 W all-around | | | |
| **Rule 30(b)**<br>Anchored<br>7 m and <50 m | W all-around | | | |
| **Rule 30(c)**<br>Anchored<br>100 m | 2 W all-around<br>All deck lights | | | |
| **Rule 30(d)**<br>Aground<br>50 m | W all-around forward<br>Lower W all-around aft<br>R/R all-around<br>(if practicable INLAND) | | | |
| **Rule 30(d)**<br>Aground<br><50 m and 12 m | W all-around<br>R/R all-around<br>(if practicable INLAND) | | | |
| **Rule 30(f)**<br>Aground<br><12 m | W all-around | | | |
| **Rule 31**<br>Seaplane<br>Underway | Masthead<br>Sidelights<br>Sternlight | None | | |

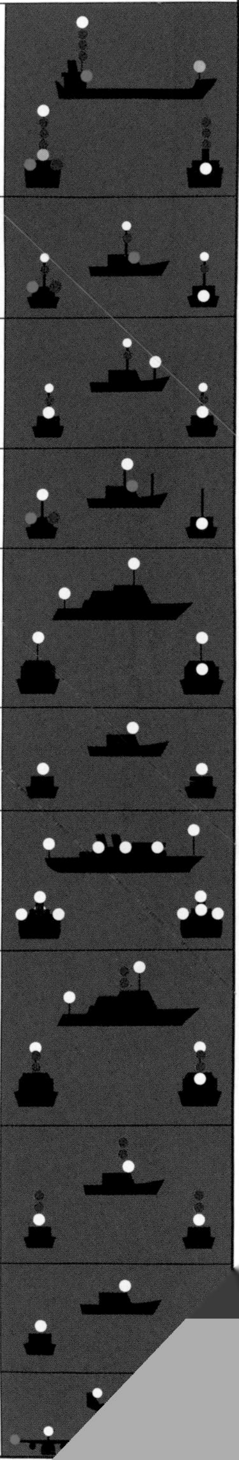

# Sound Signals *(Rules 32–37)*

• = 1-sec. blast; — = 4- to 6-sec. blast. Repeated every 2 min.

**INTERNATIONAL**

Meeting or crossing and action required (no answer required):
- I am altering my course to starboard •
- I am altering my course to port • •
- I am operating astern propulsion • • •

Overtaking in narrow channel or fairway and action required (agreement required before action initiated):
- I intend to overtake you on your starboard — — •
- I intend to overtake you on your port — — • •
- I agree to be overtaken — • — •

Warning—I dont understand your intentions • • • • •

Approaching a bend in a channel —

**INLAND**

Meeting or crossing within ½ mile and action is required (agreement by the same signal required):
- I propose leaving you to my port •
- I propose leaving you to my starboard • •
- I am operating astern propulsion • • •

Overtaking in narrow channel or fairway and action required (agreement by same signal required before action):
- I propose overtaking you on your starboard •
- I propose overtaking you on your port • •
- I agree to be overtaken as proposed • or • •

Warning—I don't understand your intentions • • • • •

Approaching a bend in a channel or leaving berth —

**IN RESTRICTED VISIBILITY** **(INTERNATIONAL & INLAND)**

Power vessel making way —

Power vessel underway but stopped — —

Manned tow — • • •

Pilot vessel—optional signal • • •

Not under command, restricted in ability to maneuver, constrained by draft, sailing, fishing, towing or pushing, fishing at anchor, or restricted at anchor — • •

Anchored:
- <100 m—ring bell rapidly for 5 sec. once per min.
- ≥100 m—ring bell 5 sec. forward, then gong 5 sec. aft

Aground: 3 bell claps + rapid 5-sec. bell + 3 claps; repeat all 1/min.
- ≥100 m—add gong 5 sec. aft
- <12 m Inland option—horn, bell, or gong once per 2 min.

# What to Do in Fog *(Rule 19)*

| Fog Situation | What You Should Do |
|---|---|
| Regardless of traffic | Maintain safe speed; power-driven vessels sound one 5-sec. blast every 2 minutes. Most other vessels sound one 5-sec. and two 1-sec. blasts every 2 minutes. |
| Hear sound signal forward | Slow to bare steerageway or stop. |
| [illegible]dar target forward | Slow; do NOT turn to port unless you are overtaking the target vessel. |
| [illegible]t aft or abeam | Maintain speed; do NOT turn toward the target vessel. |

# Light & Shape Definitions
## *(Rule 21)*

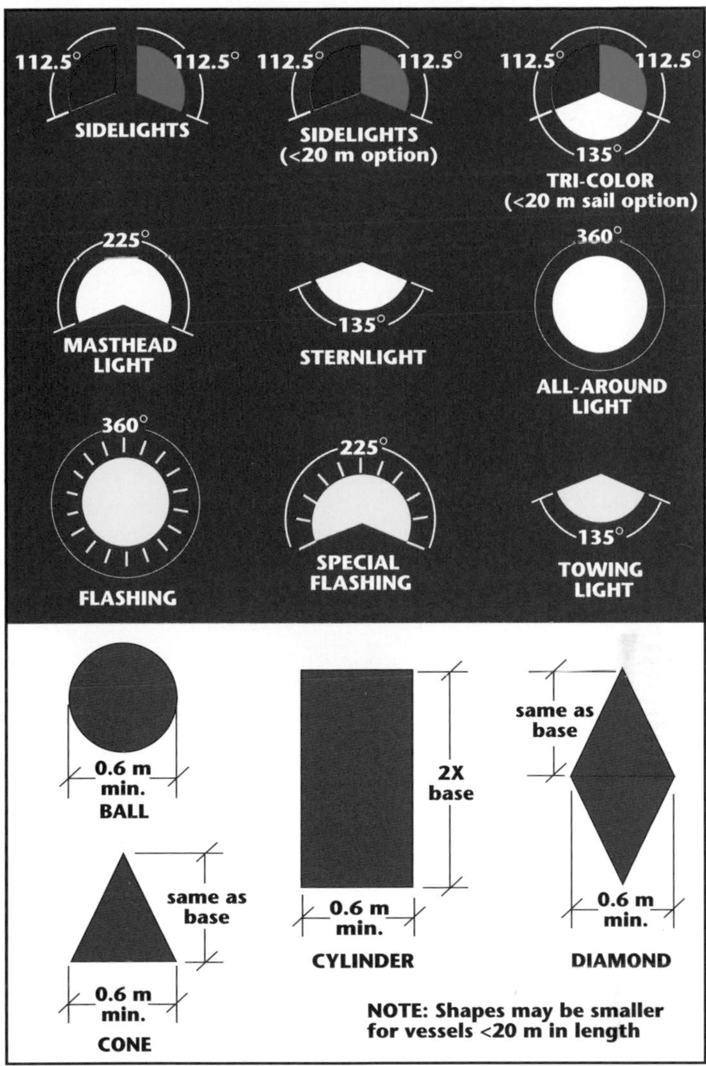


# Visibility of Lights *(Rule 22)*

| Type of Light | Vessel Length, m | Visibility, nm |
|---|---|---|
| Masthead | under 12<br>12 to 20<br>20 to 50<br>50 or more | 2<br>3<br>5<br>6 |
| Side | under 12<br>12 to 50<br>50 or more | 1<br>2<br>3 |
| Stern, Towing, and All-around | under 50<br>50 or more | 2<br>3 |

# At-a-Glance Guide

## Situation: What You Need to Do

ARE YOU IN OR ENTERING A CHARTED TRAFFIC SEPARATION SCHEME ?

YES → **RULE 10**

If using, stay in lane in direction of the arrows on chart

If crossing, do so at 90° and stay clear of vessels in lanes

If sailing, fishing, or <20 m in length, you may use an inshore zone, but you must not impede a vessel that is following a lane

Don't anchor in or near the ends of traffic lanes

If risk of collision occurs, use the rules below

NO ↓

ARE YOU IN A NARROW CHANNEL OR FAIRWAY?

YES → **RULE 9**

If crossing, don't impede vessels using the channel

If sailing, fishing, or <20 m in length, don't impede a vessel using the channel

If overtaking, first obtain agreement by sound signals

Otherwise, keep to the starboard edge of the channel

NO ↓

ARE YOU OVERTAKING OR BEING OVERTAKEN BY ANOTHER VESSEL?

YES → **RULE 13**

If overtaking, stay clear; use sound signals if necessary

If you have any doubt, assume you are overtaking

If being overtaken, stand on; answer to sound signals

NO ↓

ARE YOU ONE OF TWO POWER-DRIVEN VESSELS MEETING HEAD-ON?

YES → **RULE 14**

Both vessels alter course to starboard and pass port-to-port. On the GREAT LAKES and WESTERN RIVERS only, down-bound vessel should propose method of passage using INLAND sound signals.

VHF is OK instead of sound signals under Inland Rules. No answer required under COLREGs.

NO ↓

# to Rules 9–18

## Illustration of the Rule

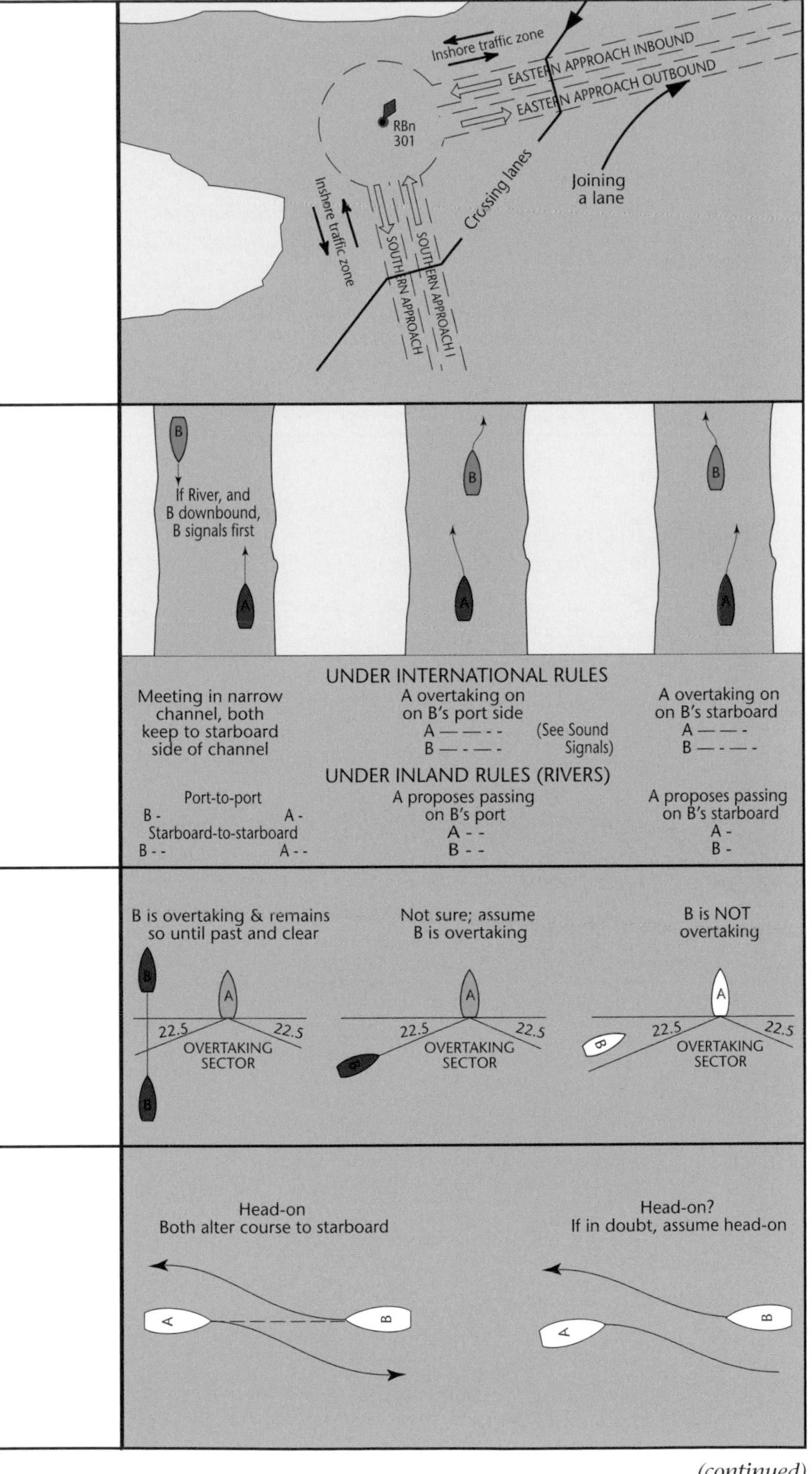


*(continued)*

# At-a-Glance Guide

## Situation: What You Need to Do

ARE YOU ONE OF TWO POWER-DRIVEN VESSELS CROSSING PATHS?

YES

**RULE 15**

If other vessel on your starboard, keep clear; pass aft

If other vessel on your port, maintain course and speed

**RULE 17**

If the give-way vessel is not giving way, the stand-on vessel MAY slow or turn to starboard to avoid collision

If collision can no longer be avoided by action of the give-way vessel alone, the stand-on vessel MUST take whatever action she thinks will best avoid collision, including a turn to port

NO

ARE YOU ONE OF TWO SAILBOATS MEETING?

YES

**RULE 12**

If on different tacks, the port-tack vessel stays clear

If on same tack, the windward vessel stays clear

If you are on port tack and you are uncertain about the tack of the vessel to your windward, stay clear

NO

IS THE OTHER VESSEL A DIFFERENT TYPE?

YES

**RULE 18**

Stay clear of vessels higher than you on the list at right

To claim their special status, vessels must display shapes during the day and lights sunset to sunrise

See pages 98–103 and 105 for shapes and lights

NO

YOU HAVE MISSED SOMETHING

Slow to bare steerageway or stop and review the At-a-Glance Guide from the top

Contact the other vessel on VHF Channel 13 or Channel 09 to clarify both vessels' intentions

## Illustration of the Rule

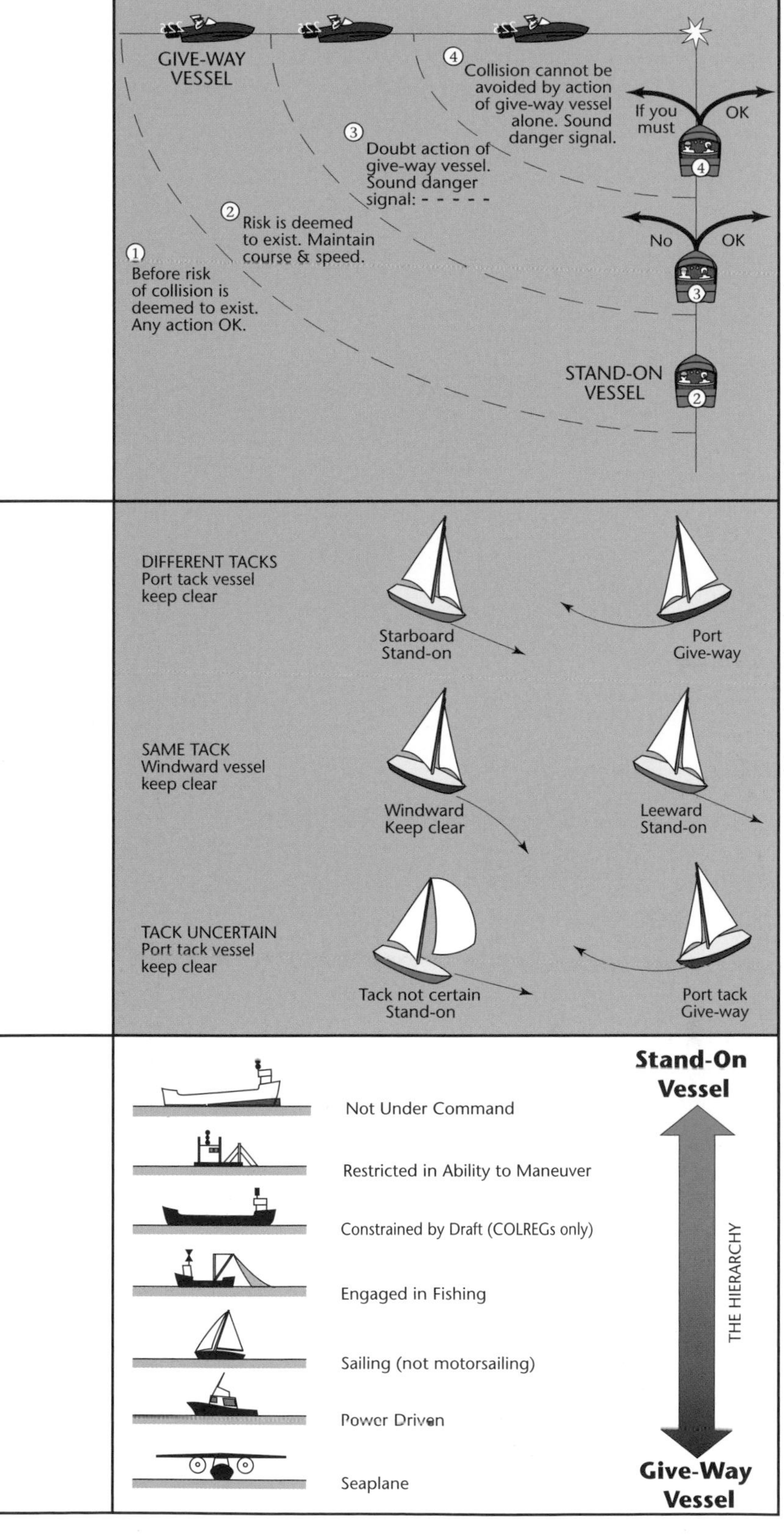

CHAPTER 7

# Knots, Splices, and Line Handling

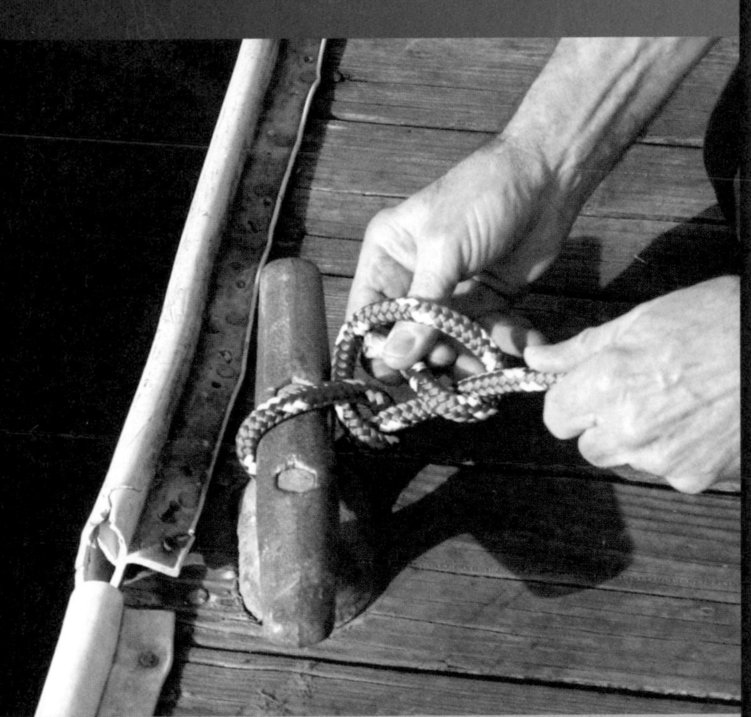

Charlie Wing

# Rope Construction

**Rope Fiber.** Virtually all rope today is manufactured of synthetic materials. Natural fibers have been replaced by chemically engineered fibers with a wide range of desirable characteristics, including high strength-to-weight ratio, high or low elasticity, infinite fiber length, and abrasion, rot, and UV resistance. The table below lists the leading fibers and their characteristics. Nylon and polyester predominate on boats.

**CHARACTERISTICS OF FIBERS**

| Material | Breaking Strength[1] | Stretch % | Abrasion Resistance | Specific Gravity[2] | UV Resistance | Relative Cost |
|---|---|---|---|---|---|---|
| Polypropylene | 1530 | 18–22 | Fair | 0.91 | Fair | Low |
| Nylon | 2600 | 30–35 | Excellent | 1.14 | Good | Med |
| Polyester (Dacron®) | 3470 | 15–20 | Excellent | 1.38 | Excellent | Med |
| Hi-Tenacity Polyethylene (Spectra®) | 8160 | 2.3–3.9 | Excellent | 0.97 | Fair | Hi |
| Aramid (Kevlar®) | 8500 | 1.5–4.5 | Fair | 1.44 | Fair | Hi |
| Hi-Tenacity Copolymer (Technora®) | 10700 | 1.5–4.5 | Fair | 1.44 | Fair | Very Hi |
| Liquid Crystal Polymer (Vectran®) | 11600 | 3.5–4.5 | Very Good | 1.40 | Fair | Very Hi |
| Hi-Tenacity Polyethylene (Dyneema®) | 12000 | 2.0–4.0 | Excellent | 0.975 | Very Good | Very Hi |

*Notes: [1]Breaking strength of single-braid 5/16" rope [2]Floats in fresh water if <1.00; salt water if <1.025*

**Construction.** Rope is either cable-laid or braided. Right-handed (the usual) **cable-laid** rope consists of fibers twisted clockwise into yarns, yarns CCW into strands, and 3 strands CW to form the rope. In **braided rope**, fibers are twisted into yarns, 2–4 yarns laid together as strands, and the strands braided into rope. Braided rope may have a uniform cross-section (single-braid), a braided core inside a braided cover (double-braid), a core of straight yarns inside a braided cover (parallel-core), or, in the case of polypropylene, a hollow core inside a braided cover.

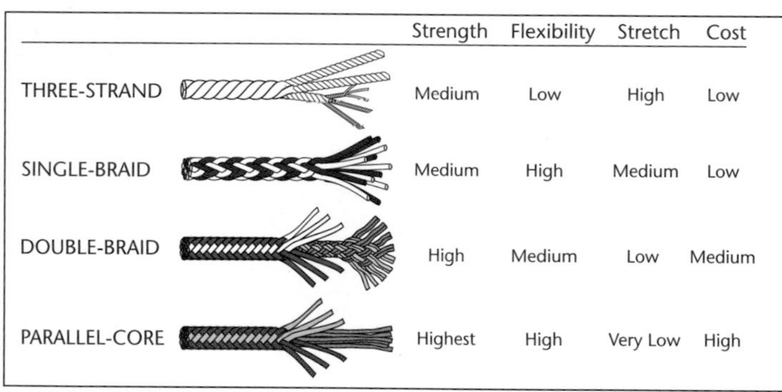

| | Strength | Flexibility | Stretch | Cost |
|---|---|---|---|---|
| THREE-STRAND | Medium | Low | High | Low |
| SINGLE-BRAID | Medium | High | Medium | Low |
| DOUBLE-BRAID | High | Medium | Low | Medium |
| PARALLEL-CORE | Highest | High | Very Low | High |

**APPROXIMATE BREAKING STRENGTHS OF ROPES**

| Diameter, inches / millimeters | 3/16 / 5 | 1/4 / 6 | 5/16 / 8 | 3/8 / 9.5 | 7/16 / 11 | 1/2 / 12 | 5/8 / 16 | 3/4 / 19 |
|---|---|---|---|---|---|---|---|---|
| Polypropylene Hollow-Braid | 550 | 980 | 1530 | 2200 | 2990 | 3910 | 6110 | 8800 |
| Polypropylene 3-Strand | 725 | 1290 | 2010 | 2900 | 3940 | 5150 | 8050 | 11600 |
| Nylon Single-Braid | 940 | 1670 | 2600 | 3750 | 5100 | 6660 | 10400 | 15000 |
| Nylon Double-Braid | 1090 | 1940 | 3040 | 4375 | 5950 | 7770 | 12100 | 17500 |
| Nylon 3-Strand | 940 | 1670 | 2600 | 3750 | 5100 | 6660 | 10400 | 15000 |
| Polyester Single-Braid | 1140 | 1900 | 3000 | 4200 | 5500 | 7000 | 11000 | 15300 |
| Polyester Double-Braid | 1200 | 2000 | 3000 | 4400 | 6600 | 8500 | 14400 | 20000 |
| with Spectra or Kevlar Core | 2300 | 3800 | 5700 | 7600 | 10200 | 12800 | 21800 | 28800 |
| with Vectran or Technora Core | 2720 | 4500 | 8000 | 10000 | 15000 | 18000 | 31000 | 42300 |
| Polyester Braid with Parallel Core | 1600 | 2700 | 4400 | 5500 | 7400 | 9600 | 15000 | 21600 |

## Selecting Rope for Lines

When selecting a type of rope, keep in mind the desired characteristics for the application. Strength per diameter or weight is rarely the determining factor. For example:

**Anchor rodes** require high stretch (to reduce shock loading) and high abrasion resistance (chafe is the leading cause of rode failure), but not great flexibility. Choose 3-strand nylon.

**Dock lines:** require moderately high stretch and strength, flexibility (for cleating), and high abrasion resistance. Choose braided (single or double) nylon, with polyester cover as an option.

**Dinghy painters, life-ring lines, and ski-tow ropes** must float so they don't get caught in the propeller. Choose polypropylene.

**Halyards** must not stretch or sail shape will be lost. Choose a polyester braid with a low-stretch core.

**Sheets and vangs** must be strong and flexible, but also moderately stretchy to absorb shock loads. Choose an all-polyester braid.

**DOCK LINES**
(Based on 3-strand or braided nylon)

| Boat Length | Bow/Stern Lines | Spring Lines | Rope Diameter |
|---|---|---|---|
| to 27' | 20' | 25' | 3/8" |
| 28–36 | 25 | 35 | 1/2 |
| 37–45 | 30 | 45 | 5/8 |
| 46–54 | 35 | 50 | 3/4 |
| 55–72 | 40 | 70 | 1 |

**ANCHOR RODES**
(Recommended rode consists of 15 feet of chain plus 200 feet of 3-strand nylon)

| Boat Length | Chain Size | Rope Dia. |
|---|---|---|
| to 25' | 3/16" | 1/4" |
| 26–35 | 1/4 | 1/2 |
| 36–45 | 5/16 | 5/8 |
| 46–54 | 3/8 | 3/4 |
| 55–72 | 1/2 | 1 |

**LINE GUIDE FOR THE CRUISER AND CASUAL RACER**

| Application | Polyester Single-Braid (e.g., Regatta) | Polyester Double-Braid (e.g., Sta-Set) | Polyester Braid/ Parallel Core (e.g., Sta-Set X) | Polyester Braid/ Vectran Core (e.g., Sta-Set X+) |
|---|---|---|---|---|
| Main/Genoa Halyard | Not Rec. | Good | Excellent | Excellent |
| Main Sheet | Excellent | Excellent | Fair | Good |
| Genoa/Jib Sheets | Very Good | Excellent | Very Good | Very Good |
| Reefing Lines | Good | Excellent | Excellent | Good |
| Spinnaker Halyard | Not Rec. | Very Good | Excellent | Excellent |
| Spinnaker Sheets | Good | Very Good | Excellent | Good |
| Spinnaker Guys | Not Rec. | Good | Excellent | Excellent |
| Foreguy/Topping Lift | Good | Excellent | Very Good | Good |
| Vang | Good | Excellent | Good | Fair |
| Control Lines | Very Good | Excellent | Good | Fair |
| Runner Tails | Not Rec. | Good | Very Good | Very Good |
| Furling Lines | Excellent | Very Good | Fair | Fair |

**RUNNING RIGGING SIZE GUIDE** (Based on polyester double-braid)

| Application | Boat Length to 20' | 20–25' | 26–30' | 31–35' | 36–40' | 41–45' | 46–50' | 51–60' |
|---|---|---|---|---|---|---|---|---|
| Main Halyard | 1/4" | 5/16" | 3/8" | 7/16" | 1/2" | 9/16" | 5/8" | 3/4" |
| Genoa Halyard | 1/4" | 5/16" | 3/8" | 7/16" | 1/2" | 9/16" | 5/8" | 3/4" |
| Main Sheet | 5/16" | 5/16" | 3/8" | 7/16" | 1/2" | 1/2" | 9/16" | 9/16" |
| Genoa Sheets | 5/16" | 5/16" | 3/8" | 7/16" | √1/2" | 9/16" | 5/8" | 5/8" |
| Reefing Lines | 1/4" | 5/16" | 3/8" | 7/16" | 7/16" | 1/2" | 1/2" | 9/16" |
| Spinnaker Halyard | 1/4" | 5/16" | 3/8" | 7/16" | 1/2" | 9/16" | 5/8" | 3/4" |
| Spinnaker Sheets | 1/4" | 1/4" | 5/16" | 3/8" | 7/16" | 1/2" | 9/16" | 5/8" |
| Spinnaker Guy | 5/16" | 5/16" | 3/8" | 7/16" | 1/2" | 5/8" | 3/4" | 3/4" |
| Foreguy/Topping Lift | 1/4" | 1/4" | 5/16" | 3/8" | 7/16" | 1/2" | 9/16" | 9/16" |
| Vang | 1/4" | 1/4" | 5/16" | 3/8" | 7/16" | 1/2" | 9/16" | 9/16" |
| Control Lines | 3/16" | 1/4" | 5/16" | 3/8" | 7/16" | 1/2" | 9/16" | 9/16" |

# Cleating and Coiling

**Cleating.** Take a single round turn around the base of the cleat, then engage the horns in a single figure-8. To leave unattended, make the last turn a half hitch for security. A lead-in angle of 10–20° prevents jamming.

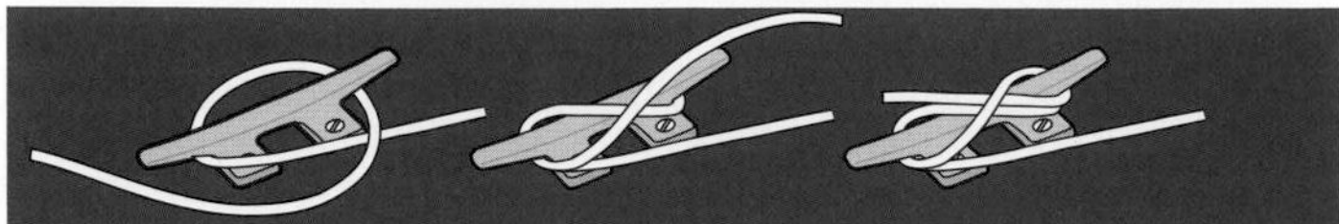

**The Sea Gasket Coil** is ideal for coiling lines not in use, such as dock lines. After coiling the line and wrapping the coil with a couple of turns, reach through the coil and pull a loop from the running end up and over the top of the coil. Pull on the running end to cinch the loop.

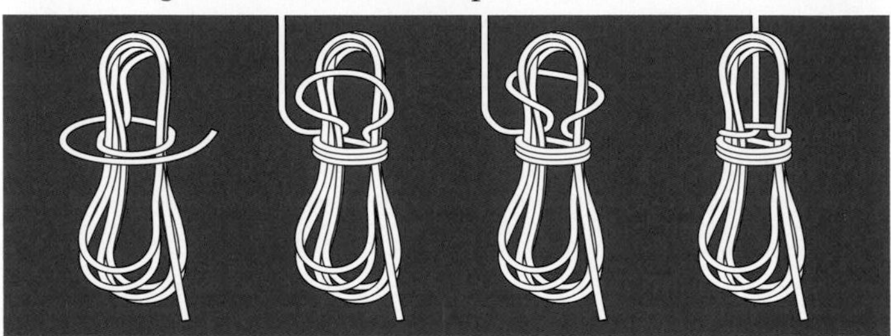

**The Halyard Coil** keeps the long halyard tail off the deck. After cleating, simply coil the halyard, pass a loop from the cleat through the coil, give it a couple of twists and hang the coil from the twisted loop.

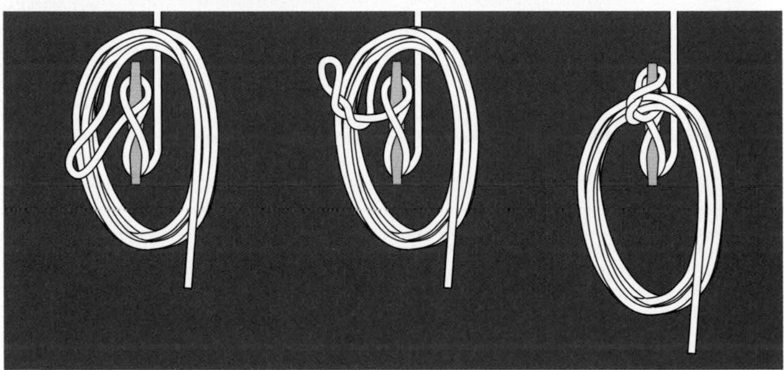

**Faking Down** a long line (such as an anchor rode) is simple to do and prevents tangling as it is paid out.

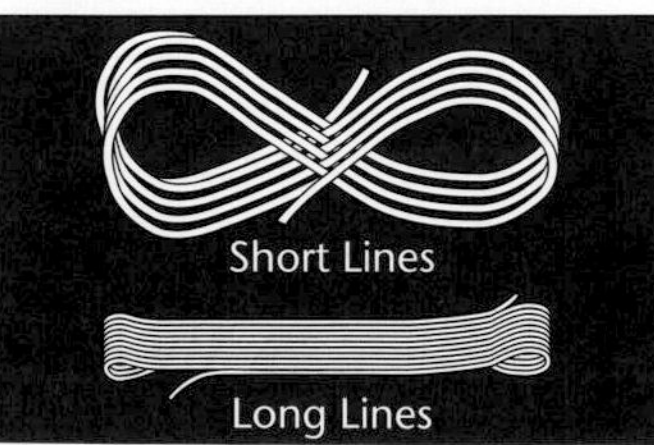


**Flemishing** the end of a line makes for a neat appearance and keeps the deck clear.

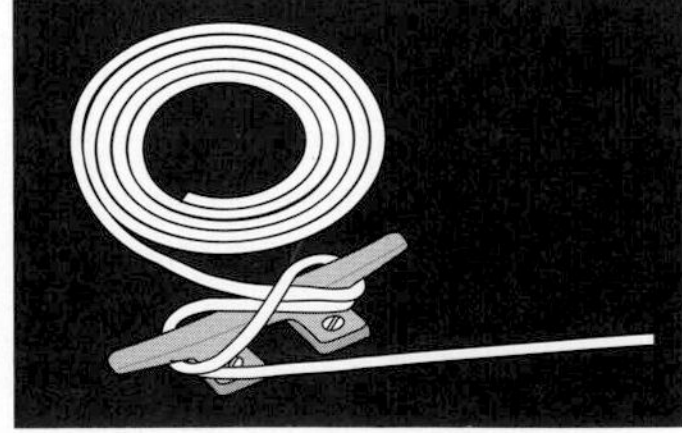

# Dock Lines and Their Uses

**DOCK LINE NAMES**

1. Bow Line
2. Bow Breast
3. Forward Spring
4. After Bow Spring
5. Forward Quarter Spring
6. After Spring
7. Stern Breast
8. Stern Line or After Quarter Spring
9. Outer Stern Line

**MOST COMMON**

1. Bow Line
3. Forward Spring
6. After Spring
8. Stern Line, or
9. Outer Stern Line

## Backing Away From Dock

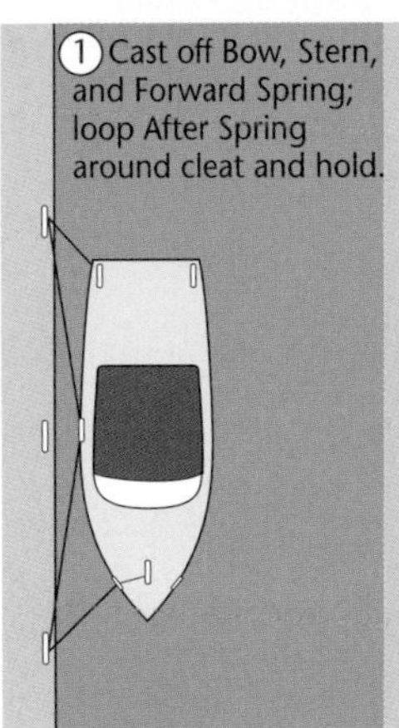

(1) Cast off Bow, Stern, and Forward Spring; loop After Spring around cleat and hold.

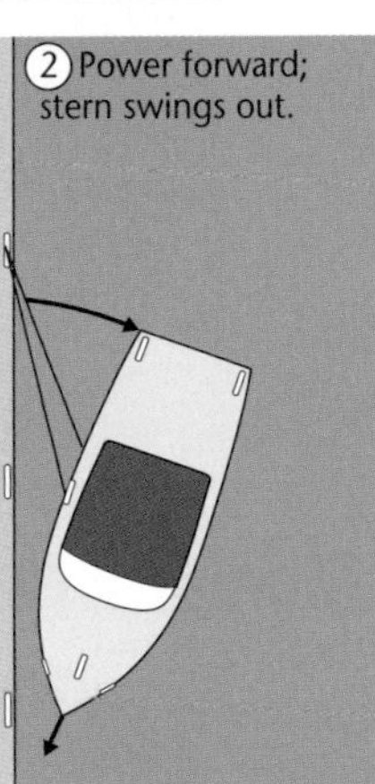

(2) Power forward; stern swings out.

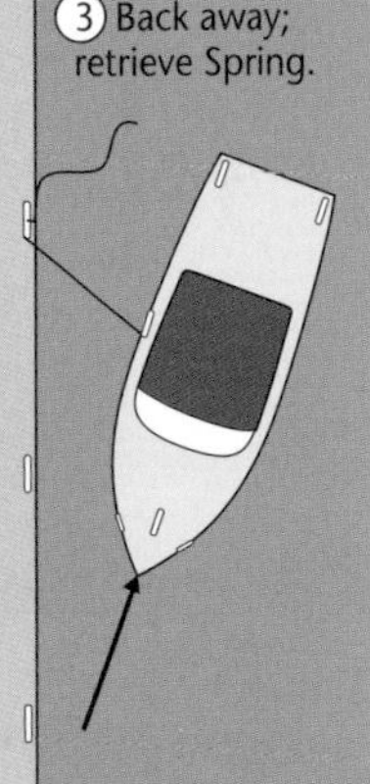

(3) Back away; retrieve Spring.

## Powering Away From Dock Forward

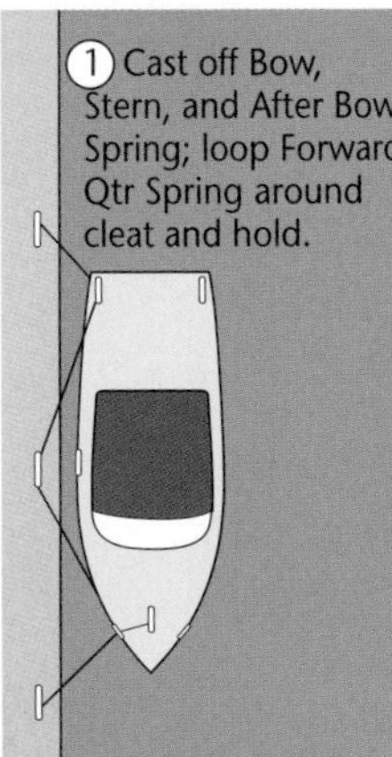

(1) Cast off Bow, Stern, and After Bow Spring; loop Forward Qtr Spring around cleat and hold.

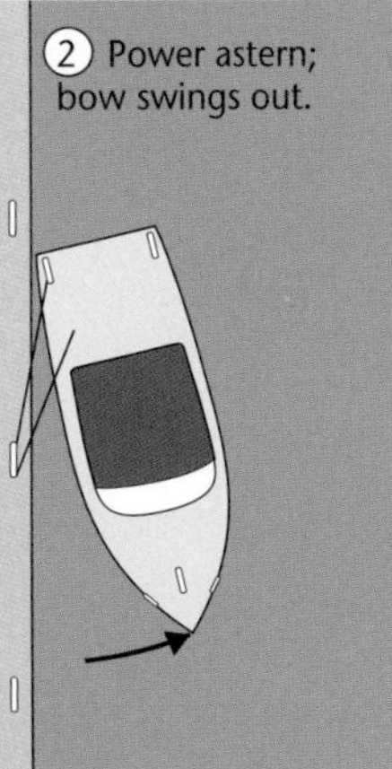

(2) Power astern; bow swings out.

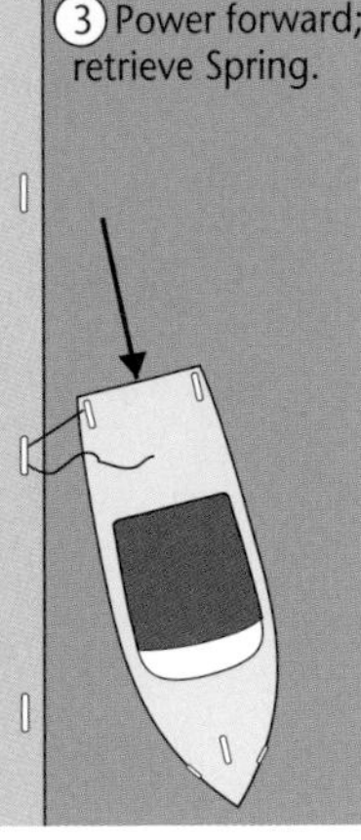

(3) Power forward; retrieve Spring.

## Landing in Tight Quarters

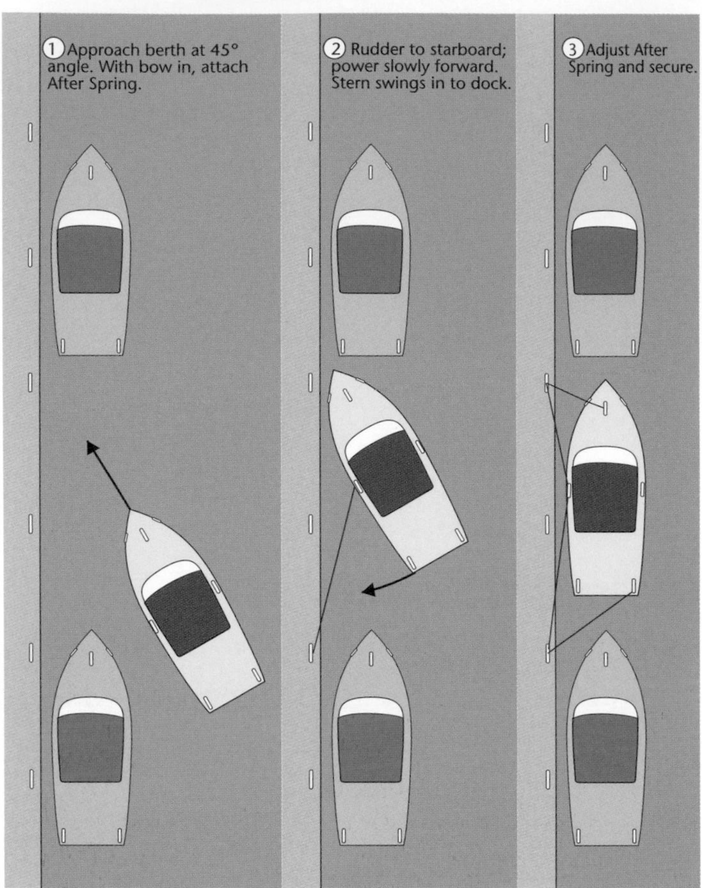


## Backing Around Corner of Pier

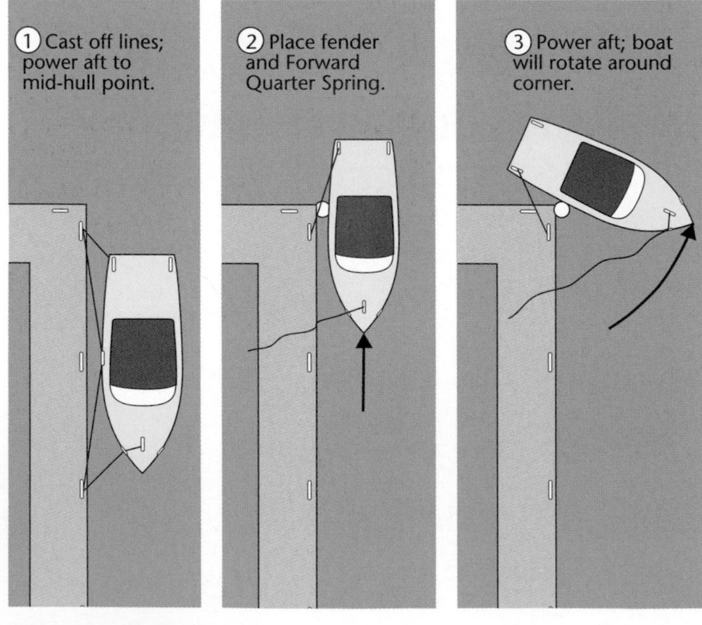

# Towing Operations

## Towing Alongside

In calm waters and in tight quarters, towing alongside (towing on the hip) gives maximum control to the towing vessel. The bow ① and stern ② lines keep the two vessels pressed together, while the towing strap ③ effects the forward tow, and the backing line ④ allows slowing.

Positioning the tow vessel's rudder and propeller(s) aft of the towed vessel's stern maximizes the maneuverability of the pair.

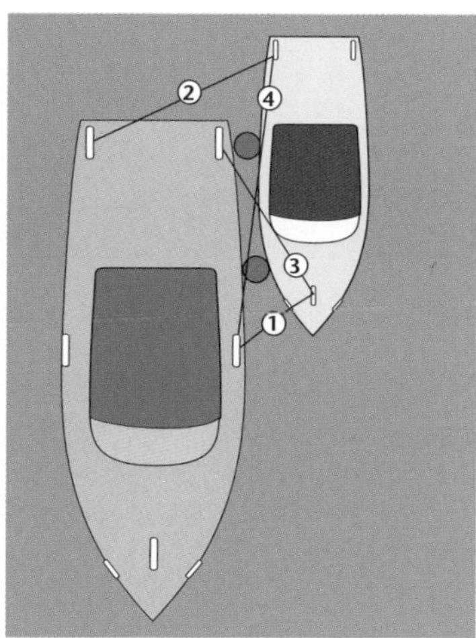


## Towing In Line

In rough waters and for long tows in open waters, towing in line is more satisfactory. A proper tow setup consists of:

① A pair of lines from the strongest points of attachment on the towed vessel, leading forward through the bow chocks. On a sailboat these may be the genoa winches aft or, where keel-stepped, the mast.

② A shackle, connecting lines ① in a bridle.

③ Low-stretch towing line (not 3-strand nylon) adjusted to keep the vessels in step with the waves.

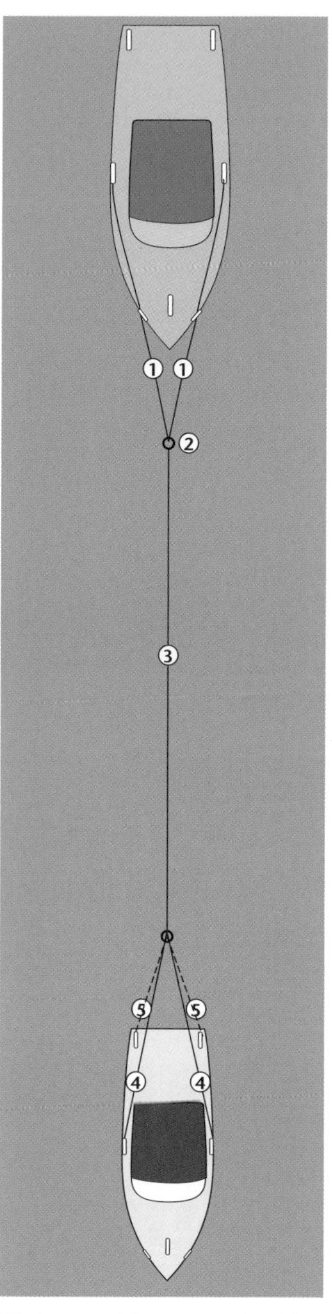


④ A pair of lines attached forward of the towing vessel's rudder and connected in a bridle.

⑤ A bridle from the stern cleats is acceptable, but reduces the maneuverability of the towing vessel.

# About Knots

### Knotting Terminology

The end of the rope used to tie a knot is its **running end**; the opposite end—usually fixed—is its **bitter end**. The section of rope around which the knot is tied is the **standing part** and a loop in rope is a **bight**.

Knots usually fall into one of three categories:

**Bends** connect two different ropes, or a rope and an anchor ring.

**Hitches** fasten the end of a rope to an object such as a piling.

**Knots** tie ropes to themselves, as in making a loop in one end.

## Tying Knots

**Square or Reef Knot:** good for tying reefing points, but may slip and always jams under high load.

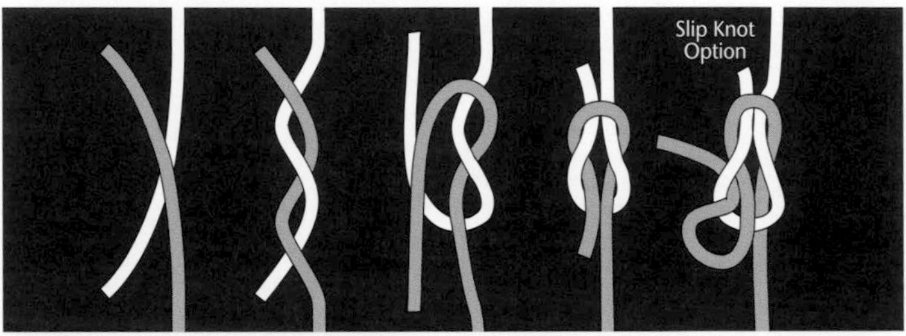


**Bowline:** single most useful mariner's knot. Never slips, no matter how great the load.

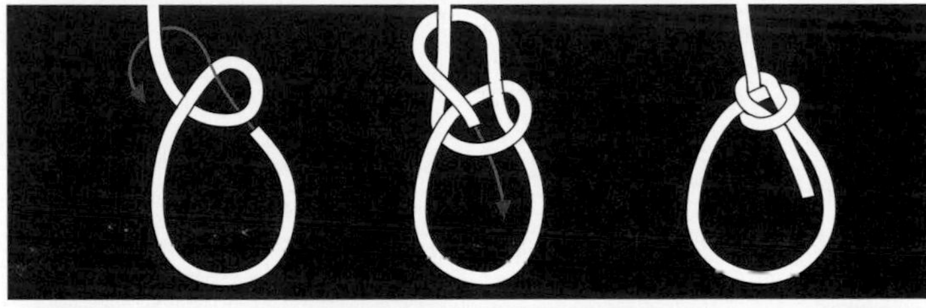

**Bowline on a Bight:** double the strength of a bowline and can be used as an emergency bosun's chair.

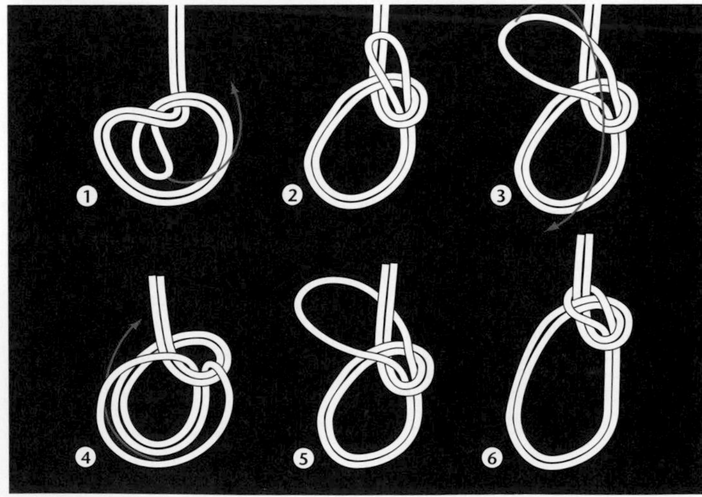

**Sheet Bend:** for connecting two different size ropes. Simpler, but not as secure as the Carrick Bend, below.

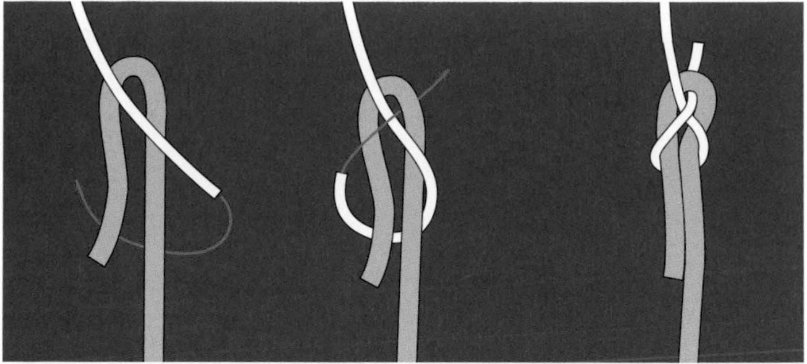

**Carrick Bend:** best for tying ropes of different sizes and/or types. Used in towing operations. Seizing ends keeps knot open for ease in untying.

**Anchor Bend** (Fisherman's Bend): except for an eye splice around a thimble, the best way to secure a rode to an anchor. Seizing increases security.

**Figure-8:** used to keep line ends from escaping blocks. Bulkier and less prone to jam than simple overhand knot.

**Round Turn and 2 Half Hitches:** allows adjustment of length and tension on a line. A third half hitch increases friction and holding power.

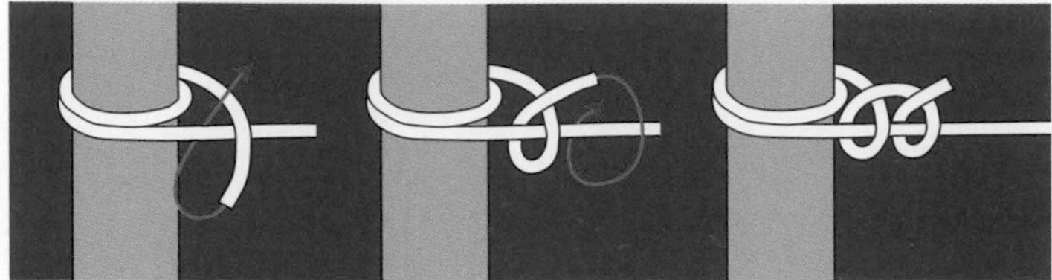

**Clove Hitch:** for tying docklines to posts or pilings or for hanging fenders from stanchion bases. Easily adjusted and never jams.

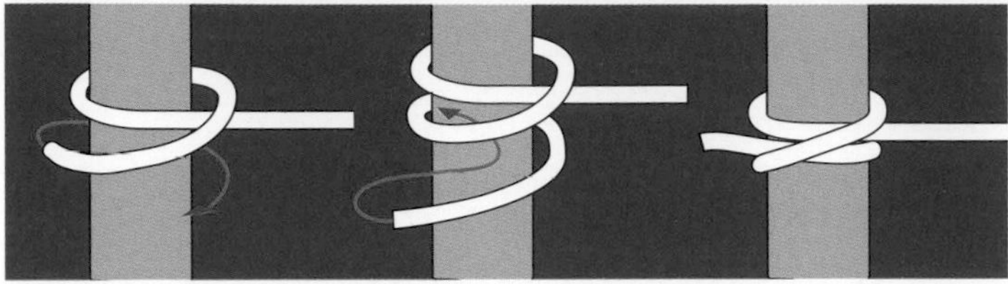

**Rolling Hitch:** grip increases as tension is applied. Used to remove strain from larger line while the line is adjusted.

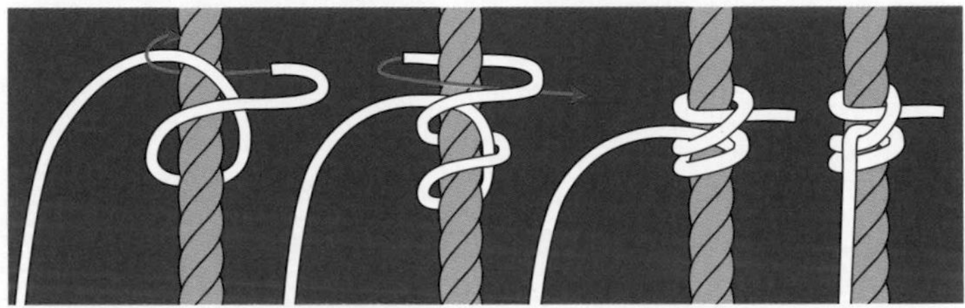

**Becket Hitch or Bend:** tied the same way as a Sheet Bend except to a line with an eye. The Double Becket is far more secure than the Single.

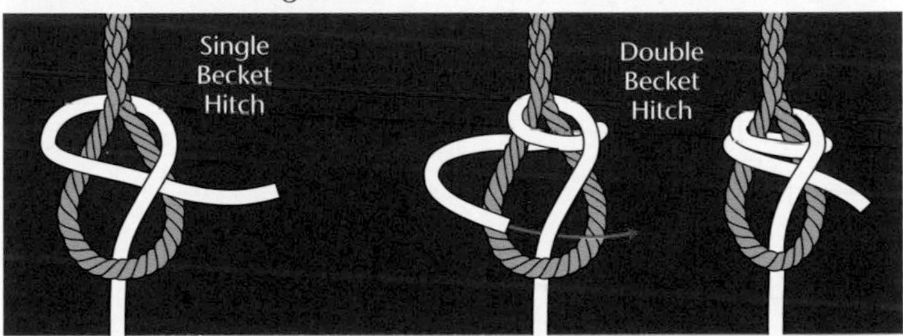


**Trucker's Hitch:** provides mechanical advantage of two when tightening. Best hitch for securing loads.

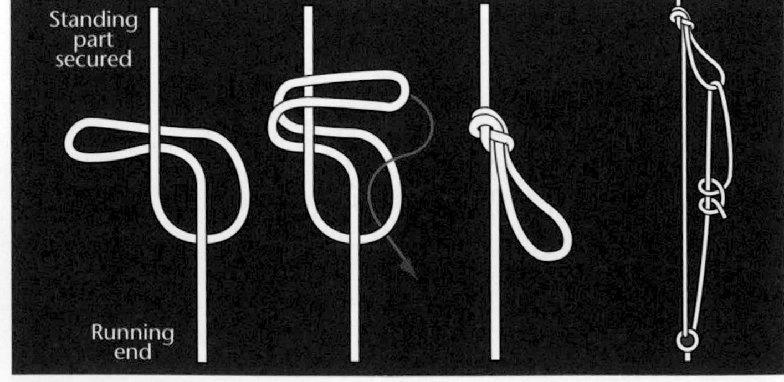

## Whipping

**Plain Whipping:** simple to produce, but temporary. Start by forming a loop of whipping cord (also called twine or "small stuff") with apex ½" from the end of the rope. Wrap the running end of the cord around the loop 8–10 times, working toward the apex. Pass the cord's running end through the loop, then pull on the bitter end until loop disappears under the turns. Clip the cord ends.

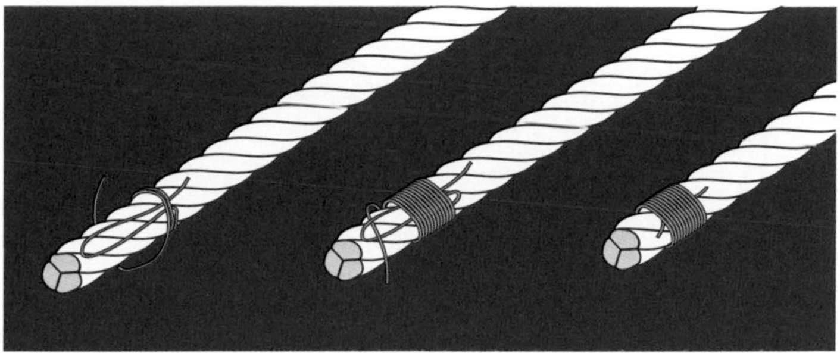

**Sailmaker's Whipping:** permanent. This version doesn't require use of a sailmaker's needle. Start by unlaying the end of a 3-strand rope about 1 inch and pass a loop of whipping cord around one of the strands, then relay the strands. Whip the rope 8–10 times toward its bitter end with the long end of the cord. Place the original loop back over its strand and pull tight using the cord's short end. Lay the long end back along the strands and tie the cord ends with a reef knot, and clip.

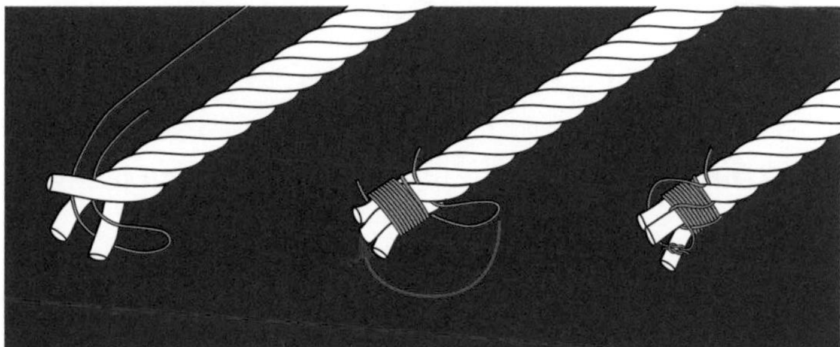

**Sewn Whipping:** can be used on braided as well as 3-strand rope. Start with two stitches through the rope. Tightly whip the rope 8–10 times toward its bitter end. Keeping the whipping taut, pass the needle through ⅓ (120°) of the rope and pull the cord taut. Now pass the needle through the rope at the other end of the whipping and tighten. Repeat until you have three double stitches spaced at 120° around the whipping. Take one final stitch and clip cord ends.

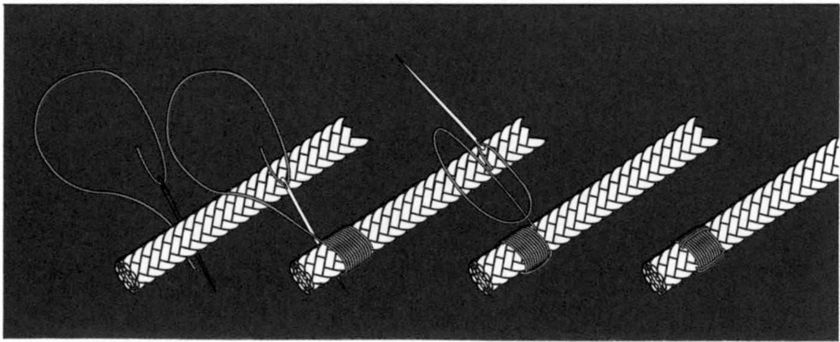

# Splices

## 3-Strand Splices

**Long Splice:** doesn't increase rope diameter (for running through blocks) but weaker than the Short Splice.

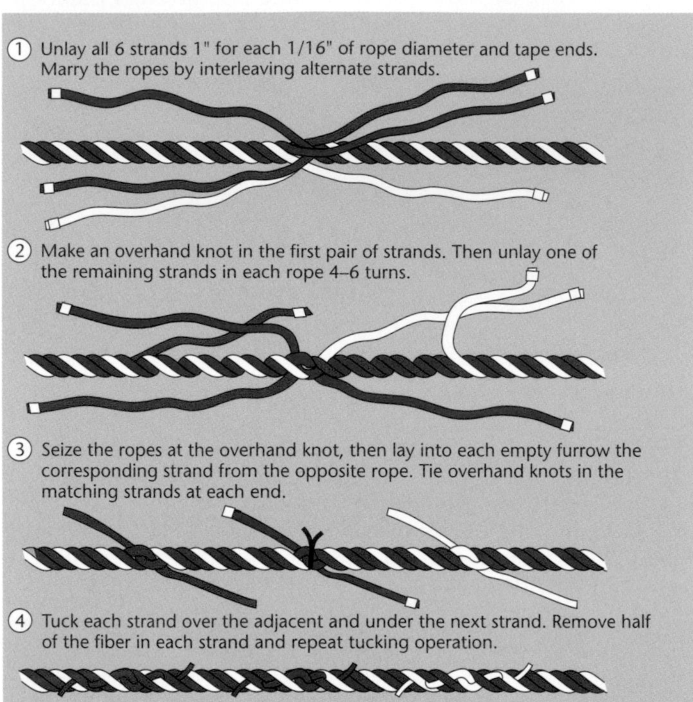


**Short Splice:** retains full strength of the rope, but increases diameter by 40 percent.

① Unlay all 6 strands 1" for each 1/16" of rope diameter and tape ends. Tape ropes to prevent further unlaying, and marry the ropes.

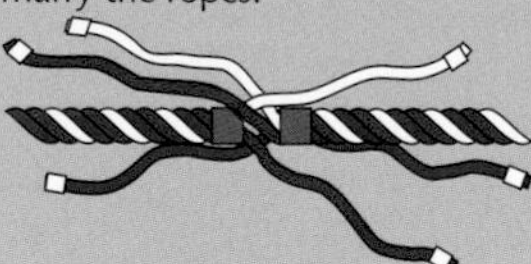

② Remove one of the rope tapes. Cross a strand end over its adjacent and under the next.

③ Continue tucking strand over and under for a total of 4 tucks (6 for nylon).

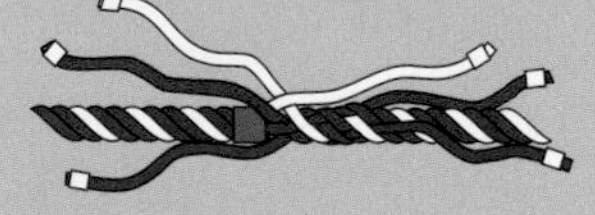

④ Repeat Steps 2 and 3 for second strand.

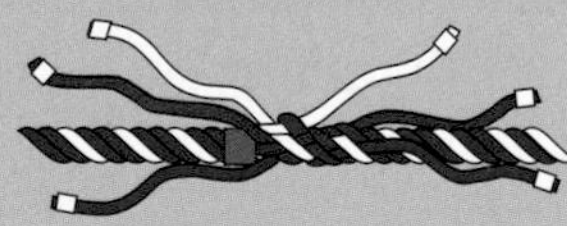

⑤ Repeat for third strand against the lay.

⑥ Remove remaining tape and pull on loose strands to snug splice. Repeat Steps 2–5 going in opposite direction.

**Eye Splice:** most useful splice. Retains 90 percent of rope's strength, compared to 50 percent for most knots.

**Back Splice:** alternative to whipping rope end; increases rope diameter by 40 percent and provides a handle.

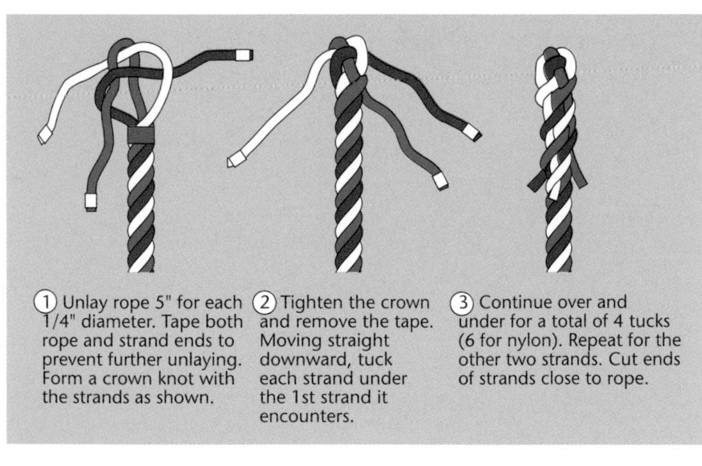

## Double-Braid Eye Splice

An eye splice in double-braid rope is complicated and time-consuming, but the end result is strong, permanent, and attractive. This splice can be made around a thimble for a mooring pendant or anchor rode.

This is a splice which cannot be achieved without a tubular fid—a hollow tube having a pointed end and interior barbs for catching inserted line. The size of the fid must be proportional to the size of the line being spliced:

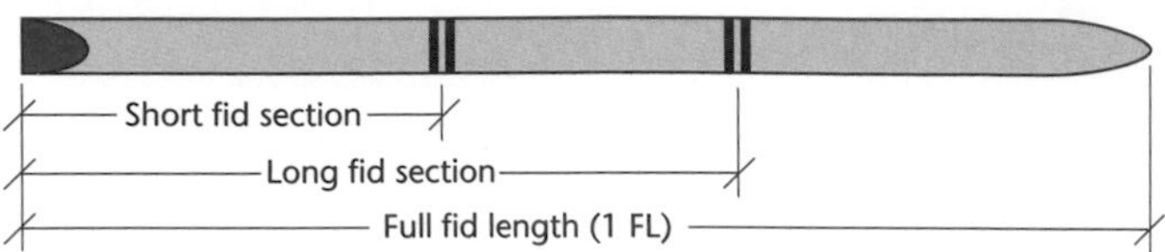


**Lengths of Tubular Fid Sections**

| Rope Diameter in. (mm) | Short Section in. (mm) | Long Section in. (mm) | Full Length in. (mm) |
|---|---|---|---|
| 1/4 (6) | 2 (51) | 3 1/2 (89) | 5 1/2 (140) |
| 5/16 (8) | 2 1/2 (64) | 4 1/4 (108) | 6 3/4 (171) |
| 3/8 (9) | 3 (76) | 4 3/4 (120) | 7 3/4 (197) |
| 7/16 (11) | 3 1/2 (89) | 6 (152) | 9 1/2 (241) |
| 1/2 (12) | 4 (101) | 7 (178) | 11 (279) |
| 9/16 (14) | 4 1/2 (114) | 8 (203) | 12 1/4 (311) |
| 5/8 (16) | 5 (127) | 9 1/2 (241) | 14 (356) |
| 3/4 (19) | 5 3/4 (146) | 11 (279) | 16 (406) |

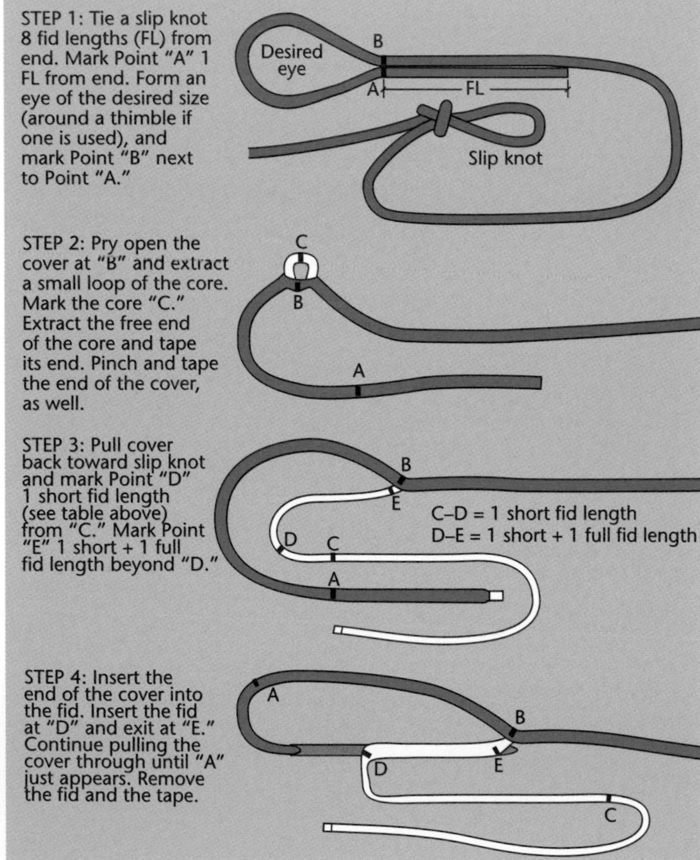

STEP 5: Now taper the exposed cover. Starting at "A" mark every 7th pic (pair of parallel ribs) running at one angle. Then count off 4 pics from "A," and mark every 7th pic running at the opposing angle. Cut one strand at each mark and remove the cut strand ends. Pull the tapered cover back until the end just disappears.

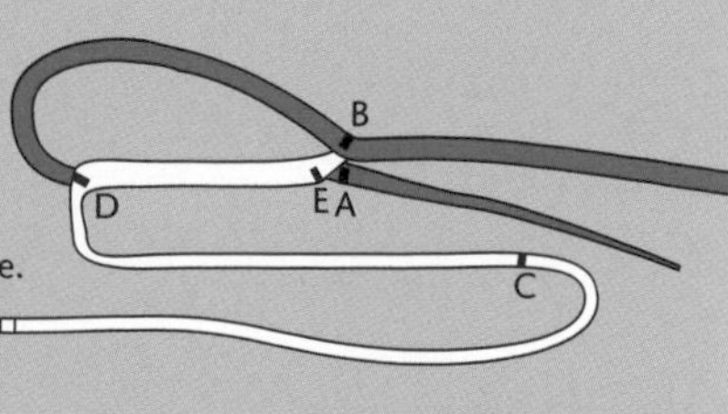


STEP 6: Insert the free end of the core into the fid. Insert the fid at "A" and exit at "B."

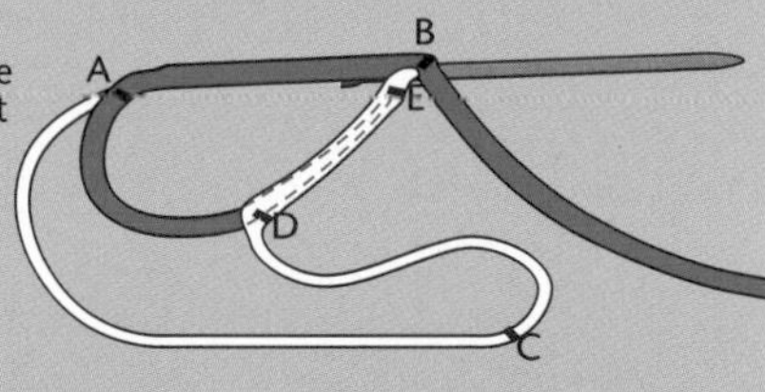


STEP 7: Pull on the core's free end until cover and core eyes match in size.

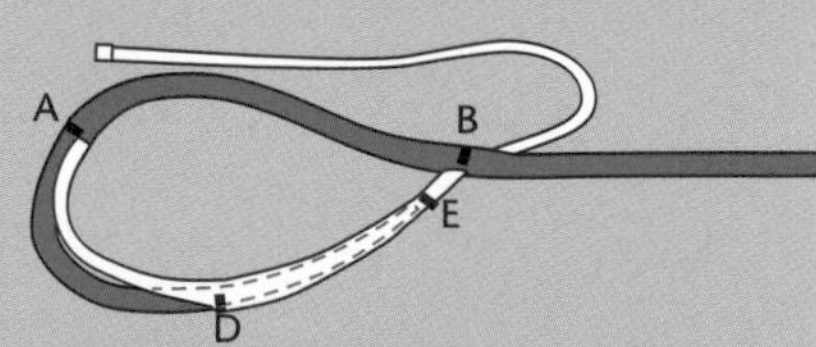


STEP 8: Insert the core end into the fid again, reinsert the fid at "B," and push it as far as you can into the rope's standing part. Pull the fid and core through the cover and cut off the excess core.

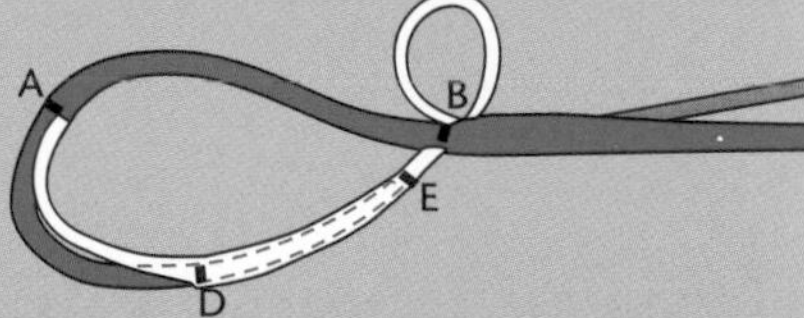


STEP 9: Grip the slip knot and work the cover toward the eye so that "E" and "D" disappear. Continue up to Point "A."

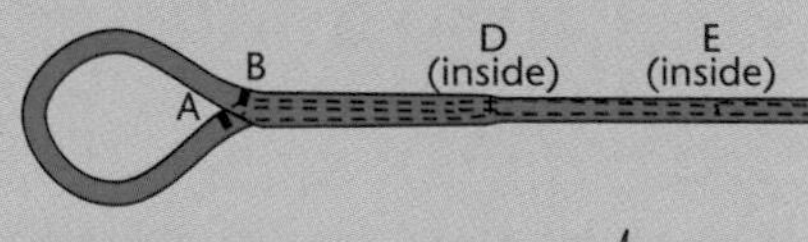


STEP 10: Secure the splice with waxed twine.Take 5 stitches through the throat of the splice, leaving a long tail. Switching the needle to the tail, take another 5 stitches at 90° to the first row of stitches.

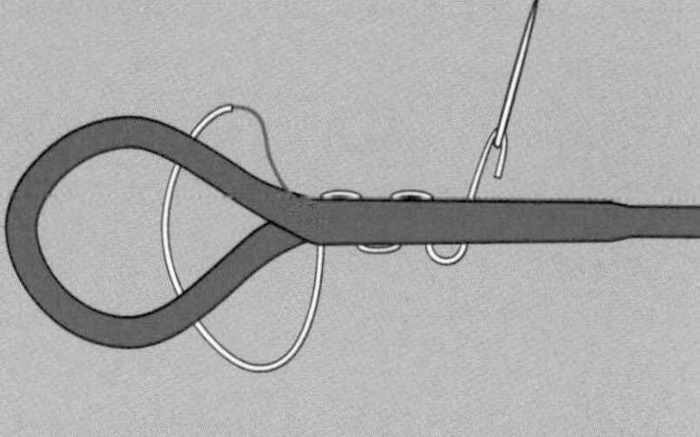

STEP 11: Tie the ends of the twine in a reef knot, and trim the ends.

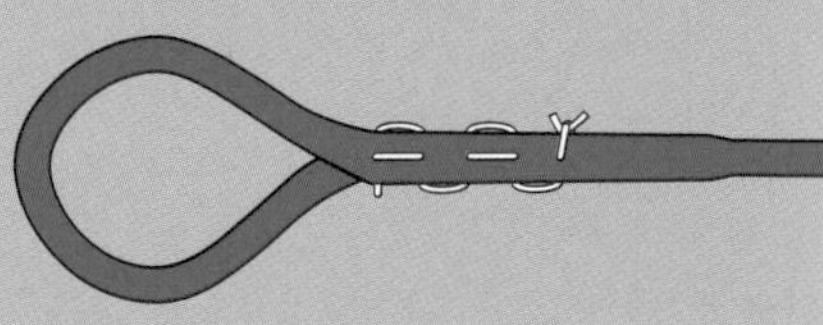

CHAPTER 8

# Anchoring

Peter Nielsen

# Which Anchor?

Anchors come in great variety. The anchor you might use for a short, sheltered stop is not necessarily the one to use for anchoring overnight. Coastal cruising sailors and powerboaters should carry two anchors of different designs—a primary anchor that you trust to hold your boat in a boisterous anchorage, and a secondary to deploy as a backup when the primary won't do the job alone. Many boats carry a third, lighter anchor to use as a fair-weather "lunch hook" and for other occasional duties. Here's a quick rundown of types:

## Plow Anchor and Scoop Anchor

CQR

**Holds best in:** Firm sand, thick mud, rock, coral, weed
**Not so good in:** Silt, sloppy mud, gravel
**Stowability:** Usually stows well on a bow roller; hard to stow belowdecks
**Comments:** Excellent all-around anchor; the most common primary anchor on sailboats with bow rollers. Designed to bury deeply and provide high holding power in firm substrates. Tends to reset itself quickly when broken out or after a change in the direction of pull. Awkward to stow except on a bow roller, so not often found on small cruising sailboats or powerboats. Most will orient themselves point down when hauled up on a bow roller, making them self-stowing as well as self-launching. Scoop anchors differ from plows in their concave upper blade surface, which enhances their holding power. Popular examples are:

**CQR.** Hinged-shank plow. One of the oldest anchors still in general use. Immensely popular. Beware poorly made copies. Best if heavier for a given size of boat than most other plows.

**Delta.** Fixed-shank plow. Valued by sailors and powerboaters for rapid setting, good holding power, and reasonable cost. Awkward to stow and won't fit some bow rollers.

**HydroBubble.** This plow has a plastic float to ensure that the blade meets the bottom at the desired angle. Sets quickly, holds well, and breaks down for storage, but creates an awkward fit on many bow rollers.

**Spade.** This scoop anchor has gained wide acceptance among cruising sailors in recent years. Concave blade and weighted tip provide excellent penetrating and holding power in most bottoms. Can be dismantled for storage.

**Rocna** and **Manson Supreme.** These new scoops have a roll bar rather than a weighted tip to orient the blade's sharp point into the seabed. Set quickly. Expensive and awkward to stow (except in a bow roller).

## Claw Anchor

Bruce

**Holds best in:** Rock, weed, coral, sand
**Not so good in:** Soft mud, soft sand
**Stowability:** Awkward to stow except on bow roller
**Comments:** Like a plow, a good all-around choice as primary or secondary anchor on any boat over 30 to 35 feet. For best substrate penetration, heavier is better. Popular examples are:

**Bruce.** Rivals the CQR among sailors' longtime favorites. Beware poorly made copies.

## Pivoting-Fluke Anchor

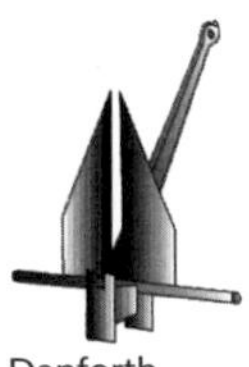
Danforth

**Holds best in:** Sand, soft mud
**Not so good in:** Rock, grass, clay, weed
**Stowability:** Light and easy to stow on deck or in a locker
**Comments:** Features a pair of blades set at right angles to the shank and hinged to penetrate the bottom whichever way the anchor lands. Unexcelled holding-to-weight ratio once dug in, but can be slow to dig in or to reset after tripping. Sometimes prone to trapping lumps of weed or rocks between blade and shank, rendering it useless. Typically the primary anchor on a boat of less than 30 feet without bow-roller stowage. Ideal on larger boats for stern anchor, lunch hook, or kedging when aground. Can also serve as storm anchor, tandem anchor, or in other uses of a secondary anchor. Every boat should carry one. Popular examples include the West Marine Perfomance, plus:

**Danforth.** Like the CQR and Bruce, has spawned countless imitators. Provides excellent straight-line holding power. Often superior to plows in mud and sand.

**Fortress.** Lightweight aluminum. Consistently scores very highly for holding power in anchor tests. Breaks down for convenient storage.

## Other Designs

fisherman

The **fisherman** anchor is excellent for taking a quick hold in rocks and for penetrating thick weed but needs to be much heavier than an equivalent plow or Danforth. It is awkward to handle, needs to be dismantled for stowage, and can be broken out too easily if a bight of the rode wraps around the fluke or stock. Four-pronged **grapnel** anchors are good in rocky bottoms but are too inherently weak to be used as a main anchor.

If you're going to be anchoring a lot, it's a good idea to carry two anchors of different designs. Shown here (clockwise from top left): Delta, Spade, HydroBubble, Fortress (assembled and disassembled).

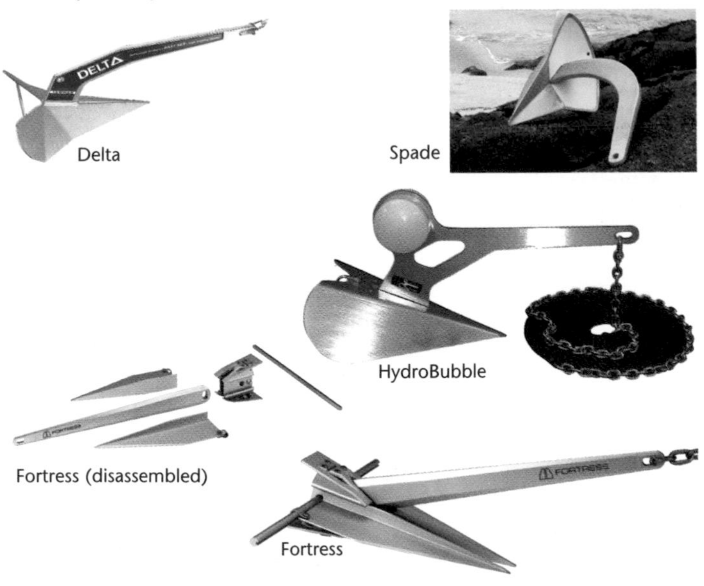

Delta
Spade
HydroBubble
Fortress (disassembled)
Fortress

# What Size Anchor?

The loads on a boat and its *ground tackle* (the combination of anchor, rope, and chain) are ever-changing and dynamic. Wind and current make a boat sheer about at the end of its anchor rode. Waves make a boat's bow pitch up and down, jerking at the ground tackle. It is the ability of an anchor to withstand such jerking and snatching from varying directions, and to rebury swiftly should it be plucked from the bottom, that is critical.

According to anchor manufacturers' recommendations, the primary or secondary anchor for a 34-foot cruising sailboat could be a 22-pound Delta, a 35-pound CQR, a 33-pound steel Spade, a 15-pound aluminum Spade, a 10-pound Fortress, an 8.5-pound Danforth, or a 16-pound Bruce. Holding power is determined not by weight but by design and the surface area of the blade or flukes. For instance, Spade claims identical holding power for its steel and aluminum anchors, which have identical dimensions apart from weight. Weight, however, is certainly a factor in getting an anchor to dig in and set on a hard bottom, and unless an anchor digs in and sets quickly, its holding power is immaterial.

For decades, the anchoring maxim was "1 pound of anchor for every foot of boat." You could do worse than to follow that maxim today, at least for a plow or claw anchor.

### Recommended Minimum Primary and Secondary Anchor Sizes for Sail or Power (pounds)

| BOAT LENGTH (FT.) | DELTA | CQR | SPADE (STEEL/ ALUM.) | WEST MARINE PERFORMANCE | FORTRESS (ALUM.) | DANFORTH DEEPSET | BRUCE (CLAW) |
|---|---|---|---|---|---|---|---|
| 20–25 | 14 | 25 | 22/10 | 6 | 4 | 5 | 11 |
| 25–30 | 22 | 25 | 33/15 | 14 | 7 | 8.5 | 11 |
| 30–35 | 22 | 35 | 33/15 | 14 | 10 | 8.5 | 16 |
| 35–40 | 35 | 35 | 44/20 | 25 | 15 | 13 | 22 |
| 40–45 | 44 | 45 | 44/20 | 40 | 15 | 20 | 33 |

**Stern** or **kedge** anchors are the exceptions to the pound-per-foot guidelines for anchor weight. You may have to row these out in a dinghy or carry them out by hand, so you want no more weight than necessary. A pivoting-fluke anchor on an all-nylon rode makes an ideal kedge.

A plow anchor (in this case a Rocna) setting itself in firm sand during beach testing.

# Ground Tackle

The other elements of your ground tackle include the rode and connectors. The rode will be rope, chain, or a combination of the two.

**Rope.** There is only one rope material suitable for an anchor rode—nylon. No other fiber offers such a combination of strength and shock absorption. Traditionally, three-strand nylon has been the rope of choice, but the 8- to 12-strand single-braid nylon (also known as multiplait nylon) now marketed under such brand names as Mega Braid and Brait is an even better alternative, able to absorb more shock energy before failure and less prone to kinking and binding in chain pipes.

BENEFITS OF ROPE

- Elasticity lessens shock loads that can jerk an anchor out of the seabed
- Light and easy to stow
- Inexpensive and easy to replace

DRAWBACKS OF ROPE

- Need to guard against chafe
- Requires greater scope than chain
- Allows boat to sail around its anchor

**Chain.** For anchor rodes, most boaters use one of four kinds of open-link galvanized chain. *Proof coil* is made from low-grade carbon steel and is the most economical chain for anchor rodes. *BBB* has shorter links and is better than proof coil for windlasses. *High-test* or G40 has a higher strength-to-weight ratio and is made from high-tensile carbon steel. *Alloy chain* is made from steel alloy and is even stronger (and more expensive) than high-test.

BENEFITS OF CHAIN

- Cannot chafe through
- Great strength
- Extra weight on seabed absorbs shock loads and reduces need for long scope
- Boat does not sail around so much on anchor

DRAWBACKS OF CHAIN

- Extra weight can be hard to handle without a windlass and can affect boat trim
- Expensive
- Doesn't absorb shock loads in extreme conditions

By way of example, let's compare nylon and chain rodes for a 32- to 36-foot boat (see the table on page 132):

| TYPE AND SIZE OF RODE | AVERAGE BREAKING STRENGTH (lbs.) | HORIZONTAL ENERGY ABSORPTION (ft.-lbs. per 100 ft.) | WEIGHT (lbs. per 100 ft.) |
|---|---|---|---|
| 5⁄16" BBB chain | 7,600 | 0 | 115 |
| 1⁄2" 3-strand nylon | 5,750 | 67,665 | 6 |
| 1⁄2" nylon Brait | 6,300 | 114,452 | 6 |

## Rope or Chain—What's Best for You?

You often see offshore cruising sailboats and trawler yachts anchored on all-chain rodes, but most powerboaters and coastal cruisers use a combination of chain at the anchor end and nylon at the boat end. The chain augments the anchor weight and keeps the pull on the anchor as horizontal as possible. A commonly accepted ratio is 6 inches of chain for each foot of boat length, but a foot of chain for each foot of boat length is better, and a 50- or 60-foot chain allows a much shorter scope to be used than if the boat were anchored with mainly rope rode. Boaters in generally shallow waters (like the U.S. East Coast) can usually get away with using less chain (and even less rope) than those plying deeper waters (e.g., the West Coast or Great Lakes).

**Recommended Rode Sizes**

| BOAT LOA (FT.) | NYLON RODE DIAMETER | CHAIN DIAMETER BY TYPE | WEIGHT (lbs. per 100 ft.) (ALL-NYLON/ALL-CHAIN/ ALL-HT CHAIN) |
|---|---|---|---|
| Up to 25 | 3/8"/9mm | 3/16" Proof Coil | 3.5/50 |
| 27 to 31 | 7/16"/11mm | 1/4" Proof Coil/BBB | 5/76–81 |
| 32 to 36 | 1/2"/12mm | 5/16" Proof Coil/BBB, 1/4"/HT | 6.5/115–120/70 |
| 37 to 44 | 9/16"/14mm | 3/8" Proof Coil/BBB, 5/16"HT | 8.2/166–173/106 |
| 45 to 50 | 5/8"/16mm | 3/8" Proof Coil/BBB/HT | 10.5/166–173/154 |
| 51 to 62 | 3/4"/18mm | 3/8" Proof Coil/BBB/HT | 14.5/166–173/154 |

## Connectors

Connect your chain to the anchor with a strong shackle (the working load should be stamped on it), preferably galvanized—stainless steel shackles are often weaker than galvanized ones. Making the shackle one size larger than the chain (e.g., 5/16" shackle for 1/4" chain) is a good precaution. Wire the shackle pin so that it can't unscrew itself ①. Do not use a carabiner-type quick link unless you have a small boat that doesn't put much load on its anchor. A stainless steel swivel between chain and anchor is a potential weak link, so if you feel you must use one (in an area of reversing currents, for example), make it top-quality. Always fit a shackle between swivel and anchor to ensure that it articulates properly.

Lengths of chain can be connected with a joining link, but a single length is stronger. There are two equally strong ways to connect rope to chain: with a rope-to-chain splice ② or with an eye splice (around a thimble) and strong galvanized shackle ③. The former approach is mandatory if you have a windlass.

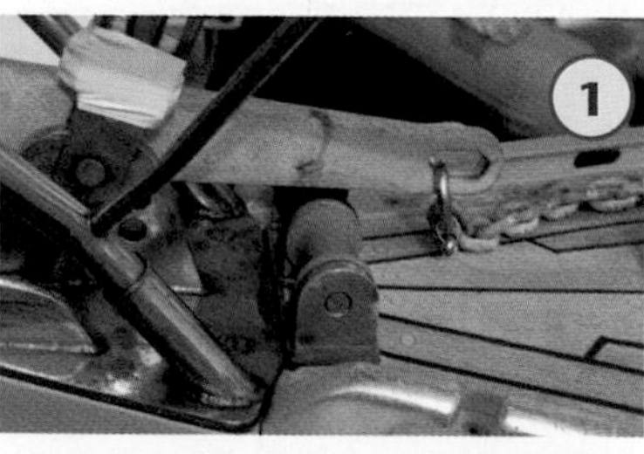

# Choosing an Anchorage

If you will only be anchored for a couple of hours in settled weather, your biggest worries will be making sure you have enough water underneath you and that the anchor has dug in. But for a longer stay:

- Consult your chart to find out how much depth there is around the anchorage, and the makeup of the bottom. (***S*** = sand; ***M*** = mud; ***Cy*** or ***Cl*** = clay; ***Si*** = silt; ***St*** = stones; ***G*** = gravel; ***P*** = pebbles; ***Cb*** = cobbles; ***Sh*** = shell; ***Co*** = coral; ***S/M*** = sand over mud; ***Wd*** = weed.) Avoid unmarked rocks or shoals and obstructions on the bottom that could foul your anchor.
- Check the weather forecast—will the anchorage provide shelter from the forecast wind direction?
- Look at how other boats are oriented. If their bows are not all pointing into the wind there is likely some current running, and this will influence your choice of where to anchor.
- Choose a spot that will have enough depth at low water—at least 6 feet under the keel. The less depth you anchor in, the smaller your swinging circle will be. If you know the local times and heights of low water and high water, you can estimate the height of tide when you anchor using the Rule of Twelfths. The rule assumes, given a 6-hour tidal range, that the tide rises or falls by one-twelfth of its overall range in the first hour, two-twelfths in the second, and so on, in this pattern: 1, 2, 3, 3, 2, 1.
- If possible, anchor on a flat bottom.
- Try to anchor where the effects of swell or wind are minimized.
- Make sure your boat can swing to its anchor without fouling other anchored boats, hitting obstructions, or grounding.
- Take compass bearings of safe routes out of the anchorage in case you have to leave at night.

These boats have taken clearing bearings on dangers at the entrance.

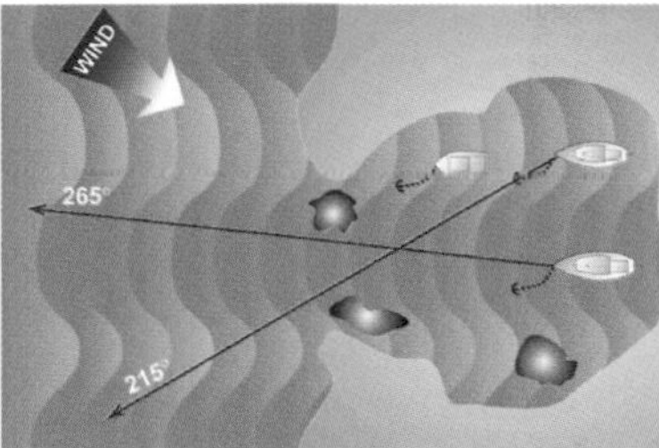


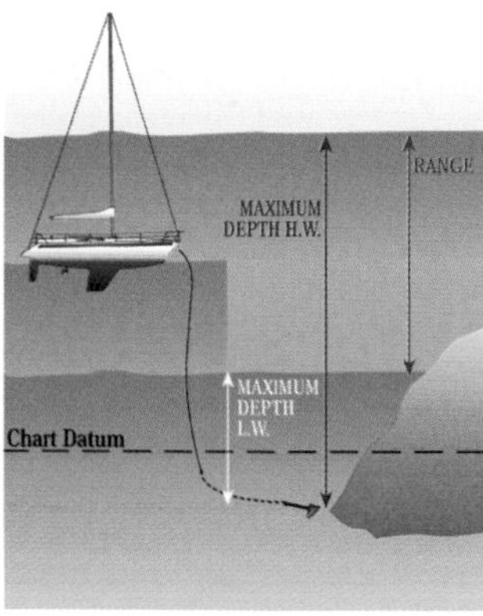


You need to know how much depth you'll have under your keel at low water. The depths marked on your chart and the heights of tide predicted in tide tables both relate to chart datum. If the height of tide at low water is predicted to be +1.0 foot, you can add 1 foot to the charted low-water depth. Allow for the range of tide when determining how much scope you need.

# Anchoring Among Neighbors

Make a circuit of the anchorage to choose a good spot and check out depths and hidden dangers. Now take a close look at your neighbors. Different boats lie differently to their anchors. If possible, anchor next to boats that are similar to yours, and check whether they are anchored with chain or rope.

Observe the unwritten code of conduct. The first boat to arrive gets its choice of prime spots. The last to arrive is the first to move when boats swing too close. Also, don't drop your anchor over someone else's, don't anchor too close abeam of another boat, and respect your neighbors—don't play loud music or make unnecessary noise.

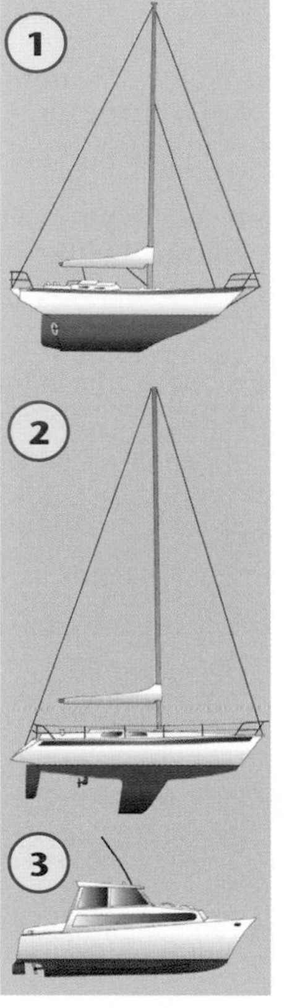


① A long-keeled, heavy-displacement sailboat will tend to lie quietly in most conditions, especially if anchored with all-chain rode.

② A sailboat with fin keel and spade rudder will tend to range from side to side at anchor.

③ A powerboat with little of its hull underwater will typically sail about all over the place when wind and tide are opposing each other, especially if it is on a rope rode.

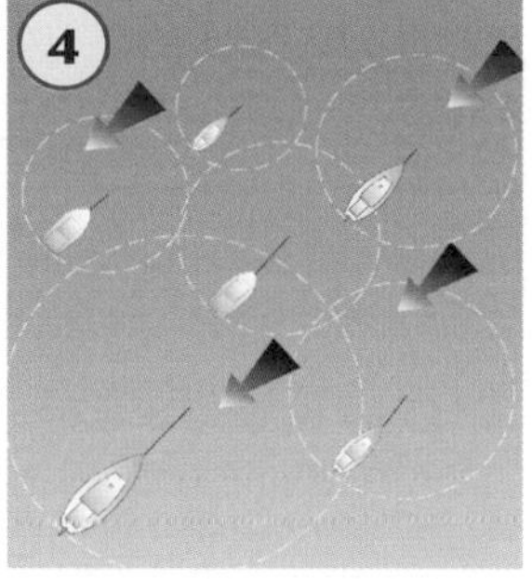


④ Synchronized swinging circles, when all boats move together to the changing wind or tide, make for a peaceful anchorage.

Unfortunately, while boats will lie predictably when wind and current are in the same direction ⑤, they will be all over the place when the wind and current oppose each other ⑥.

In a river, try to anchor where the prevailing wind blows across the river ⑦. Otherwise you will spend much of your time in an undesirable wind-against-tide situation ⑧.

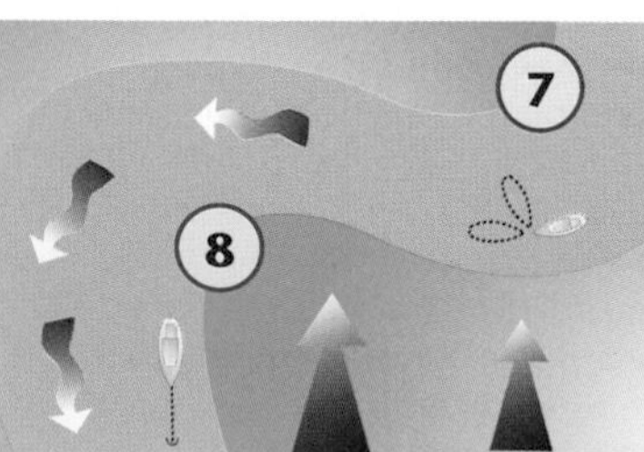

# Anchoring Under Power

The procedure for setting an anchor under power is so simple that it is amazing so many people get it wrong so often. The same rules apply to power- or sailboats.

- Head into the wind or current, whichever is stronger.
- Bring the boat to a dead stop.
- As the boat begins to gather sternway, ease the anchor to the bottom either hand over hand or with the windlass. Do not just let the rode run out uncontrolled ①.
- Apply a touch of throttle in reverse to get the boat moving astern. If it is windy, this won't be necessary.
- Pay out the rode as the boat drifts back, keeping a slight tension on it so it forms a line across the seabed. The boat will probably lie broadside to the wind ②.
- When you have paid out about half your intended scope, snub the rode until you feel resistance from the anchor, then resume easing it out ③.
- Keeping tension on the rode, pay out another quarter of the scope, then snub again momentarily.
- With the boat still moving astern, secure the anchor rode when the desired scope has been paid out. The boat's weight should dig the anchor in solidly; the anchor rode will rise out of the water in a straight line ④.
- To make doubly sure the anchor is well dug in, back down with the engine at half throttle for 30 seconds. The boat should move forward on the rode when you ease the throttle.
- If you don't get your anchor to set the first time, try again. If it still won't set, try another spot.

**Common mistakes:** letting chain pile up on top of the anchor; letting the anchor go while the boat is still moving forward; going astern so quickly that the anchor does not have a chance to dig in; anchoring too close to other boats.

**Most common mistake of all:** failing to let out enough scope (see page 136).

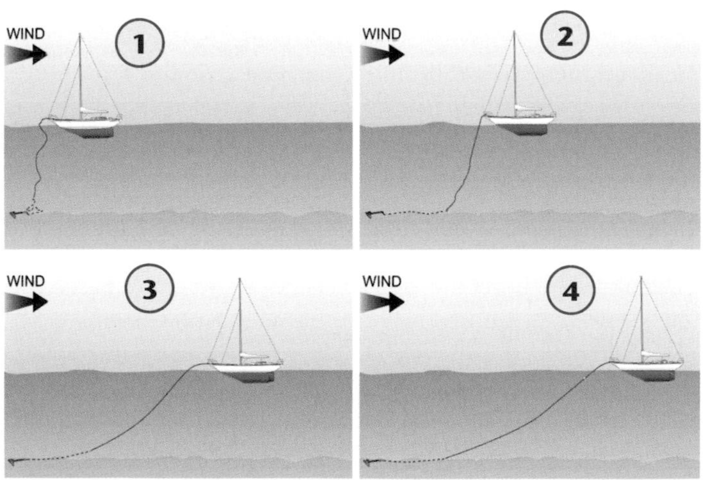

# Anchoring Under Sail

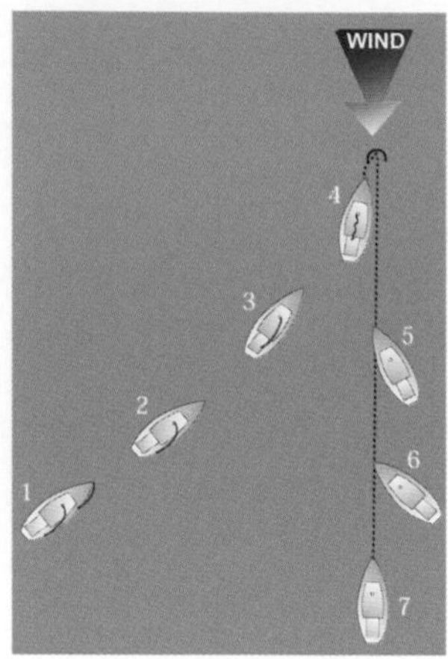


**Upwind:** Roll up the headsail as you approach the chosen spot on a close or beam reach. Steer into the wind and let the mainsail luff until the boat stops. Drop the anchor as the boat begins to make sternway, and pay out the desired scope as on page 135. You can lower the mainsail as the boat falls back.

**Downwind:** Drop the main and play the jibsheet to spill wind and slow the boat as you approach the chosen spot. Roll up the jib completely as the anchor is let go. If you have a rope rode, be careful not to overrun it and get it tangled with your keel or rudder. As you snub the rode, put the helm over so that the boat swings around. The weight of the boat coming onto the rode should dig in the anchor.

# Scope

**Scope** is the ratio of rode length to water depth plus freeboard (i.e., the height of the bow above the water added to the depth of water). If you anchor at low tide, add the expected rise of tide.

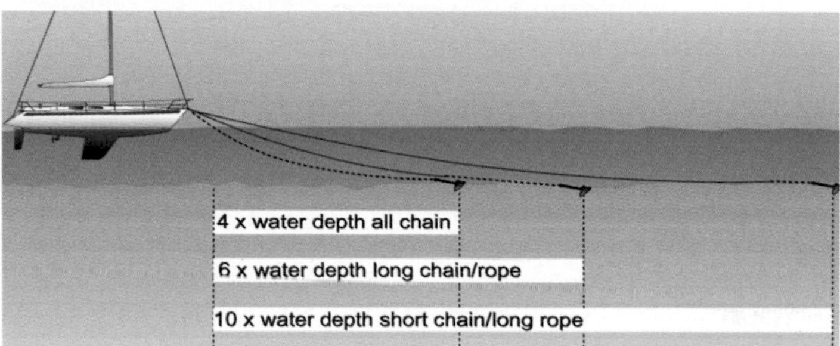


For instance: 5' height of bow + 15' depth + 6' rise of tide = 26'. At the recommended 4:1 scope (all chain) you would let out 104' of rode; at 6:1 (chain/rope), 156'; and at 10:1 (all rope) a whopping 260'.

Adapt these rules of thumb to prevailing circumstances. In a crowded anchorage in settled conditions, you should get by with 3:1 scope on an all-chain rode or 4:1 or 5:1 on a rope/chain combo. Conversely, as the wind and seas increase, let out more rode to increase your scope.

Catenary—the sag in a chain rode caused by the weight of the chain—helps dampen loadings on the anchor and keep a horizontal pull on it.

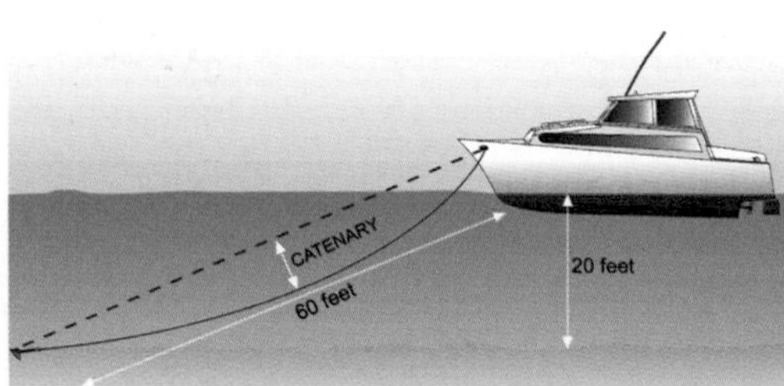

# Dragging Anchor

Sometimes the anchor won't set even after several attempts. You can either try a different anchor or move to a different spot. Even after you think the hook is set, it may drag when the wind increases or the tide changes and the anchor fails to reset.

## How to Tell When You're Dragging

Immediately after anchoring, line up a couple of landmarks or seamarks on either side of the boat. Two objects in line with each other comprise a range; as long as the two objects stay aligned, one behind the other, you can be sure you are not dragging.

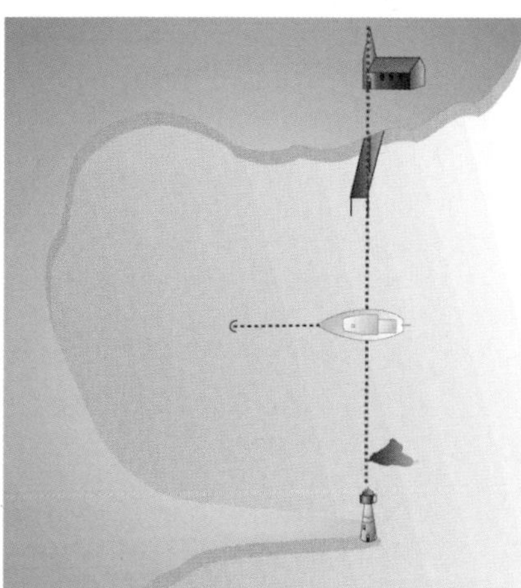

The pier and church steeple make a range to starboard. The rock and lighthouse make a range to port.

**You are probably dragging if:**

- The two objects in a range are no longer aligned
- Anchored boats appear to be overtaking you
- The rode rises up out of the water and then goes slack again
- The boat sheers to one side and does not swing back again
- The boat lies side-to the wind
- You can feel the rode vibrating beneath your hand or bare foot

## What to Do When You're Dragging

The first thing to try, if you are dragging into shallow water but are far enough from shore for safety, is to let out more rode (inadequate scope is the #1 reason anchors drag). Often this is all that's required. If you are among other boats, dragging into deep water, or too close to shore, get the anchor up immediately. If your anchor has pivoting flukes, make sure they have not been jammed by a pebble or starfish, and take special care when you try again to make the anchor dig in properly. If you still drag, your anchor may not like the bottom, so it is best to move to another part of the anchorage. On a windy night in an exposed anchorage, the crew may have to take turns keeping "anchor watch." Be careful when you're raising anchor with other boats close abeam. If it's windy the bow of your boat will fall off quickly when the load comes off the anchor, and you will have to use a lot of throttle to keep control.

# Anchoring Tips and Tricks

**Weight on rode.** An excellent way to reduce your swinging circle in a constricted anchorage is to lower a weight down the rode ①. This can be a dedicated metal weight weighing a minimum of 20 pounds, shackled to the anchor rode, or you can use your kedge anchor. Rode weights also improve holding in strong winds.

**Riding sail.** A riding sail, attached to the backstay and sheeted in tight, acts as a weather vane to keep the boat facing into the wind ②. It greatly decreases a boat's tendency to sail around its anchor. They are commercially available or you can make your own.

**Anchor trip line.** When anchoring over rocks or obstructions, you can attach a trip line to the crown of the anchor. If the flukes get stuck, the trip line should release them. The other end of the line goes to a small float ③ that should be clearly marked so that other boats don't mistake it for a mooring buoy. In a crowded anchorage, it makes sense to bring the trip line back on board your boat so that it doesn't foul other boats ④.

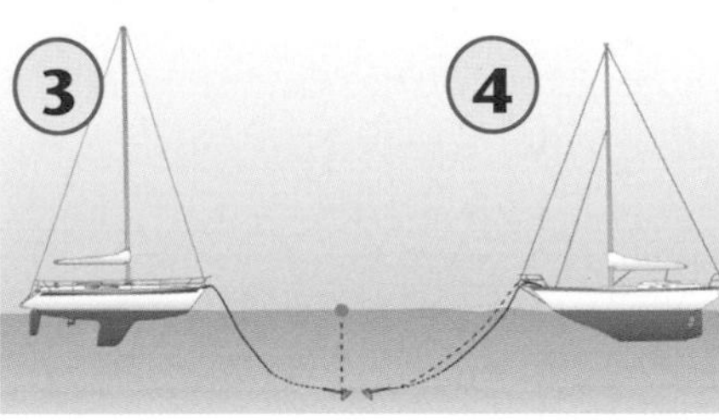

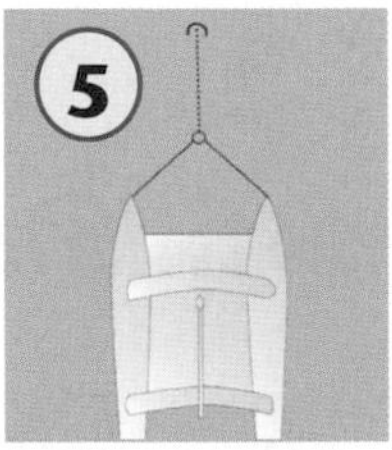

**Multihull anchoring.** Catamarans and trimarans tend to sail around their anchors more than monohulls. This tendency can be minimized by rigging an anchor bridle ⑤.

**Anchoring from the stern.** In calm, settled conditions, it is possible to anchor from the stern in order to get the breeze flowing through the cockpit and into the cabin. The best way to do this is to lead the main anchor rode back to the stern and cleat it there ⑥. When it is time to leave, or if the wind increases, uncleat the anchor rode so that the boat comes head to wind, then retrieve the anchor ⑦.

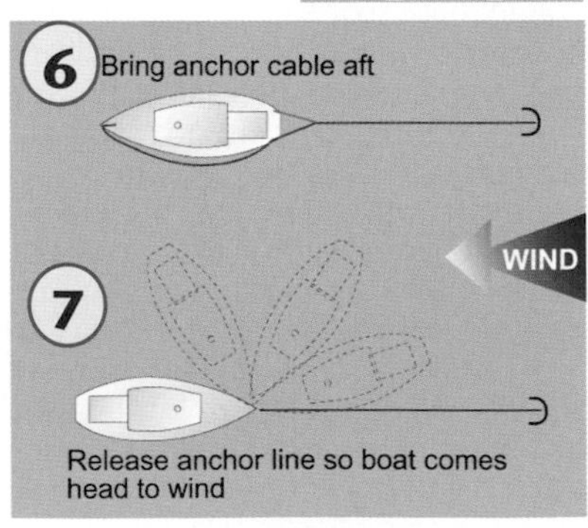


Anchoring

**Anchor rollers.** On small boats where weight distribution is important, it is often not feasible to keep an anchor on the bow, but if your boat is big enough and coastal cruising figures in your plans, a dedicated bow roller ⑧, ⑨ and anchor locker will be a blessing. Aftermarket anchor rollers are readily available, and fitting them is within the scope of a competent do-it-yourselfer.

**Left:** Double bow roller.
**Below:** CQR stowed in bow roller. Danforth stowed in bow-pulpit bracket.

If your boating habits take you into waters where you will often need to set a stern anchor, you will also get good use out of a stern anchor roller ⑩, which can be bolted to the taffrail.

**Chafe protection.** Nylon rode has many virtues, but resistance to abrasion isn't one of them. A ½"-inch anchor rode can chafe through in a matter of hours when the bow is pitching up and down in a rough anchorage. A length of fire hose (discards from the local fire station or commercial equivalent) is an excellent chafe preventer. Second best is a length of flexible vinyl water hose (used in plumbing). The only practical way to get these onto a nylon anchor rode is to split them lengthwise, and this means they'll work loose more easily. The best solution is to slide the fire hose or water hose over a snubbing line, which is then rolling-hitched to the anchor rode.

**Marking your rode.** How do you know how much rode you've got out unless you mark it? Commercially made rode markers are available from West Marine, or you can make your own. Plastic cable ties work well on either chain or nylon. They don't interfere with windlass operation and are available in different colors so you can come up with your own code. Leave the tails long; they can cut your fingers if trimmed too short, and they'll be easier to feel in the dark. Webbing markers are another alternative. There's no need to mark the rode more than every 25 or 30 feet.

**A spring line on the anchor.** Some anchorages are inherently rolly. Often the boat will ride more comfortably if you fasten a line from the stern quarter to the anchor rode with a shackle or rolling hitch, then ease the rode until the boat presents its bow to the swell rather than the wind ①.

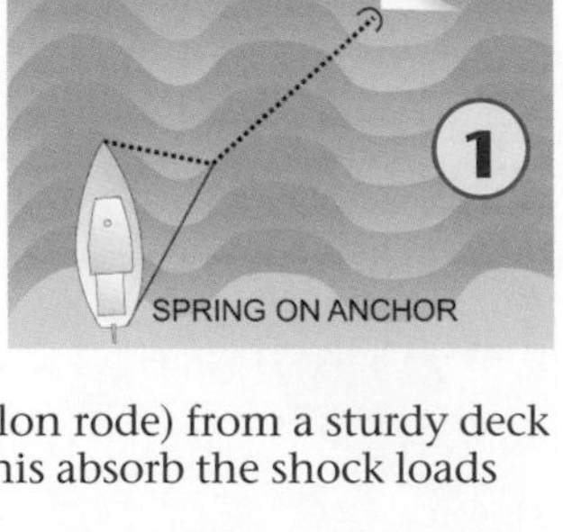


**Anchor snubber.** If anchoring with all-chain rode, you should rig a nylon snubber line (sized like a nylon rode) from a sturdy deck cleat to the chain ②. Not only will this absorb the shock loads the chain would otherwise transmit to windlass or anchor cleat, it prevents the rumblings of the chain dragging across the bottom as the boat swings from being transmitted to the hull. The snubber should be about 30 feet long so that you can lengthen it as the wind increases. It can be fastened to the chain with a rolling hitch or with a chain claw.

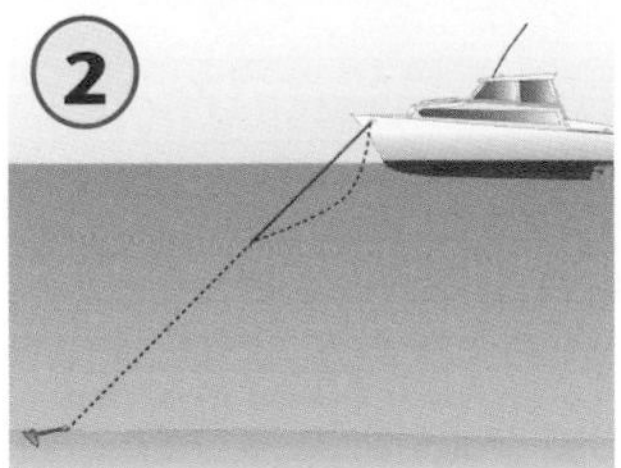


**Taking a line ashore.** It is often possible to anchor in narrow coves with little swinging room by taking lines ashore ③. The boat should always face open water in case you have to leave in a hurry. Drop the anchor, back into the desired spot, then take lines ashore with a dinghy. This is a good technique to use where the bottom drops away steeply from the shore.

**Keeping your rode in order.** If you don't have a dedicated chain locker, the best way to keep your anchor rode ready to run is by faking it into a bucket ④. This will ensure that it will pay out without tangling or kinking. Tie the bitter end of the rode to the handle of the bucket, leaving enough free so that it can be cleated off before you drop the anchor.

**Setting two anchors.** Sometimes it is a good idea to set two anchors. For example, you might want to limit your swinging circle so as to anchor closer to shore; you might be anchoring in a river or narrow cut where the current reverses; or you might want extra security because strong winds are forecast.

The most common way of doing this is to drop your main anchor first ⑤, then fall back until you have paid out

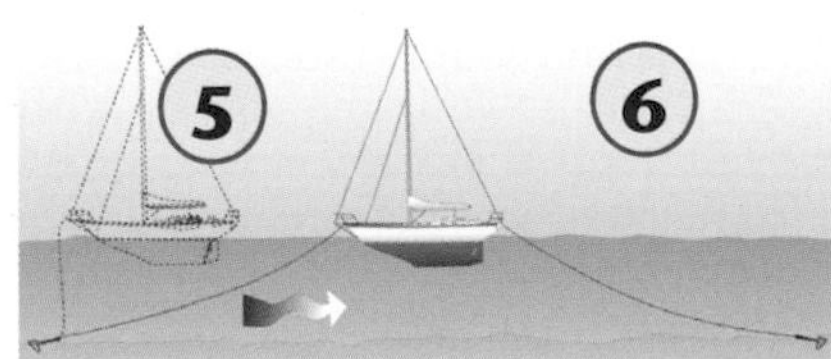

double the desired scope. Release the stern anchor, then pull the boat forward on its bow anchor rode until the scopes are equalized ⑥. Remember that the heavier anchor is always set in the direction of the strongest current, which flows from upchannel if anchoring in a river. When it's time to leave, weigh the downstream anchor first; if the bow is facing downstream, take the stern anchor rode forward outside the lifelines and cleat it off at the bow. Then let the boat swing head to current before dropping back to retrieve the anchor.

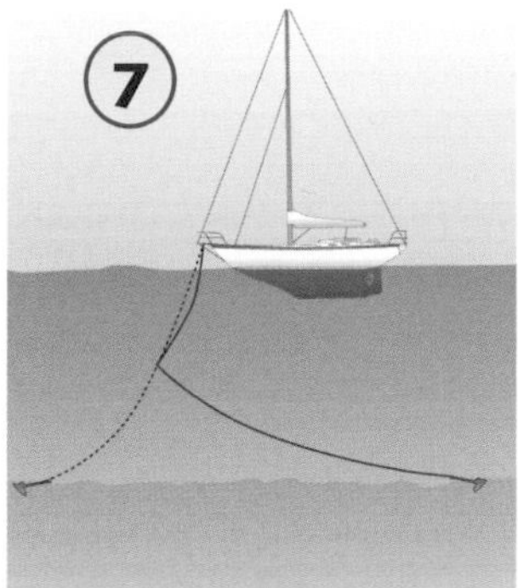


The fore-and-aft moor works well most of the time in confined waters. When the wind is blowing from abeam, however, it puts a huge strain on the anchors and may well break out one of them. At such times you can set bow and stern anchors as above, then carry the stern anchor rode forward and secure it at the bow. This configuration is known as a **Bahamian moor**. The stern anchor rode may foul the keel when the boat swings unless you weight it or secure it to the main rode well below keel depth ⑦.

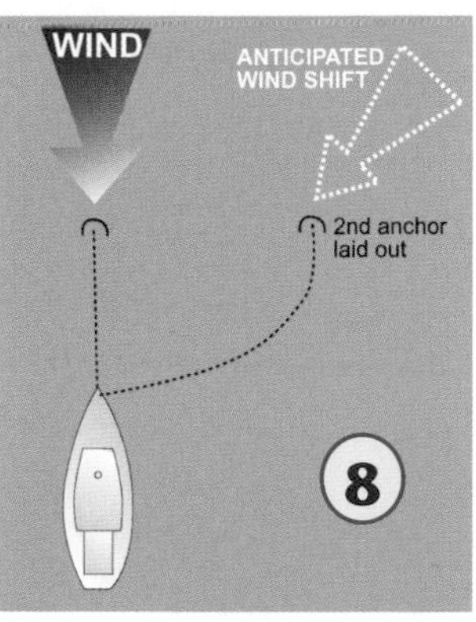


If you are in an exposed anchorage and a change in wind direction is forecast, you can lay out a second anchor from the bow in the direction of the anticipated wind shift ⑧. This is best done with the dinghy. When the wind shift arrives, equalize the two rodes so that they share the strain.

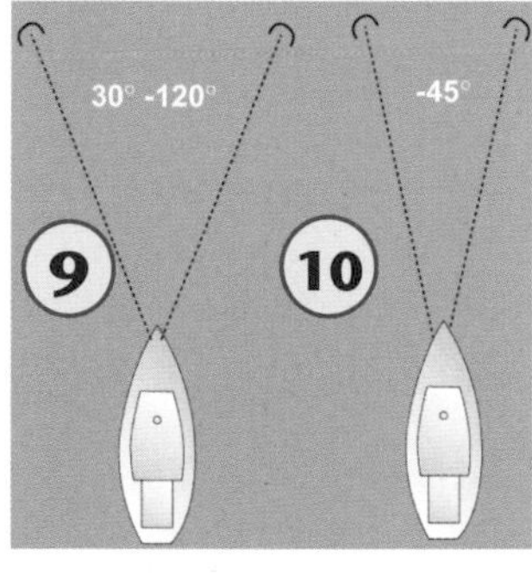


Sometimes you might want to set two anchors from the bow to reduce your swinging circle. An angle of up to 120 degrees between them is fine in light to moderate winds ⑨, but in strong winds the angle should not exceed 45 degrees, and 30 degrees is better ⑩.

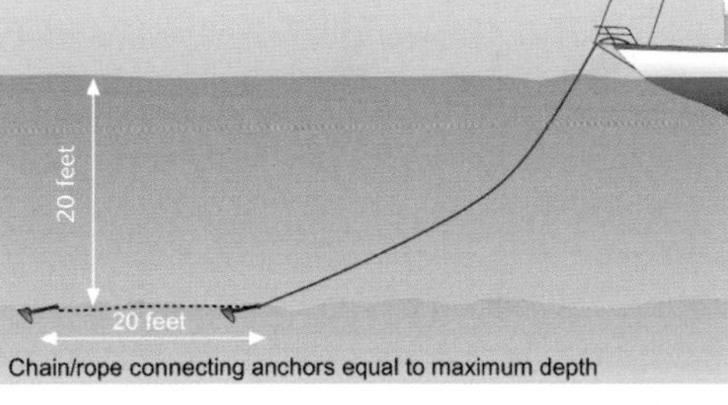


Finally, some long-distance sailors recommend setting **tandem anchors** in strong winds. The technique involves shackling a lighter anchor to the crown of the main anchor. Unless you do this with a length of chain at least equal to the depth at high water, you will find it very awkward to retrieve the second anchor. You need to get the main anchor on deck or in its roller before lifting the second one.

CHAPTER 9

# Onboard Weather Forecasting

Bob Sweet

# Be Your Own Forecaster

Meteorologists monitor large-scale weather systems and, using computer models, are able to predict with fair regional accuracy what lies ahead for those in a system's path. Before heading out on the water, you should by all means obtain a local forecast, and update it on board if you can. This is your earliest indicator of what may be heading your way. Pages 152 and 153 list some sources of weather forecasts.

But these regional forecasts don't always match the conditions you encounter on the water. For one thing, the precise path of a low-pressure center will significantly impact what happens where you are. For another, a regional forecast cannot account for variations across the region of coverage. On land it rarely matters whether the actual local wind strength is 15 or 25 knots, but on the water it certainly does. Then too, a topographically enhanced sea breeze or a locally generated thunderstorm cannot be covered adequately in a regional forecast. And forecasts prepared for offshore waters—where there are few monitoring stations—may be several hours out of date by the time they reach you.

You'll be better prepared for what's coming if you use your own observations to modify and refine official forecasts. This chapter, which focuses on the temperate regions where most boats operate—between 30 and 60 degrees north and south latitudes—will provide the background you need.

Over the centuries, mariners have developed weather proverbs for interpreting their observations. We'll find out why these four, in particular, have proved reliable:

Red skies at night, sailor's delight; red skies in the morning, sailors take warning . . . (see page 146).

A wind from the west means weather's fair; a wind from the east, foul weather's near . . . (see page 146).

Mackerel sky, 12 hours dry . . . (see page 151).
The higher the clouds, the better the weather . . . (see page 150).

# Highs and Lows (Depressions)

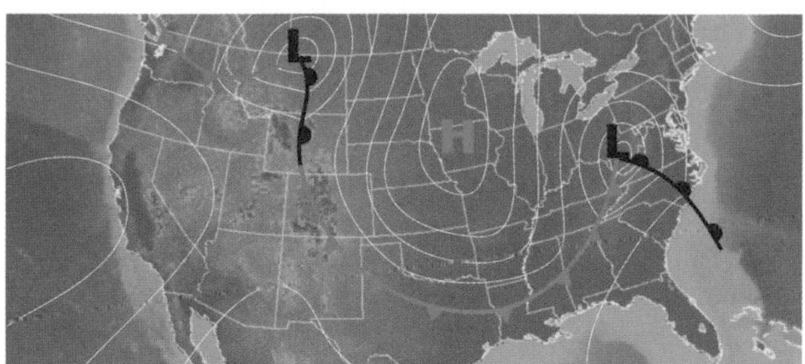


Weather maps show the locations of high- and low-pressure centers, around which are lines of equal atmospheric pressure called *isobars*. (The maps also show fronts. See page 146.) Winds blow from high-pressure centers toward lows, but the Earth's rotation deflects the winds so that they tend to follow the isobars at higher altitudes. Due to friction with the Earth's surface, however, ground-level winds over land cross the isobars at about a 30-degree angle toward the low. Over water, where there is less friction, surface winds blow at a lesser angle to the isobars—about 15 degrees toward the low.

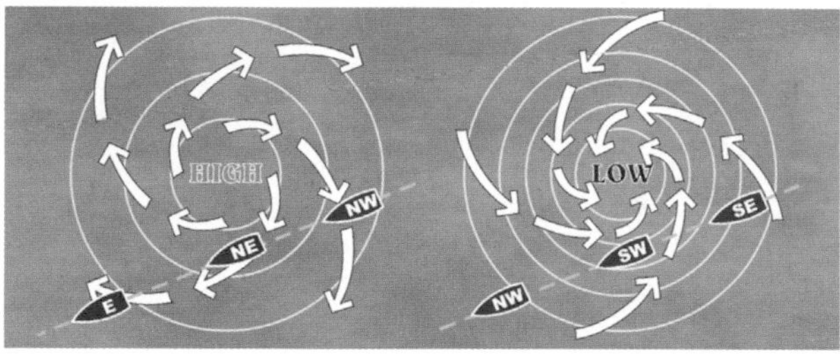


In the Northern Hemisphere, winds are deflected to the right by the Earth's rotation and thus spiral outward from highs in a clockwise direction and inward toward lows in a counterclockwise direction. The opposite is true in the Southern Hemisphere, where winds are deflected to the left. Highs can be likened to hills, lows to hollows, and isobars to the contour lines on a topographic map. When the isobars are closer, the slope is steeper and the resultant winds are stronger.

Generally, isobars are more closely spaced around a low than a high, which means the winds will be stronger in a low. Highs are typically broad, ranging up to a thousand miles or more across, while lows tend to be more compact, perhaps 400 or fewer miles across. Within a high, air from the atmosphere is sinking and therefore stable; the air in a low is rising and therefore unstable. Simply stated, bad weather is associated with lows, or depressions, and fair weather with highs.

| | HIGH | LOW |
|---|---|---|
| Weather | Generally fair | Stormy, precipitation |
| Temperature | Stable – long periods | Cool to warm changing to colder |
| Motion (avg) [~West to East] | Winter: 565 nm/day<br>Summer: 390 nm/day | Winter: 600 nm/day<br>Summer: 430 nm/day |
| Winds | Moderate, rising near edge | Strong and changeable with possible high seas |
| Pressure [Typical] | Rapid rise on approach, slow decline on retreat | Rapid fall on approach, slow rise on retreat |
| Clouds | Sparse, mostly near periphery | Wide variety, all altitudes |

# Passage of a Low

Since bad weather is usually associated with lows, knowing where the center of a low lies relative to your location can tell you a great deal about what to expect. Weather systems move generally west to east, steered along a boundary of major air masses by the planet's high-altitude jet streams—so if a low is to your west, you are likely to experience deteriorating weather as the low approaches. If the low is to your east, the weather is likely to improve as the low moves away. Since clear air refracts sunlight into the red spectrum, this is the reason the red skies proverb proves correct 70% of the time: red skies to the east at sunrise mark retreating clear weather, while red skies to the west at sunset herald its approach. Jet stream locations and the average speed of advance of a low (see page 145 table) vary by season.

To find the direction to a nearby low in the Northern Hemisphere, face the wind and extend your arm to your right. According to Buys Ballot's law, the low pressure will be slightly behind your outstretched arm—15 degrees behind over water, up to 30 degrees over land. In the Southern Hemisphere, use your left arm instead.

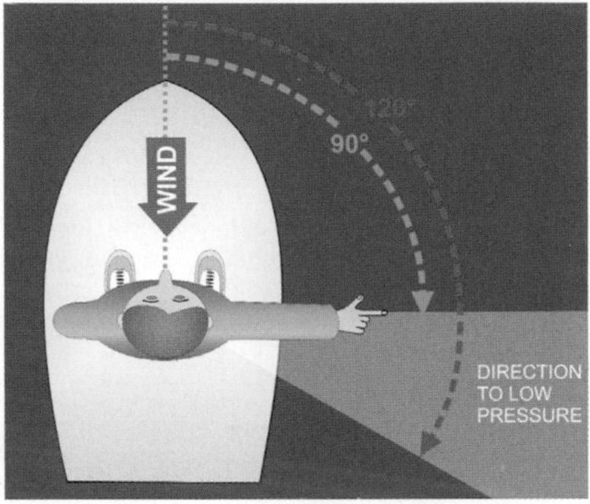

Detecting the center of a low in the Northern Hemisphere.

## Frontal Weather Systems

The lows that drive our middle-latitude weather form along the boundaries between two adjacent air masses—for example, between the cold, dry air mass that persists over Canada and the warm, moist air mass that recurs over the southern U.S. A low is born when a kink forms along this boundary and begins a counterclockwise rotation (Northern Hemisphere). East of the kink, southerly warm air starts to override colder air to the north and east, while to the west, northerly cold air pushes south and east, displacing the warmer air ahead of it. The resultant frontal boundaries (called *fronts*) separating regions of cool or colder air from warm assume the shape of an inverted V with the low at its apex, as in the page 147 graphic.

The newly formed system migrates eastward, steered by the overhead jet stream that follows and defines the air mass boundary, until the low dissipates several days later. The isobars surrounding the low show distinct bends along fronts, marking abrupt shifts in wind direction there.

A front is named for the relative temperature of the advancing air behind it. A warm front (red line on weather maps) denotes warm air overriding cooler air ahead, while a cold front (blue line) marks cold air overtaking warmer air ahead.

The weather sequence you experience with the passage of a low depends in large measure on whether the low passes to your north or south.

# Advancing Weather System

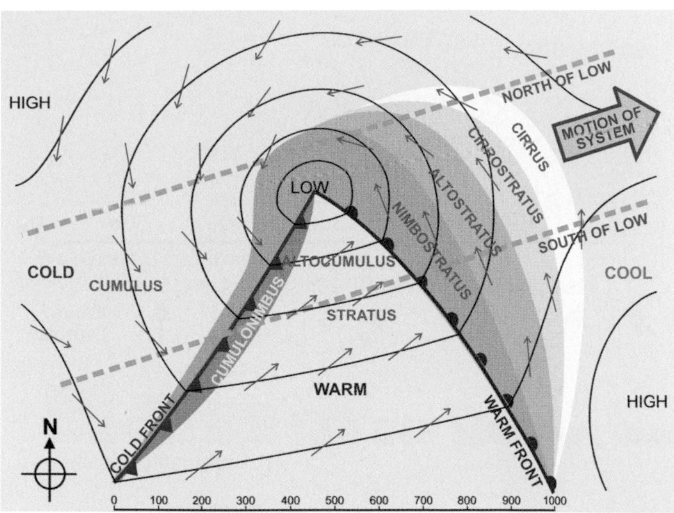


When a low passes poleward of you (i.e., to your north in the Northern Hemisphere), both fronts are likely to pass overhead as shown here by the lower dashed green line. In this illustration the black lines are isobars. The lowest pressure is within the small circle around the low, and each isobar moving outward from the center represents another 4-millibar (mb)[1] increase in pressure. As the system moves overhead, you can visualize the corresponding change in pressure by observing the isobars that pass by. The blue arrows indicate wind direction at each location, with the wind shifts clearly visible. The characteristic progressions of cloud types heralding the approach of each type of front are also labeled. A vertical cross-section along the dashed green line is shown on pages 148 and 149 for the warm front and cold front, respectively.

If the low is moving to your south (as in the upper dashed green line), you may have a period of rain without distinct fronts, as shown at the bottoms of pages 148 and 149.

Because cold fronts move faster than warm fronts, the cold front associated with a mature low (one that is several days old) will overtake the warm front, lifting the warmer air off the ground and forming an *occluded front* (purple line on weather maps) of moderating weather characteristics. The occluded front will usually dissipate within a day or so, and the low itself may dissipate soon thereafter, having traveled several thousand miles since its formation.

The red half circles along a warm front depiction and blue triangles on a cold front point toward the front's direction of advance. Occasionally two fronts meet and oppose each other, forming a *stationary front* that is depicted by alternating segments of cold- and warm-front symbols.

[1]Standard atmospheric pressure at sea level equals 1013 mb, or 29.92 inches of mercury. The actual sea level pressure varies between 925 and 1060 mb (27 to 31 inches).

## Advancing Warm Front

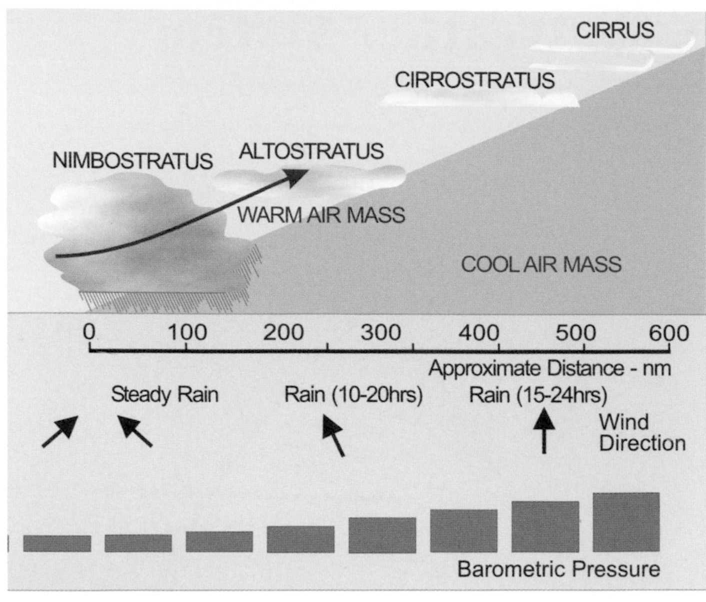


In a warm front, the overtaking warm air rises gradually up and over the cold air, forming a long wedge or incline. When a Northern Hemisphere low is passing north of you, you will see high cirrus clouds (see page 150) up to 24 hours or 600 miles ahead of the warm front, followed by cirrostratus, and the barometer will begin to fall. Up to half a day later, the winds will *back* (change in a counterclockwise direction) from south to southeast, and altostratus clouds will begin to move in under the cirrostratus. As the ground-level warm front continues its approach, the clouds will get steadily lower and thicker while the barometer continues a steady fall. Precipitation will begin up to 200 miles or more ahead of the front. As the front passes, the temperature will rise and the winds will *veer* (clockwise change in direction) from southeast to southwest. Within the warm sector, the wind direction will be fairly steady from the southwest (Northern Hemisphere) while the barometer will be somewhat steady. The skies may clear and the temperature will remain mild. Follow along the lower green line on page 147 to see the progression of isobars and winds.

## North of the Low

If you are poleward of an approaching low (upper green line in the page 147 graphic), you will not experience a warm or cold front. Instead, there will be an indistinct transition between the cool air ahead of the low and the colder air behind it, with nimbostratus clouds and steady rain likely. The approaching low will cause changes like those of an approaching warm front, except that the winds will back from east to northeast as the low passes to the south, and there will be no warm sector. Barometric pressures will fall gradually with the approach, then rise as the low moves off, while the winds gradually back into the northwest. The infamous *nor'easters* of the northeast U.S. result when a low stalls near the coast. The northeast winds north of the low dump moisture picked up from the sea.

## Advancing Cold Front

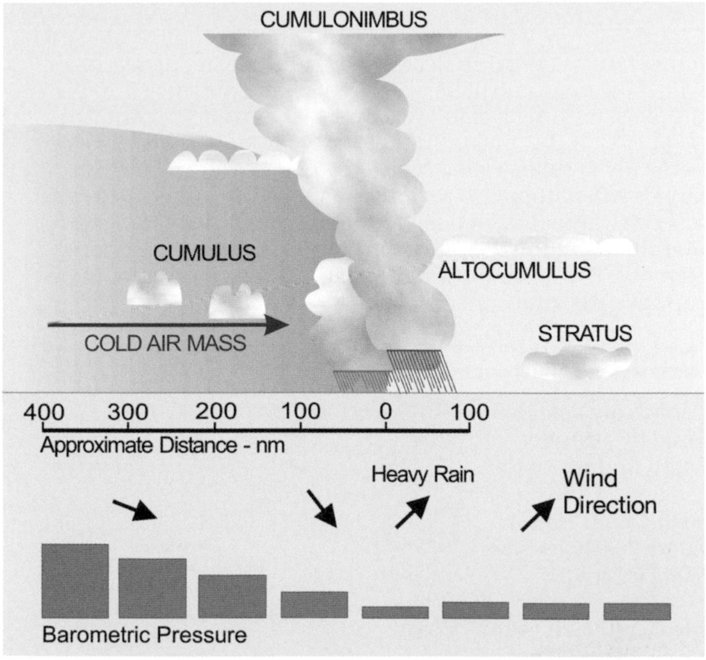


The interval of relative stability within the warm sector will end with the approach of the cold front. Unlike the slow transition of a warm front, the cold air behind a cold front is shouldering the overtaken warmer air abruptly aloft. This rising warm air cools and can no longer hold all its moisture, becoming highly unstable. Dangerous squall lines can develop 100 miles or more (i.e., several hours) in advance of the front. High storm clouds will pile up, leading to gusty winds, squalls, and possible thunderstorms as the front approaches. The barometer may fall immediately ahead of the cold front, perhaps rapidly—caused by the narrow band of rising air. The period of rain will be brief but could be severe. As the cold front passes, the winds will veer from southwest to northwest with gusts, and the temperature will drop. Cumulonimbus clouds will give way to nimbostratus, followed by clearing. Pressures will rise quickly. Clear, cool, dry weather is the norm, but those gusty northwest winds can continue. An assortment of clear-weather cumulus clouds may be seen.

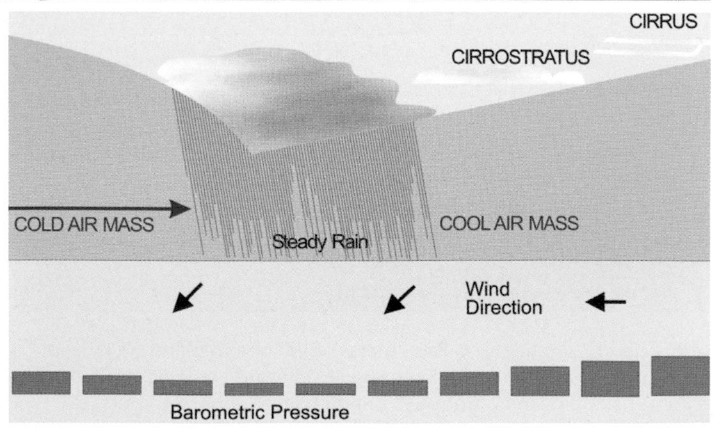

# Cloud Formation

Clouds form when water vapor condenses in cooling air. Since temperatures fall fairly steadily with altitude, rising warm air will cool, and some of its water vapor will condense into water droplets, forming a cloud when it reaches its dew point (see page 157). If the air continues to rise, the clouds will develop vertically (a shape called *cumuloform*). If the air stops rising, the clouds will flatten into a *stratiform* shape. How high and how fast the warm air rises depends upon what is pushing it aloft, and thus cloud shapes are a direct indicator of atmospheric stability. The more vertically developed the clouds, the more unstable the atmosphere.

## Cloud Types

Clouds are categorized by altitude: high, middle, or low.

**High Clouds (Cirro):** Above 20,000 feet consist of ice crystals

**Medium Clouds (Alto):** 6,500 to 20,000 feet consist of water droplets

**Low Clouds:** Below 6,500 feet consist of water droplets

**Name Clues:** Cumulo—bumpy (unstable); Stratus—flat (stable); Nimbo—rain

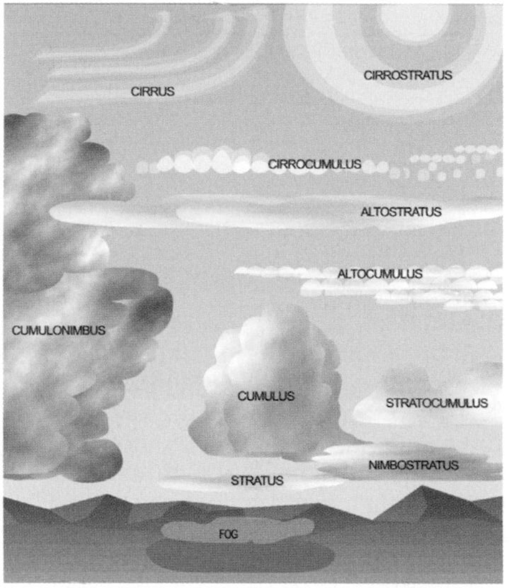


## High Clouds

Above 20,000 feet, the water droplets become ice crystals. This makes high clouds wispy and insubstantial. The sun or moon viewed through these clouds will have a halo around it but will not be obscured. High clouds, called *cirro*, come in three varieties, depending on their shapes.

Cirrus clouds, sometimes called "mares' tails," are thin and wispy and often precede a warm front. They usually indicate immediate fair weather, but the approaching front will bring change within 24 hours.

Cirrostratus are flat, like a mild veil across the sky, and suggest that the coming warm front is 12 to 24 hours away.

Cirrocumulus, often called a mackerel sky, are thin and bumpy. These clouds are lower than cirrostratus. They are usually seen in winter and indicate fair but cold weather.

## Middle Clouds

Clouds found between 6,500 and 20,000 feet are called *alto*. They are likely to be thicker than the high clouds, are often associated with light rain, and come in two varieties.

Altostratus, at the upper altitudes for middle clouds, are flat and blue-gray in color. When they thicken, long-lasting precipitation often follows.

Altocumulus are fluffy and bumpy. They often appear late in the day and produce brilliant red sunsets. When observed on a warm, humid morning, look for late afternoon thunderstorms.

## Vertical Clouds

Some clouds develop vertically to such a degree that they transcend the low, middle, and high categories. Such clouds usually form from convectively rising, extremely warm, moist air or from warm air forced aloft by a cold front.

Cumulonimbus are often associated with thunderstorms and squalls. These clouds can extend from low altitudes to the upper edge of the troposphere at 45,000 feet. This great vertical development is a sure sign of atmospheric instability.

Cumulus clouds often have significant vertical development (up to 16,000 feet), but are widely spaced and associated with fair weather. They are often left over from cumulonimbus clouds that have dissipated.

## Low Clouds

Clouds at altitudes under 6,500 feet are likely to be even denser than alto clouds and are often associated with steady rain. Low clouds are sometimes called, collectively, *strato*.

Stratocumulus are low, lumpy, gray, and quite thick, and often foretell rain preceding a front.

Nimbostratus, thick and dark gray, usually bring sustained precipitation with winds NE to S.

The lowest of these clouds, stratus, are a uniform gray and bring steady but often light rain and drizzle.

Clouds at ground level are fog.

## Where Can I Get Weather Forecasts?

Weather forecasts are available from many sources, both government and commercial. The NOAA National Weather Service (NWS) provides forecasts across the U.S. and much of the globe. These predictions are available on the Internet at www.nws.noaa.gov. Regional NWS offices develop local forecasts and operate weather radars to observe storms. These radars and the local forecasts can also be viewed on the Internet. NWS also operates NOAA Weather Radio, which broadcasts local forecasts, including marine forecasts, on VHF radio frequencies. Marine VHF radios enable you to quickly select one of these frequencies, and this is the principal means of obtaining forecast updates on U.S. waters.

Commercial sources include local and national newspapers and media (TV and radio), which develop their own forecasts from NOAA data. Often, local media and services operate their own radars and meteorological equipment to enhance their forecasts. Several services provide round-the-clock forecasts on

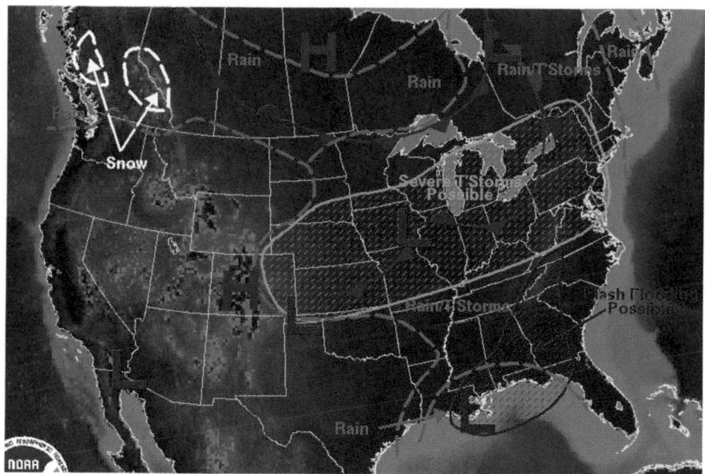


NOAA 24-hour forecasts indicate frontal patterns and pressure centers, as in this map of the U.S.

TV, and more recently via satellite. For example, *The Weather Channel* and *XM Weather* broadcast weather information that can be received via a special receiver and displayed on a computer or chartplotter aboard your boat.

Offshore, the principal source of weather information is HF (shortwave) radio via voice or modem (for data or fax). NOAA's Ocean Prediction Center (OPC) is the mariner's weather lifeline. They provide forecasts for the high seas from 65°N to 15° S (except for the Indian Ocean) via radiofacsimile and shortwave radio broadcasts. The U.S. Coast Guard provides radio forecasts in both voice and text (using special printing or display devices) on HF and MF bands, and voice messages on VHF Channel 16 (coastal). USCG also supports NAVTEX, which is part of the GMDSS (Global Maritime Distress and Safety System), providing MF text coastal forecasts to shipboard text receivers out to about 250 miles at sea. Contact www.navcen.uscg.gov for details. A number of global services are available via HF SSB marine radio for offshore mariners—most by subscription.

While NOAA provides broad global coverage, there are many other sources of forecasts and current marine weather data, both government and commercial. For example, around Canadian waters, Environment Canada (weatheroffice.ec.gc.ca/marine) provides marine forecasts. Around the United Kingdom, the Met Office (www.metoffice.com) is the official government source and the BBC is another source (www.bbc.co.uk/weather). The Bureau of Meteorology provides weather forecasts around Australia (www.bom.gov.au). A number of commercial companies provide excellent resources on the Internet, easily found via a web search.

**COLD FRONT**—advancing cold air

**WARM FRONT**—advancing warm air

**STATIONARY FRONT**—front has stopped advancing

**OCCLUDED FRONT**—cold front has overtaken warm front—still advancing

**TROUGH ("TROF")**—isobars make a sharp turn around a low, much like a front, and weather conditions are much like a front

# Making Your Own Forecast

The foregoing elements of onboard forecasting can be combined in various ways to understand what your observations are telling you. Let's look first at the signs of stable or changing weather.

| | Continuing Good Weather | Indicators of a Change |
|---|---|---|
| **Skies** | Clear, light to dark blue, bright moon, contrails dissipate | Hazy, halo (sun or moon), thick lingering jet contrails |
| **Clouds** | Few, puffy cumulus or high thin clouds, higher the better | Veil of clouds, clouds at multi-layers & directions, cirrus |
| **Winds** Seas | Generally steady, little change over day; sea swells same direction | Strong winds in early AM, wind shift to S; seas confused, varying directions |
| **Temperature** | Stable; heavy dew or frost at night | Marked changes; increase in humidity |
| **Dew Point** | Marked spread between dew point & temperature = no fog | Close spread: probable fog if temperature drops |
| **Barometer** | Steady, rising slowly | Falling slowly |
| **Sunrise** | Gray sky at dawn or sun rising from clear horizon | Red sky, sun rises above horizon due to cloud cover |
| **Sunset** | Red sky, sun ball of fire " or sets on a clear horizon | Sun sets high above horizon, color purplish or pale yellow |

Forecasters have great difficulty predicting a low's precise path, but Buys Ballot's Law (see page 146) gives you the local perspective. Here's how to refine a regional forecast with your own observations:

## APPROACHING LOW

**CLOUDS: high cirrus, gradually lowering and thickening**
**WIND: backing to SE—possibly increasing**
**BAROMETER: begins to fall (2 to 10 mb in 3 hours)**
**SEAS: Offshore swell increases, with decreasing period**

**What to Expect:**
**RAIN: within 15–24 hours**
**If low is W to NW, passing to your north, you will see fronts**
**If low is W to SW, passing to your south, you will not see distinct fronts**

## APPROACHING WARM FRONT

**CIRRUS OR MACKEREL CLOUDS: front > 24 hr away**
**LOWERING AND THICKENING CLOUDS (ALTOSTRATUS, NIMBOSTRATUS): front < 24 hr away**
**RAIN: begins lightly, then becomes steady and persistent**
**BAROMETER: falls steadily; faster fall = stronger winds**
**WINDS: increase steadily, stay SE**
**VISIBILITY: deteriorates, especially in rain**

### PASSING WARM FRONT

**SKY:** lightens toward western horizon
**RAIN:** breaks
**WIND:** veers from S to SW, may decrease
**BAROMETER:** stops falling
**TEMPERATURE:** rises

### WITHIN WARM SECTOR

**WIND:** steady, typically SW, will strengthen ahead of cold front
**BAROMETER:** steady—may drop shortly ahead of cold front
**PRECIPITATION:** mist, possible drizzle

### APPROACHING COLD FRONT

**WIND:** SW increases; line squalls possible > 100 mi ahead of front
**BAROMETER:** begins brief fall, could be rapid
**CLOUDS:** cumulonimbus build to W
**TEMPERATURE:** steady
**RAIN:** begins and intensifies, but duration short (1–2 hr typical)

### PASSING COLD FRONT

**WIND:** veers rapidly to NW, gusty behind front
**BAROMETER:** begins to rise, often quickly
**CLOUDS:** cumulonimbus, then nimbostratus, then clearing
**TEMPERATURE:** drops suddenly, then slow decline
**RAIN:** ends, gives way to rapidly clearing skies, possibly with leftover altocumulus

# Special Weather Topics

## Wind Chill

The following wind chill table will give you an idea of the apparent temperature when radiational cooling due to wind is factored in. Wind speed means apparent wind on deck (the vector sum of true wind and your boat's forward motion). Especially in spring and fall, wind chill is directly related to onset of hypothermia.

| Wind (mph) | Temperature (°F) | | | | | | | | | | | | | | | | | |
|---|---|---|---|---|---|---|---|---|---|---|---|---|---|---|---|---|---|---|
| | 40 | 35 | 30 | 25 | 20 | 15 | 10 | 5 | 0 | -5 | -10 | -15 | -20 | -25 | -30 | -35 | -40 | -45 |
| 5 | 36 | 31 | 25 | 19 | 13 | 7 | 1 | -5 | -11 | -16 | -22 | -28 | -34 | -40 | -46 | -52 | -57 | -63 |
| 10 | 34 | 27 | 21 | 15 | 9 | 3 | -4 | -10 | -16 | -22 | -28 | -35 | -41 | -47 | -53 | -59 | -66 | -72 |
| 15 | 32 | 25 | 19 | 13 | 6 | 0 | -7 | -13 | -19 | -26 | -32 | -39 | -45 | -51 | -58 | -64 | -71 | -77 |
| 20 | 30 | 24 | 17 | 11 | 4 | -2 | -9 | -15 | -22 | -29 | -35 | -42 | -48 | -55 | -61 | -68 | -74 | -81 |
| 25 | 29 | 23 | 16 | 9 | 3 | -4 | -11 | -17 | -24 | -31 | -37 | -44 | -51 | -58 | -64 | -71 | -78 | -84 |
| 30 | 28 | 22 | 15 | 8 | 1 | -5 | -12 | -19 | -26 | -33 | -39 | -46 | -53 | -60 | -67 | -73 | -80 | -87 |
| 35 | 28 | 21 | 14 | 7 | 0 | -7 | -14 | -21 | -27 | -34 | -41 | -48 | -55 | -62 | -69 | -76 | -82 | -89 |
| 40 | 27 | 20 | 13 | 6 | -1 | -8 | -15 | -22 | -29 | -36 | -43 | -50 | -57 | -64 | -71 | -78 | -84 | -91 |
| 45 | 26 | 29 | 12 | 5 | -2 | -9 | -16 | -23 | -30 | -37 | -44 | -51 | -58 | -65 | -72 | -79 | -86 | -93 |
| 50 | 26 | 19 | 12 | 4 | -3 | -10 | -17 | -24 | -31 | -38 | -45 | -52 | -60 | -67 | -74 | -81 | -88 | -95 |
| 55 | 25 | 18 | 11 | 4 | -3 | -11 | -18 | -25 | -32 | -39 | -46 | -54 | -61 | -68 | -75 | -82 | -89 | -97 |
| 60 | 25 | 17 | 10 | 3 | -4 | -11 | -19 | -26 | -33 | -40 | -48 | -55 | -62 | -69 | -76 | -84 | -91 | -98 |

Frostbite Times: 30 minutes / 10 minutes / 5 minutes

## Thunderstorms and Squalls

Thunderstorms are of two origins: air mass or frontal. The former is created when warm, moist air rises over land, usually during hot, humid summer days. When the resulting cumulonimbus clouds mature, the storm begins, and may bring squalls to coastal waters. It soon dissipates.

Frontal thunderstorms and squalls are associated with the near-vertical wall of cold air in an advancing cold front, which forces warm air aloft at a rapid rate. Especially during spring and early summer, the resulting squalls can be severe, and are dangerous to boaters.

Check forecasts for the possibility of squall-line thunderstorms and be on the lookout. An advancing dark band of vertical clouds, often called a *roll cloud*, will be preceded by strong winds blowing in your direction, followed by heavy squalls from the opposite direction as the storm passes overhead. Severe lightning usually accompanies these squalls.

Severe squalls can precede the arrival of a cold front by up to several hundred miles.

## Tropical Storms

The highs, lows, and fronts that sweep west to east in the middle latitudes are absent from the tropics, which are characterized instead by the steady northeast (Northern Hemisphere) and southeast (Southern Hemisphere) trade winds, which converge near the equator in a zone of rising air and light and baffling breezes known as the *doldrums*.

Tropical disturbances take the form of low-pressure troughs or waves that move east to west with the trades, picking up heat energy from warm tropical waters. Some develop into tropical depressions (closed cyclonic circulation with surface winds less than 39 mph) or tropical storms (winds of 39 to 74 mph), and a few become hurricanes (winds higher than 74 mph; known as typhoons in the western North Pacific and cyclones in the Indian Ocean and Australia). The path of a hurricane is hard to predict even with sophisticated computer models, but you will have ample public warning of a hurricane's advance. Use that warning to get ashore and secure your boat. Vessels caught at sea in the Northern Hemisphere should strive to be on the left side of the hurricane's path (facing the direction the storm is heading), where the speed of its advance subtracts somewhat from wind speed rather than adding to it.

## What Causes Fog?

The *dew point* is the temperature below which water vapor begins to condense from air of a given humidity. If you know the dew point at ground level, you'll know the temperature at which fog will form. For example, if the current temperature is 65°F and the dew point is 61°F, a mere 4° drop in temperature, such as might occur with the approach of sunset, is likely to produce fog.

The dew point can be measured by comparing the temperatures recorded by the dry- and wet-bulb thermometers in a sling psychrometer. The instrument is swung until evaporation depresses its wet bulb reading.

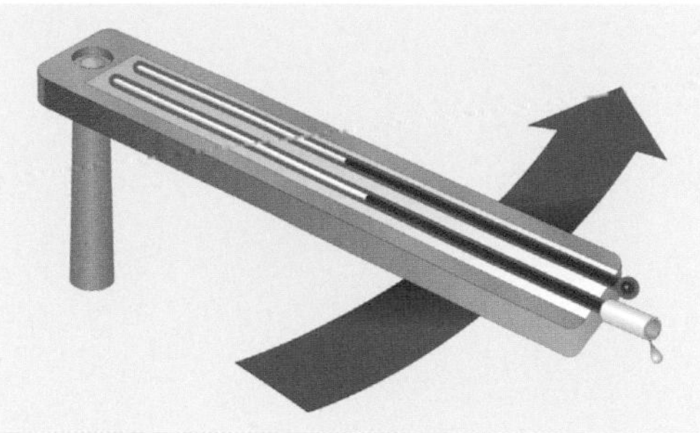

A sling psychrometer (with wet- and dry-bulb thermometers) measures the dew point.

The several types of fog that affect boaters are listed below.

| | | |
|---|---|---|
| **Advection** | *Conditions:* | light winds (5–10 Kn up to 15 Kn), warm, moist air blown over cold water—air condenses to produce fog |
| | *Clears:* | persistent fog that will clear when winds become stronger or change direction |
| **Radiation** | *Conditions:* | light winds (5–7 Kn), low lying areas, warm, moist air condensed by nighttime radiational cooling |
| | *Clears:* | fog will lift in stronger winds or burn off as soon as the area is heated by the sun |
| **Frontal** | *Conditions:* | warm front, warm rain or drizzle falling through cool air can form dense fog |
| | *Clears:* | wind shift or passage of warm front |

A barometer is a mariner's best forecasting tool. Pages 154 and 155 tell you what the readings mean.

CHAPTER 10

# Heavy Weather Sailing

John Rousmaniere

# What Is Heavy Weather?

Heavy weather is not an absolute wind speed, like (say) 30 knots. Rather, it's when the wind blows so hard and the waves are so big that *your boat* is on the verge of losing control and *you and your crew* begin to feel overwhelmed. This can be 12 knots in a small dinghy, or 40 knots in a big, heavy cruising boat.

**Heavy weather can sneak up on you.** Because the force of the wind increases with the cube of its speed, a seemingly small increase in wind strength has a big effect on wind force. So be sensitive to your boat's handling characteristics. Always be prepared to change course or **shorten sail**. Your crew should be able to reef in less than 2 minutes. Practice reefing and setting storm sails (see pages 166–69) ahead of time. **Remember this rule: "When you're thinking about shortening sail, it's already too late!"**

Here's a wary guide for shortening sail based on the Beaufort scale of wind forces. For storm tactics, see pages 170–73. NOTE: Every boat has to be handled uniquely. Many boats can usually carry more sail when running or reaching than when sailing close hauled.

| | BOAT SIZE AND TYPE | | |
|---|---|---|---|
| **BEAUFORT FORCE (wind and waves)** | **SMALL**<br>**Heavy monohull<30′**<br>**Light monohull<35′**<br>**Multihull<40′** | **MEDIUM** | **LARGE**<br>**Heavy monohull>50′**<br>**Light monohull>55′**<br>**Multihull>60′** |
| **FORCE 5**<br>Fresh breeze, 17–21 knots; 6′ seas, some whitecaps | Small jib, 1–2 reefs | Small jib, 1 reef | Medium jib, 0–1 reef |
| **FORCE 6**<br>Strong breeze, 22–27 knots; 10′ seas, extensive whitecaps | Small jib, 2 reefs | Small jib, 2 reefs | Small jib, 1–2 reefs |
| **FORCE 7**<br>Near gale, 28–33 knots; 14′ seas, some breakers | Storm jib, 3 reefs (or storm trysail) | Small jib, 2–3 reefs | Small jib, 2 reefs |
| **FORCE 8**<br>Gale, 34–40 knots; 18′ seas, heavy spray | Storm sails, storm tactics (except heaving-to) | Storm jib, 3 reefs (or storm trysail) | Storm jib, 3 reefs (or storm trysail) |
| **FORCE 9**<br>Strong gale, 41–47 knots; 23′ seas, rolling crests, dense foam | Storm sails, storm tactics (except heaving-to) | Storm sails, storm tactics | Storm sails, storm tactics |
| **FORCE 10**<br>Storm, 48–55 knots; 29′ seas, all white; survival conditions except for the best-found boats | One storm sail, storm tactics (except heaving-to) | Storm sails, storm tactics (except heaving-to) | Storm sails, storm tactics |

Waves are more dangerous than wind. Flying water packs a lot of force. Don't leave loose objects (like sails and fenders) exposed on deck, where a wave can catch and throw them into the cabin or through the lifelines, causing damage to the boat or crew.

The size of a wave depends on several factors: wind strength, wind fetch (the distance over water that the wind blows), the length of time the wind's been blowing, water depth, and current. The biggest seas are caused by winds blowing hard and long over a great fetch; but the worst waves often are the short, steep breakers that appear in the early part of a storm, in shallow water, in rapidly shifting winds, in tidal races, and anywhere the tide runs against the wind. By one estimate, a 1-knot contrary tide doubles the size of a wave, and a stronger current increases it still further. A fast-moving boat may jump off one of these waves and smash down, doing great damage to itself and the crew. Being caught beam-to by such a wave invites being rolled over or stove in by the breaker and filled with water. About one wave out of twenty is a "rogue" that runs at an angle across the others, sometimes stirring up unusually steep, breaking seas.

Therefore, it pays to anticipate areas of rough water and either slow down or steer around them.

Wind against current kicks up a steep chop in a tidal race.

**Sailing in a blow is most dangerous when the wind is astern.** That's when you're going fastest, when the crew is most exuberant and likely to be careless, when their backs are turned to the waves, and when a small mistake at the helm or the appearance of even a tiny rogue wave can toss the boat over on its side in a wild broach (see page 166).

Author steers downwind in the 1979 Fastnet Race storm. All elements were in the 50s—wind and water temperatures (Fahrenheit), wind speed (knots), and the occasional wave height (feet).

# Preparing for Bad Weather

Signs of approaching bad weather include a falling barometer, a swift change in wind speed or direction, ocean waves from a new direction, a mass of dark clouds in the west, fierce lightning, and warnings over the radio or Internet (see *Onboard Weather Forecasting*, Chapter 9). If any of these appears, take the time to carefully gather all the information you can. Sketch a weather chart showing the location of the approaching weather front or center of low pressure, and carefully consider your options. You want to dodge the storm, but may not have time to get to port.

Running off in the Southern Ocean.

## Underway Offshore

**Plan your strategy.** Sail away from the storm, especially the "dangerous quadrant" on its right front (left front in southern hemisphere). To predict the path of a low-pressure storm system, use Buys Ballot's Law: when you face the wind in the northern hemisphere, low pressure is on your right and high pressure on your left. (This is because wind circulates counterclockwise around a northern hemisphere low. The low will be on your left in the southern hemisphere, where wind circulates clockwise around a low.) As a rule, except when the wind is south to southwest, keep the wind in the northern hemisphere on your starboard side in order to sail away from the approaching storm.

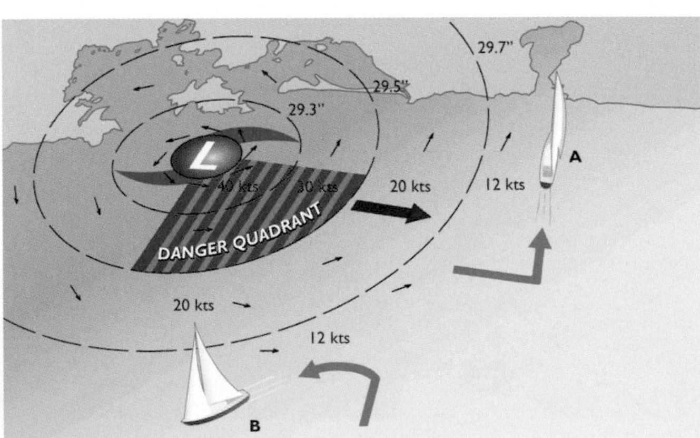


Boat A has time to reach harbor. Boat B tacks out to sea and away from the dangerous quadrant (shaded).

**Prepare the boat and crew.**

**1. Check fuel.** Now's the time to switch to a full tank.

**2. Shorten sail** (see page 166).

**3. Suit up.** With the skipper setting the example, everybody puts on foul-weather gear, life jackets, and (if they have them) safety harnesses, which must always be hooked on when on deck. (See page 172.) Rig grab lines in the cockpit and cabin. Take seasickness medication.

**4. Batten down.** Shut and dog (bolt down) hatches and ports, install washboards in the companionway. Take loose gear off the deck. If you have protective panels to put over large windows, do it now—especially on the leeward side—to keep windows from breaking should the boat fall on its side. Below, secure personal items, food, dishes, etc. in lockers (which must be shut tight). While the boat's still steady, cook some hot food and heat water to put in thermoses.

## Underway, Squalls Near Shore

Follow steps 1–4 above.

When black clouds appear and sweep your way, expect a squall. After plotting your position, decide if you have time to return to harbor. (To estimate the distance to a squall in miles, time the interval between the flash of lightning and the sound of the thunderclap, then divide by 5.) Because squalls are unpredictable, it's often safest to stay in open water, well away from land, shoals, and other boats.

## In Harbor

If your boat is in the harbor when a storm approaches, prepare it carefully.

Squall clouds warn of an approaching wind.

**1. Reduce windage.** Any exposed area makes the boat sail around its anchor or dock lines, snapping them. Strip off *everything:* all sails (including roller-furled sails), the Bimini, ventilators, awnings, the Lifesling, etc. Deflate the dinghy and put it in the cockpit. A hard-bottomed dinghy should be sunk or stored ashore.

**2. At the dock.** Double or even triple up on dock lines, using plenty of spring lines (they control surges). Tie leather or cloth chafe protection over lines and fittings. Deploy all your fenders, tying plastic milk bottles full of water to their bottoms to keep them from riding up as the boat rocks against the dock.

**3. At anchor.** Set out all your anchors with plenty of scope.

**4. Close all seacocks and other through-hull fittings.**

**5. Batten down.**

**6. Get off.** The Coast Guard and other authorities are adamant that the dumbest thing anyone can do is stay aboard a boat in a hurricane.

Squall coming: high-windage deck gear cleared away.

Dock lines doubled.

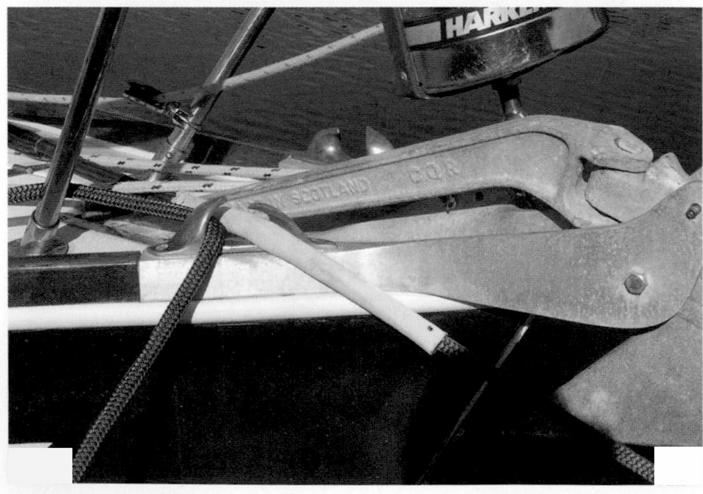


Chafe gear installed.

# Boat Care at Sea

**Check engine fuel filters often.** Rolling and pitching stir up dirt in the bottom of fuel tanks that can stop an engine.

**Keep the bilges dry.** You don't want water sloshing up into bunks. Pump every hour or half hour, and note in the log how many strokes are needed before the pump sucks dry. To keep water from coming below, tightly shut hatches and ports, close off holes at the partners (where the mast comes through the deck), and aim deck ventilators downwind.

Multiple chafe points on foredeck.

**Inspect gear often.** In rough weather, chafe (damage from rubbing) occurs remarkably quickly. In addition, halyards and other lines loosen, and tie-downs undo themselves. Take regular inspection tours around the deck and cabin.

**Rig preventers.** Rolling about in waves causes booms to fly around, and this has caused serious injuries and deaths. When a sailboat is reaching or running, even in light wind, the boom must be held out by a preventer—a line leading from the boom forward to the deck, through a block, and back to the cockpit. Secure the block to a strong point on deck, and tie the line to a reinforced point on the boom (for instance, a mainsheet block attachment). Most of the time the preventer can be rigged on deck near the leeward shrouds. When running in very large seas, however, lead the preventer forward all the way to the bow so there is little downward pull on it, and if the boom trips in the water, it will lift and not break. Lead the line back to the cockpit so it can be adjusted easily as you ease and trim the mainsheet. In rough conditions, you want to keep people off the deck as much as possible.

# Strong Wind Tactics

**Slow down.** When the boat gets uncomfortable, decrease speed. It's amazing how much better a boat rides when you slow down by just a couple of knots. Under power, throttle back on the engine. Under sail, let the traveler down or let the sails luff a little (but not too much or you'll break battens and rip sail cloth). If that doesn't work, shorten sail.

**Change your angle to the waves.** A comfortable, safe angle often is with the wind about 30 degrees forward or aft of the beam. Big waves directly on the side roll boats violently and may capsize them. Waves on the bow can cause dangerous pounding and wave-jumping. Waves from behind may lift the stern and cause the boat to broach (turn violently to one side) or even pitchpole (somersault over the bow).

**Find protection.** If the boat is still out of control, get on the tack that has the smoothest water, try stopping altogether, or find some land that provides protection.

## Shortening Sail: Reefing

Reducing sail area is often all that's necessary to steady a boat in fresh to strong breezes (17–27 knots) and 6- to 10-foot waves with whitecaps. (This is Force 5–6 on the Beaufort scale of wind forces.)

One way to shorten sail is to douse (lower) or roll up a sail. You can partially or completely roll up or lower the jib, and even sail under one sail alone. ***Warning:*** Don't sail under jib alone except in smooth water; the mainsail provides considerable fore-and-aft support for the mast in rough seas.

To reef the mainsail:

**1. Support the boom, luff the sail.** Tighten the topping lift or adjust a rigid, rod-type boom vang so the boom won't drop when the halyard is eased. Then ease the sheet until the sail luffs completely.

**2. Reef the sail's luff.** Lower the halyard and pull down the luff until its cringle (the big steel eye) is at or near the boom. (It helps to mark the halyard at this point.) Secure the cringle to the boom with a line or a metal hook. Pull the halyard so tight there are tension wrinkles in the luff.

**3. Reef the leech.** With the sail still luffing, pull on the leech reefing line to haul the leech cringle right down to the boom. This pull will be long and hard.

**4. Finally, ease the topping lift**, trim the mainsheet, and coil the halyard and reef lines.

**5. If the sail's foot is flogging**, tie in and tighten reef points—either short lines or a long line led through the grommets (small holes) along the reef.

To shake out (undo) a reef: luff the sail, cast off the reef point, throw off the leech reefing line, throw off the luff, raise the halyard, and retrim.

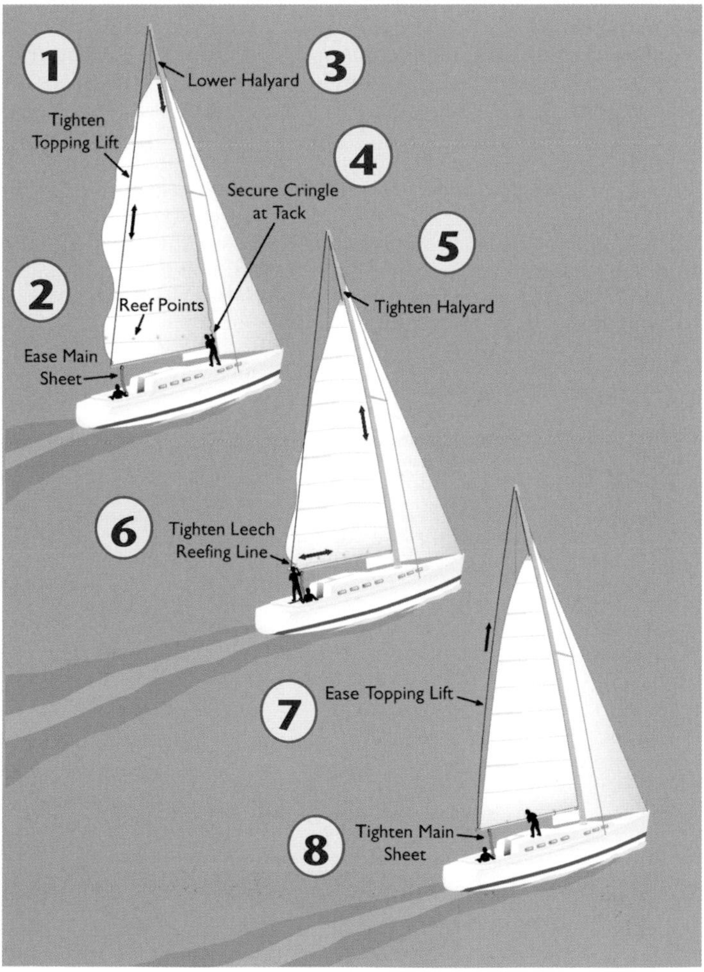

1 Tighten Topping Lift
2 Ease Main Sheet
3 Lower Halyard
4 Secure Cringle at Tack
Reef Points
5 Tighten Halyard
6 Tighten Leech Reefing Line
7 Ease Topping Lift
8 Tighten Main Sheet

**Common reefing problems:**
**The reef isn't tied in soon enough.** When you first think about reefing, it's probably already too late. Once the boat is heeled over 20 degrees most of the time, think seriously about reefing.

**The sail is too full when reefed.** The halyard or reefing lines must be tightened all the way. The leech reefing line must be far enough aft on the boom so it pulls *back* as well as down.

**The reefing lines stretch.** This means they're too small. They should be the same size as the mainsheet.

A fine, rail-down breeze. But when you heel this far, you should think about reefing.

## Shortening Sail: Storm Sails

As the wind builds, tie in a second (or third) reef, and then go to the storm sails. The storm trysail and storm jib are set low (to decrease heeling force) in place of the mainsail and regular jib. At first they look ridiculously small, but because the wind's force rises exponentially with velocity, in a strong wind they'll be enough to drive the boat. These sails have no battens, which might break.

**The storm jib** is best set alone on an inner stay (called the forestay), which keeps the sail area near the mast so the boat balances well and the sail is easy to handle without having to venture out on the bow. If you don't have a forestay, you may be able to improvise one by leading a spinnaker pole topping lift or a spare halyard to the bow cleat and tightening it hard, then hanking the storm jib to it. But the storm jib can be hoisted on the headstay if necessary, even over the roller-furled jib using loops of line that ride over the sail. The storm jib's tack should be on a pendant (short strap) that lets it ride high above any waves that may come on deck.

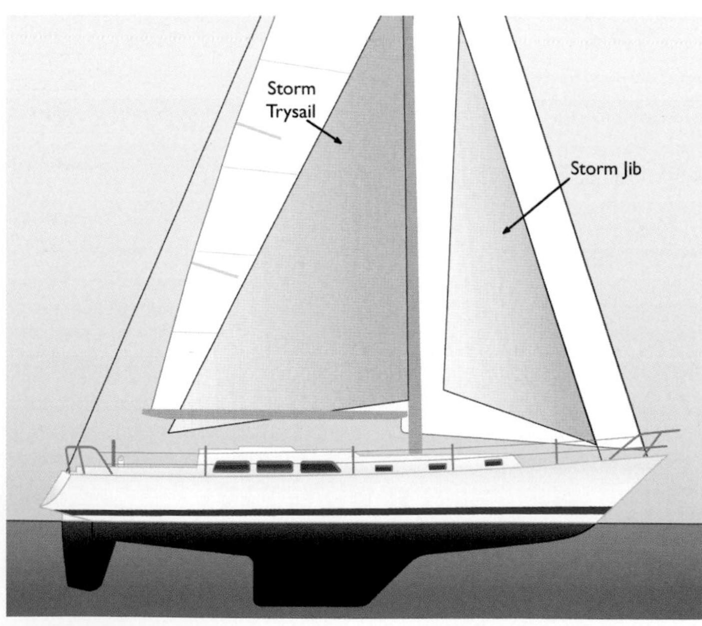

This storm jib's tack pendant should be longer.

**The storm trysail's** luff is hoisted like the mainsail's on a mast track or in a groove (true cruising boats have a separate track for the trysail). The tack is secured with a pendant so the sail is above the furled mailsail. Traditionally a trysail is trimmed through a block on the leeward rail to allow the main boom to be dropped down on deck so it won't swing around. But with the modern rod-type boom vang that holds the boom up, many sailors tie the clew of the trysail to the boom. Some of the load must be carried by the boom's strong points (for instance its end and the eyes for the reefing lines). The trysail can be trimmed in the usual way with the mainsheet and traveler so the boat can sail close-hauled.

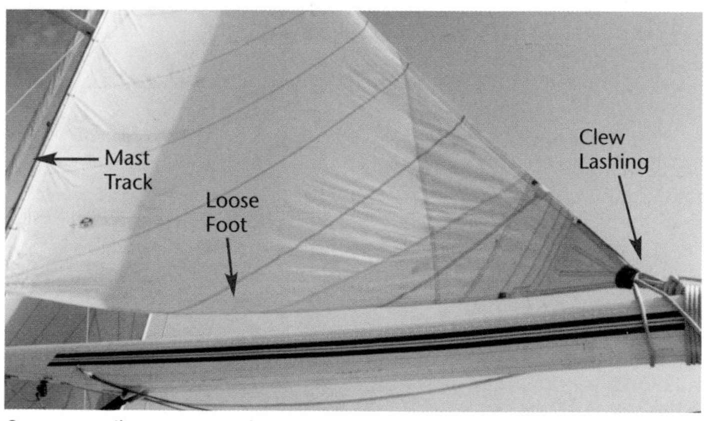


Storm trysail set on main boom and dedicated mast track.

# Gale and Storm Tactics

There are four tactics for coping with strong winds in conditions when sailing is less important than surviving: heaving-to, lying ahull, running before it, and lying to a sea anchor.

## Heaving-To

Hove-to with backed jib.

Heaving-to is an excellent tactic for nearly stopping the boat and making it more comfortable in conditions when sail can be carried, which usually means below about 50 knots (Beaufort scale Force 10)—or less in a small boat. Even in lighter wind, it's a fine way to stop while you cook a meal in big seas or wait for dawn to light your way into a strange harbor.

**To heave-to.** On a close reach at about 60 degrees off the wind, back the jib or storm jib by trimming it flat on the windward (wrong) side. (Alternatively, trim it the usual way, to leeward, and tack without casting off the sheet.) With the jib pushing the bow to leeward and the mainsail and rudder pushing it to windward (the wheel or tiller can be lashed to help achieve this), there is little force left over to push the boat ahead. The boat will jog along comfortably at less than 3 knots. Adjust the mainsheet and traveler so the boat self-steers. Since the boat will make leeway (slide downwind), heaving-to is not a good tactic when you are near a lee shore. Neither is it a safe tactic when the waves are breaking or throwing heavy spray.

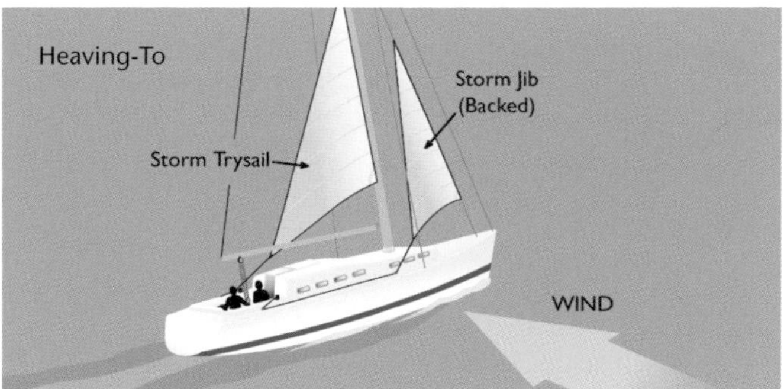


**In a variation of heaving-to called the Rod stop** (named for seaman Rod Stephens), sail on a beam reach at 90 degrees to the wind, roll up the jib (or let it luff), and push the mainsail or trysail all the way out, securing it there with a line.

## Lying Ahull

When the wind pressure on the jib becomes strong enough to force your bow off the wind despite mainsail and rudder action, heaving-to becomes unsafe. One possibility then is to lie ahull, which simply means to douse sails and let the boat drift under bare poles. This tactic permits the crew to rest, but the risk is that the boat may lie beam-to breaking seas that could roll it over. Lying ahull in big breaking seas is not recommended.

## Running Before It

Running before the wind is the only *active* storm tactic, meaning that the boat has to be actively steered. Set enough sail to carry the boat up the faces of big waves, but not so much that the boat goes too fast when running down the backs of waves and loses control. With speed up and the waves on your stern, the force of the waves is less. If you begin to lose control, tow warps (long lengths of rope with objects—like fenders or sails—tied on to increase resistance) or a drogue (a parachute or a series of small parachutes on a line). The loads on warps and drogues will be powerful. Lead their lines to winches or other through-bolted fittings, and treat them respectfully. In big breaking seas, running before the wind often is the best storm tactic for monohull boats, even though they must be steered very carefully and there is a risk of carrying the boat toward land.

Running before big seas in the Southern Ocean.

Cone configuration and bridle arrangement for a Jordan series drogue. A 30,000 lb. boat needs 300 feet of ¾" nylon line and 132 cones.

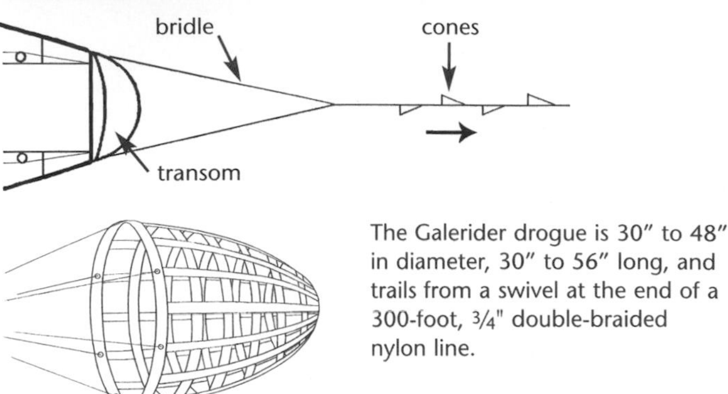


The Galerider drogue is 30″ to 48″ in diameter, 30″ to 56″ long, and trails from a swivel at the end of a 300-foot, ¾" double-braided nylon line.

## Lying To a Sea Anchor

This is the storm tactic often favored by catamarans and trimarans because their narrow, sharp bows make less resistance to waves than a monohull's wider bow. Under bare poles, the boat lies with the bow into the wind and a parachute-like device called a sea anchor deployed over the bow on the anchor rode or other long line. There is little drift downwind. The crew must be alert to changing wave patterns so the boat is not caught beam-to a big sea. A variation is to heave-to with some sail set and the sea anchor on a bridle. The loading on the lines is very high, so lead them to through-bolted fittings.

A growing body of evidence suggests that monohulls, especially those with fin keels, ride out storms more successfully trailing a drogue from the stern than riding to a sea anchor.

## Crew Concerns

Heavy weather is cold, wet, uncomfortable, and discouraging. If it's also demoralizing, the crew may give up just when you need everyone's full attention.

**Be optimistic.** Under strong, calm, cheerful but realistic, purposeful leadership, many crews have avoided passivity and survived terrible storms on the faith that something better was awaiting them at the other side. Thoughts of family and friends ashore usually provide sufficient motivation to keep sailing, as does loyalty to shipmates and the vessel.

**Maintain normal shipboard routines.** Serve hot, nutritious food, arrange meals and watches so everyone has time to sleep or at least rest, and keep the cabin neat and dry (with wet clothes and foul-weather gear well away from bunks).

**Wear personal safety gear.** With the owner and skipper setting the example, everybody should wear PFDs and (if available) safety harnesses, which prevent falls and keep people on board. Put on the harness before you come on deck and hook it in the cockpit before you step out of the companionway. Hook harness tethers into sturdy jacklines on deck or through-bolted fittings. Keep the tether short so any fall won't be long. Clip on all the time, especially when doing a two-handed job—like steering, coming in or out of the companionway, trimming sails, or moving around on deck.

**Stay dry.** Wear foul-weather gear. A dry body is a warm body, and also an effective body, because symptoms of hypothermia include slow thinking and loss of agility.

**Get your rest**. Organize the crew in short watches so nobody's exposed on deck for too long. If you can't sleep, at least lie down.

**Don't let seasickness catch you by surprise.** Take medication early, anticipate drowsiness and other side effects, drink Coke Classic to settle a queasy stomach (some people swear by ginger ale), stay well hydrated, and try to get some food down, even if it's only an unsalted cracker.

**Use hand signals.** Wind and waves are often so loud that people can't hear each other, so use hand signals. Here are examples:

***Trim or ease a line:*** Point toward or away from the person holding a line.
***Lower or hoist a sail:*** Point down or up.
***Stop:*** Open palm toward the person.
***Cleat the line:*** OK sign (form circle with index finger and thumb).
***Change course:*** Point in the new direction.

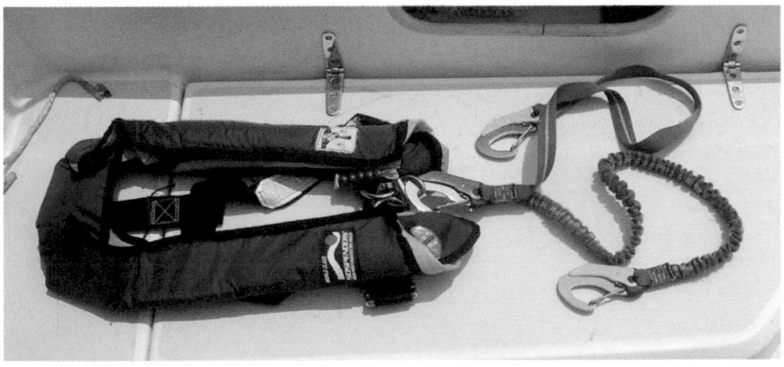

A safety harness with two tethers.

Clip your tether before going on deck.

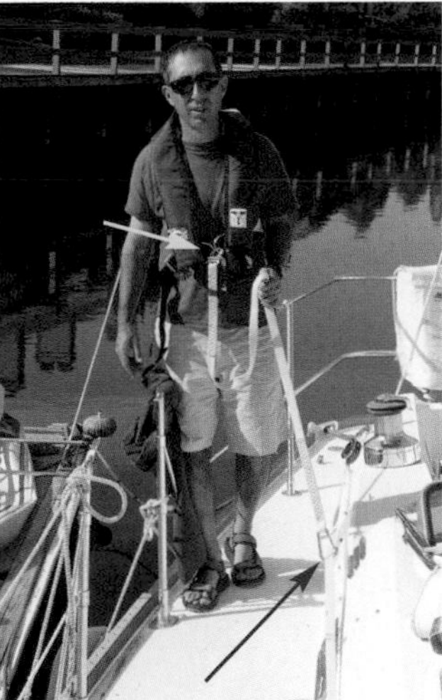

Tether clipped to jackline.

CHAPTER 11

Nigel Calder

Diesel Engine Care and Repair

# Meet Your Diesel Engine

Unlike a gas engine, a diesel engine has no ignition system or spark plugs. Instead, diesel fuel ignites "spontaneously" when sprayed into air that has been superheated by compression within a cylinder. This combustion then generates a power stroke. Thus there are three preconditions for a diesel engine to work:

1. An adequate supply of combustion air.
2. Compression of this air until its temperature rises above the ignition point of diesel (this requires a higher degree of compression in colder air than in warmer).
3. Injection of diesel fuel into this cylinder of heated air at a moment that is precisely coordinated with the movement of the pistons up and down the cylinders.

Given air, adequate compression, and proper fuel injection, a diesel engine more or less has to run. Routine maintenance is designed to guarantee these three preconditions; troubleshooting focuses on finding out which of them is missing.

Maintenance requirements and troubleshooting procedures are similar across the variety of diesel engines found in powerboats and sailboats.

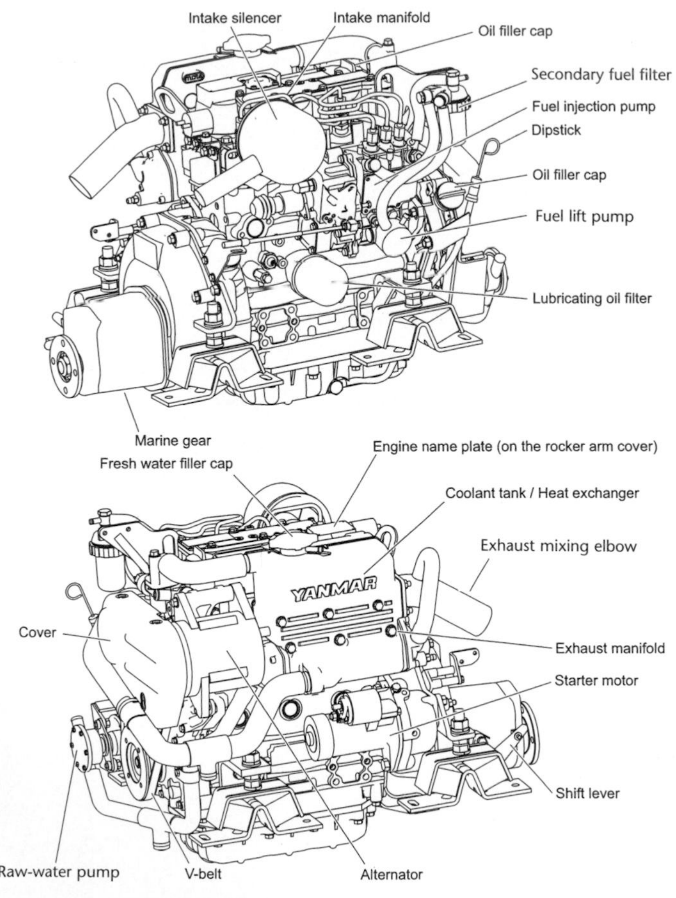

# Standard Operating Practices

Before cranking the engine with the starter motor, check the oil level ① and the freshwater level ②. Also be sure the raw-water seacock is open, the raw-water strainer is unobstructed (see page 184), any "stop" device is not activated (note: many diesels do not have a stop device), and the transmission is in neutral ③.

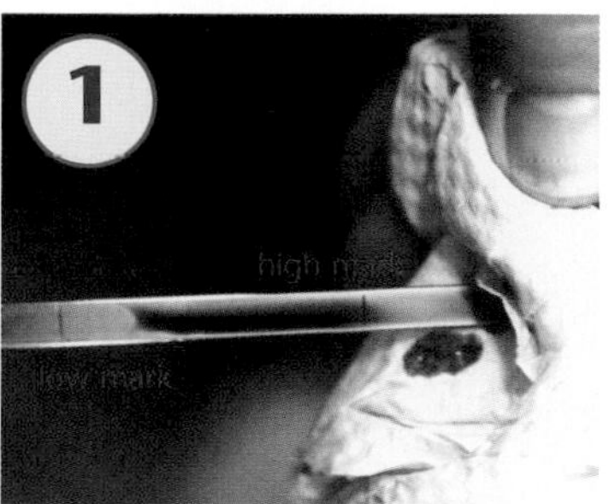

Immediately after the engine fires, be sure the oil pressure gauge is normal or the oil pressure warning light is out. Also be sure that the alternator is charging (i.e., either the ammeter shows charging or the light is out) and that cooling water is coming out of the exhaust ④. (Note: It is important to develop a sense of what constitutes normal flow.)

# Troubleshooting

**Symptom**

| Seizure | High exhaust back pressure | Hunting | Rising oil level | Excessive oil consumption | Low oil pressure | Knocks | Misfiring | Loss of power | Poor idle | White smoke | Blue smoke | Black smoke | Overheating | Low compression | Lack of fuel | Cranks, but poor starting | Will not crank | Low cranking speed |
|---|---|---|---|---|---|---|---|---|---|---|---|---|---|---|---|---|---|---|
| | | | | | | | | | | | | | | | | | ● | ● |
| ● | | | | | | | | ● | | | | | ● | | | | | |
| | | | | | | | | ● | | | | | | | | | | ● |
| | | | | | | | ● | | | ● | | | | | | ● | | |
| | | | | | | | ● | ● | | | | ● | | | | ● | | |
| | ● | | | | | | ● | ● | | | | ● | | | | ● | | |
| | | | | | | | | | | | | | | | ● | ● | | |
| | | | | | | | ● | ● | ● | | | | | | ● | ● | | |
| | | | | | | ● | ● | ● | ● | ● | | | | | ● | ● | | |
| | | | | | | ● | ● | ● | ● | ● | | ● | | | | ● | | |
| ● | | | | | | | | | | | | | ● | | | | | |
| ● | | | | | | | | | | | | | ● | | | | | |
| ● | | | | | ● | | | | | | | | ● | | | | | |
| ● | | | | ● | ● | | | | | | | | ● | | | | | ● |
| ● | | | ● | | ● | | | | | | | | ● | | | | | |
| | | | | | | | | ● | | | | | | | ● | ● | | |
| | | | | | | ● | ● | ● | ● | | | ● | | | | ● | | |
| | | | | | | | | ● | ● | | | | | | ● | ● | | |
| | | | | | | ● | | ● | ● | | | ● | ● | | | ● | | |
| | | | | | | | | | | | | ● | | | | | | |
| | | | | ● | | | ● | ● | ● | ● | ● | | | ● | | ● | | |
| | | | | | | | ● | ● | ● | ● | | | | ● | | ● | | |
| | | | | | | | ● | ● | ● | ● | | | | ● | | ● | | |
| | | | | ● | | | | | | | ● | | | | | | | |
| | | | | | | | ● | ● | ● | ● | | | | ● | | ● | | |
| | | | | | ● | | | | | | | | | | | | | |
| | | ● | | | | | | | ● | | | | | | | | | |
| | | | | | | | | | ● | | | | | | | | | |
| ● | | | ● | | | | | | | ● | | | ● | ● | | ● | | |
| ● | | | | | | | | | | | | | ● | | | | | |
| | | | | | | ● | | ● | | | | | | ● | | ● | | |
| ● | | | | | | | | ● | | | | | ● | | | | ● | |
| ● | | | ● | | | | | | | | | | | | | | ● | |

# Overview

Bn engine that does not crank almost always has an electrical problem (pages 180 and 181), but occasionally has water in the cylinders (page 182). An engine that cranks slowly and fails to start is probably not compressing the air in the cylinders sufficiently to attain ignition temperatures—the cranking speed will need to be increased. An engine that cranks at normal speeds and does not start (page 183) likely has one of the following: a fuel supply problem; an obstruction of the air inlet or exhaust; or a serious lack of compression. The latter requires a rebuild, and is particularly likely with an engine that has high operating hours, especially if it is harder to start in cold weather.

| Possible Causes |
|---|
| Battery low/loose connections |
| Engine overload/rope in propeller |
| Auxiliary equipment engaged |
| Pre-heat device inoperative |
| Plugged air filter |
| Plugged exhaust/turbocharger/kink in exhaust hose |
| Throttle closed/fuel shutoff solenoid faulty/tank empty |
| Plugged fuel filters |
| Air in fuel lines |
| Dirty fuel |
| Closed seacock/plugged raw-water filter or screen/plugged cooling system |
| Defective water pump/defective pump valves/air-bound water lines |
| Oil level low |
| Wrong viscosity oil |
| Diesel dilution of oil |
| Lift pump diaphragm holed |
| Defective injector/poor-quality fuel |
| Injection pump leaking |
| Injection timing advanced or delayed |
| Too much fuel injected |
| Piston blowby |
| Dry cylinder walls |
| Valve blowby |
| Worn valve stems |
| Decompressor levers on/valve clearances wrong/valves sticking |
| Dirt in oil pressure relief valve/ defective pressure gauge |
| Governor sticking/loose linkage |
| Governor idle spring too slack |
| Blown head gasket/cracked head |
| Uneven load on cylinders |
| Worn bearings |
| Seized piston |
| Water in the cylinders |

# Engine Cranks Slowly or Not at All

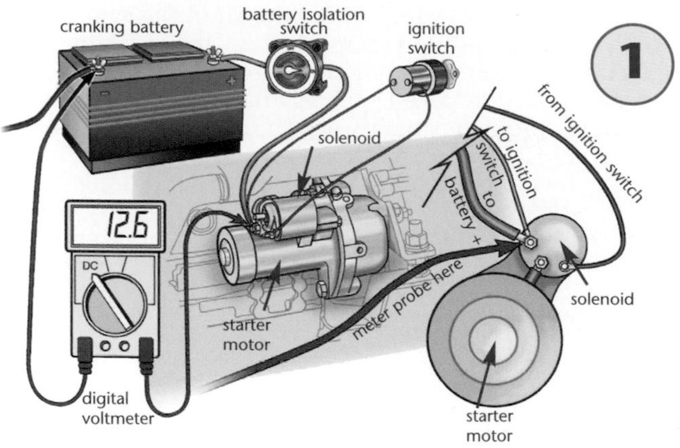


1. Turn on the ignition, but do not crank. Place the '+' probe of a DC voltmeter on the terminal at which the battery positive cable connects to the starter motor solenoid ① and the '–' probe on the cranking battery negative post (or engine block if the negative post is not accessible):
   - Higher than 12.6 volts: OK
   - 12.4 to 12.6 volts: the battery is somewhat discharged
   - 12.2 to 12.4 volts: the battery needs recharging
   - Below 12.2 volts: the battery is almost completely discharged and needs recharging
   - No volts: a battery isolation switch is probably turned off!
2. Assuming a charged battery, put the meter probes as in (1) and have someone attempt to crank the engine:
   - If the voltage remains the same, either the ignition circuit is defective or the solenoid is out of action. To investigate further, connect a jumper wire or screwdriver blade from the starter motor cable terminal on the solenoid to the ignition switch terminal (the one with a relatively small cable going into the wiring harness ②). If the engine cranks, the switch circuit is defective. If it does not crank, use a screwdriver blade to short the two big terminals on the solenoid ③. **Caution: Sparks may fly—hold the screwdriver**

**firmly to the terminals, and MAKE SURE THE SCREWDRIVER DOES NOT TOUCH THE STARTER MOTOR CASE.** If the starter motor spins (the engine will probably still not crank), the solenoid needs rebuilding (remove the end cover and check the points). No response means the battery is dead (check it again) or the starter motor is inoperative.

- If the voltage falls a volt or two but then stabilizes, feel all connections and cables in the cranking circuit (positive and negative). If any connections are warm, undo them, clean the terminals, and reconnect. If any cables are warm, they are undersized and need replacing with larger cables.

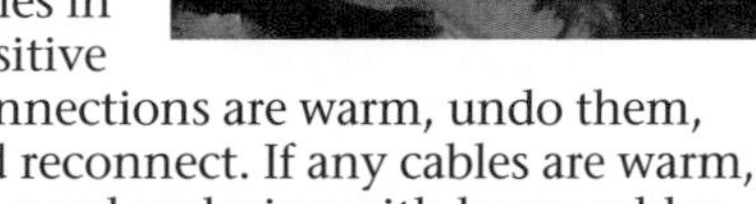

- If the voltage collapses, the battery is dead or has no remaining capacity, or the starter motor is shorted, or the engine is seized or full of water. Place a socket on the crankshaft pulley nut (see page 182) and attempt to turn the engine over. If it will not turn, the engine is seized or full of water.

Many cranking circuits on boats suffer from excessive voltage drop as a result of undersized cables. To test this, place the '+' probe of a DC voltmeter on the cranking battery '+' post, and the '–' probe on the terminal at which the starter motor '+' cable or strap attaches to the solenoid ④ and crank. Note the reading. Now place the '+' meter probe on the starter motor case and the '–' probe on the battery negative terminal ⑤ and crank. Note the reading. If either reading is above 0.5 volt, there is excessive voltage drop. Clean all the terminals and try again. If a high reading persists, fit larger cables. (Note: Given a high reading on the positive side of the circuit, before replacing the cables put the meter probes on the two large solenoid terminals and crank again. If that reading is high, the solenoid points need cleaning or replacing.)

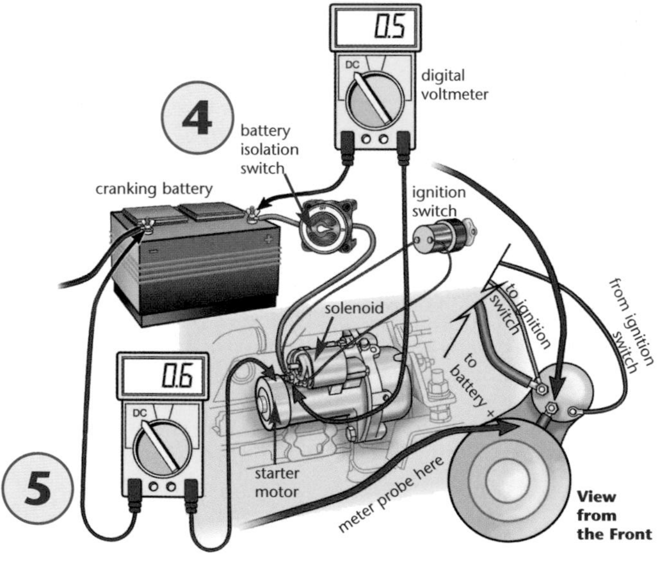

# Engine Seized Up

When a previously working engine seizes on start-up, suspect water intrusion into the cylinders. In an emergency, to clear the cylinders, CLOSE THE THROTTLE, ACTIVATE ANY "STOP" DEVICE, and flick the starter on momentarily with someone watching the crankshaft pulley:

1. If the pulley turns on the first "flick," do this repeatedly, pausing several seconds between each flick, until the engine turns normally. DO NOT AT ANY TIME HOLD THE STARTER ON UNTIL THE PULLEY TURNS FREELY—YOU WILL BREAK SOMETHING EXPENSIVE!
2. If the pulley does not turn on the first flick, *or if it stops turning at any point when the starter motor is flicked on*, STOP! You can try turning the crankshaft *in tiny increments* by placing an appropriate wrench on the crankshaft pulley nut ①. Better yet, remove the valve cover, identify the exhaust valves (those on the exhaust manifold side of the engine), find all those that are closed (the valves will not be depressed), and push a coin between the top of the valve and the rocker arm or camshaft to open the valve ②. Flick the starter motor on as above or use the wrench on the pulley nut until the engine turns normally. Remove the coins.

Once the engine is turning over, change the oil and filter. If there is any sign of water in the oil, run the engine for a few minutes and change the oil and filter again. Do this once more after 25 hours of running time.

If seawater has gotten into your engine, quite likely it either siphoned in from the raw-water system or was driven up the exhaust pipe by large seas (sailboats are especially vulnerable when under sail). To prevent these intrusions, any engine installed below the waterline requires a siphon break on the raw-water side (normally between the heat exchanger and the raw-water injection nipple into the exhaust, but sometimes between the raw-water pump and the heat exchanger) and a loop in the exhaust line that remains above the waterline at all heel angles and wave heights. Rectify as necessary.

# Engine Cranks Normally But Does Not Fire

Suspect a problem with the fuel supply or insufficient compression of the air in the cylinders. A complete obstruction of the air supply is less likely.

1. Ensure that there is fuel in the tank and any fuel valves are open.
2. Make sure any engine "stop" device is not activated. (Not all engines have such a device.)
3. Be sure the air intake and exhaust are unobstructed (is there a closed exhaust seacock?).
4. If the engine has glow plugs, check to see that they are working (the cylinder head in the immediate vicinity of each plug should be warm).
5. Open the throttle wide, crank 10 to 15 seconds, let the engine rest 2 minutes, and crank again. If the engine now fires, it probably has poor compression and needs an overhaul.
6. If the engine is cranking slowly, check the battery and cranking circuit (see pages 180 and 181). If these are OK, block the air intake while cranking and then remove the blockage while continuing to crank (this will help the engine to crank faster). NEVER BLOCK THE AIR INTAKE ON A RUNNING ENGINE.
7. Still not running? On all but common rail fuel injection systems (some modern engines—check the manual), crack an injector nut ①, open the throttle wide, crank the engine, and check for fuel periodically spurting out of the loosened connection (DO NOT DO THIS WITH A COMMON RAIL FUEL INJECTION SYSTEM):
   - No fuel? Recheck any engine "stop" device. Look for a failed electrically operated shutdown solenoid. Bleed the system (see page 188).
   - Fuel? If the engine has been getting progressively harder to start, it likely has poor compression and needs an overhaul. If the failure to start is a new event, go back to (1) and try again!

# Engine Overheats

If the raw-water flow in the exhaust is normal, check the freshwater pump belt. If that is OK, check the header tank on the freshwater side of the engine (CAUTION: let the engine cool before removing the pressure cap) ①. If the level is OK, proceed with the next paragraph.

If the raw-water flow in the exhaust is reduced or absent, shut down the engine, then check the raw-water pump belt (note: some pumps are gear driven and have no belt). If that is OK, make sure the raw-water intake seacock is open. (If it is not, the raw-water pump impeller may have been destroyed.) Next inspect the raw-water strainer ②. If it is clean:

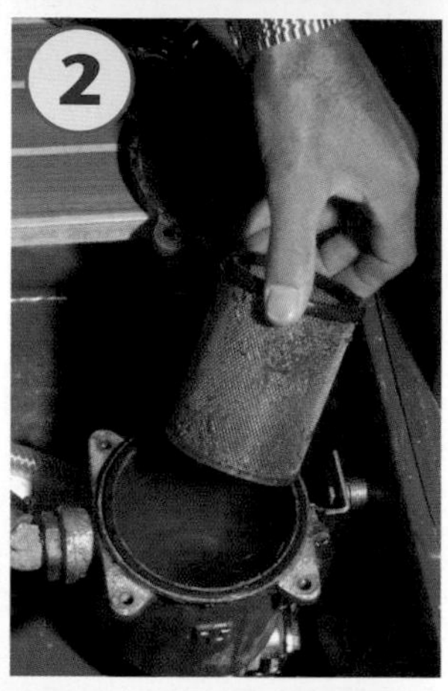

1. Close the raw-water seacock, disconnect its hose, and momentarily open the seacock to check for a strong flow. If the flow is reduced or absent, there is an obstruction at the raw-water inlet strainer on the outside of the hull.
2. Remove the raw-water pump cover and check the impeller for cracked or missing vanes ③. If any are missing, track down the pieces (they will likely be in the heat exchanger—see next item).

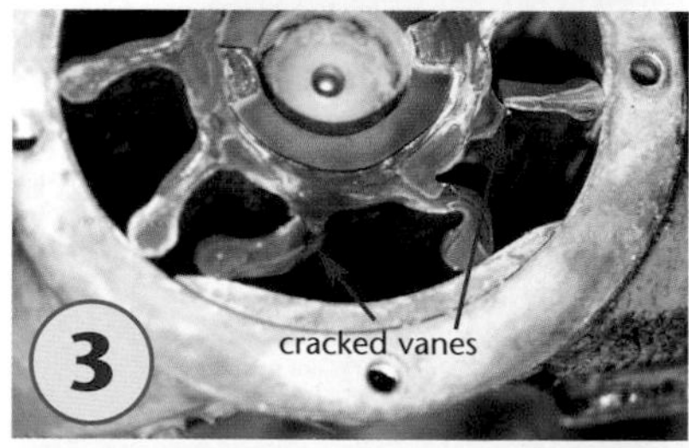


3. Check the tube stack in the heat exchanger for scaling (flaking) or obstructions (the tube stacks are often accessed by removing covers at one or both ends of the heat exchanger) ④. If necessary, have a mechanic descale an older engine.

4. Disconnect the raw-water hose from the injection nipple on the exhaust elbow and check for scaling or debris.

If an older engine only overheats when heavily loaded or after a move into warmer waters, suspect a scaled heat exchanger.

# Miscellaneous Operating Problems

## Exhaust Has Blue Smoke

A little blue smoke is normal on start-up. If it persists after the engine has warmed, the engine is burning oil and needs an overhaul.

## Black Smoke

A puff or two of black smoke on sudden acceleration is normal for an older engine. In all other circumstances, black smoke indicates improper fuel combustion:

1. Check the air filter or inlet for obstructions.
2. Break the exhaust hose loose from the water lift muffler and check for carbon fouling in the exhaust ①. (This photo shows a carbon-free exhaust exit.) If more than a thin film of carbon is present, the exhaust needs cleaning (and the cylinder head and valves also probably need servicing).
3. If the black smoke only occurs at high engine speeds, check for overloading (a line around the propeller, a heavily fouled boat bottom, too much auxiliary equipment, etc.). If this is a new boat, the propeller may be oversized.

## Misfiring

A rhythmic misfiring means that one or more cylinders are misfiring. A misfiring on start-up that stops once the engine is warm suggests that one or more cylinders are losing compression, and the engine needs an overhaul.

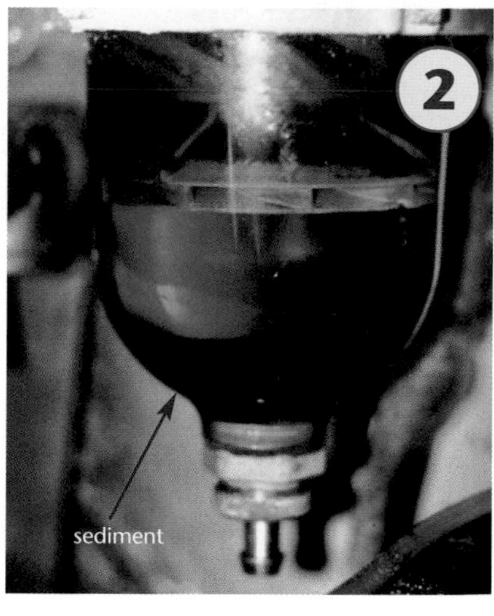


An irregular misfiring suggests dirty fuel (check for sediment in the base of the fuel filter ②), water in the fuel (check for water in the filter), or plugged fuel filters—especially if the misfiring only occurs at higher engine speeds and loads.

# Routine Maintenance

The great majority of engine problems are caused by a failure to ensure clean fuel or a failure to change the oil at the prescribed intervals.

## Clean Fuel

Dirty fuel is the #1 cause of marine diesel problems. There are four lines of defense to ensure clean fuel:

1. Adequate filtration of everything that goes into the tank. If adding fuel from dubious sources, use a Baja filter or water-separating fuel filter funnel.

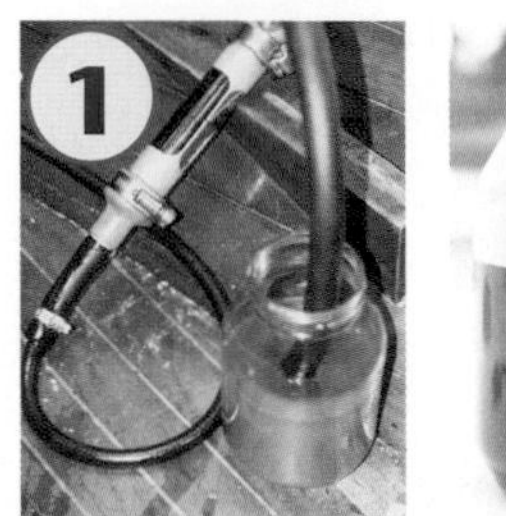

2. Take one or more fuel samples from the base of all fuel tanks at least once a year to remove any sediment and water ①, ②, or employ a commercial fuel-polishing service.
3. Change the primary fuel filter at the specified intervals ③, and clean the tank if the filter is dirty.

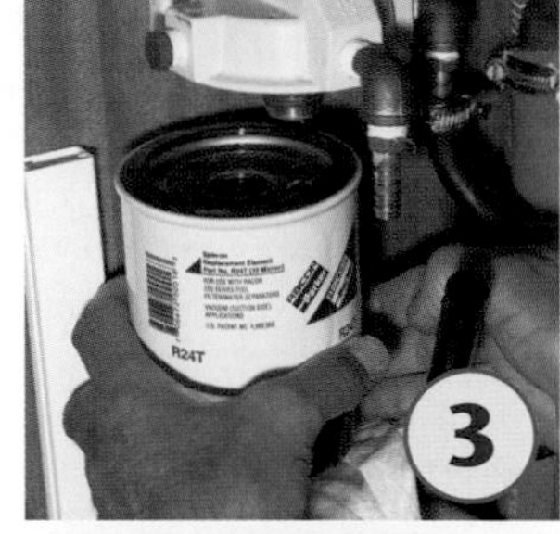


4. Change the secondary filter at the specified intervals ④. If the filter is dirty, clean the primary filter and the tank, and check the filter screen in the lift pump. (See page 188 to bleed the fuel system.)

## Additional Routine Maintenance

1. Change the air filter at the prescribed intervals (many small diesels do not have an air filter).
2. Periodically tighten the alternator belt. It should depress no more than 1/2 inch at the center of the longest belt run under moderate finger pressure ⑤.
3. Check the heat exchanger for a sacrificial zinc anode (many modern diesels do not have zinc anodes). If present, inspect it monthly until the rate of zinc loss is established. Replace the anode when it is no more than half gone.

4. See also pages 187 and 189.

## Changing the Oil

Along with ensuring clean fuel, this is essential for long engine life. A marine diesel engine needs an hour meter in the panel so you know when to do oil changes and other maintenance.

1. Run the engine until it is up to normal operating temperature.
2. Pump the oil out of the crankcase with the installed oil-change pump ⑥ or by sucking it out through the dipstick tube ⑦. Marine chandlers sell a variety of manual and electric pumps for this purpose.

3. Unscrew the oil filter with the appropriate filter wrench. In the absence of a filter wrench, use a spare alternator drive belt. Catch any spills in a disposable diaper or by placing a plastic bag around the filter ⑧.
4. Lubricate the sealing ring on a new filter with clean oil ⑨ and screw it on until hand tight. Tighten a further one-half to three-quarters turn with the filter wrench.
5. Add oil to the appropriate mark on the dipstick ⑩.

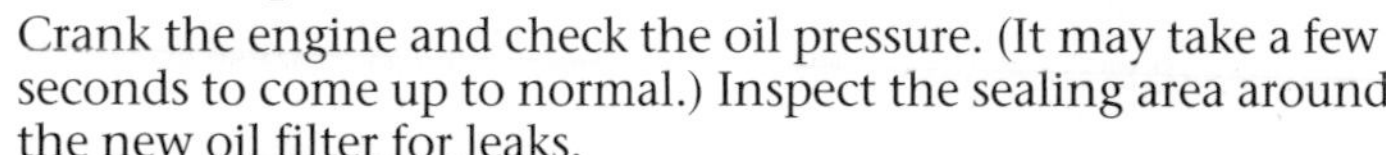

Crank the engine and check the oil pressure. (It may take a few seconds to come up to normal.) Inspect the sealing area around the new oil filter for leaks.

## Bleeding the Fuel System

Air in the fuel system will stop most diesels. Many modern diesels can be purged of air by opening the throttle wide (on a single-lever engine control, push in the button in the center of the throttle before opening it so that the transmission is not engaged) and cranking 10 to 15 seconds at a time. Allow the starter motor to cool at least 2 minutes between cranks.

With older engines, air must be removed by bleeding the fuel system as follows:

1. Check for a pump and bleed nipple on the primary filter ①. If present, unscrew the bleed nipple two or three turns and operate the pump until fuel free of bubbles spurts out.
2. If there is no pump on the primary filter, find the engine-mounted fuel lift pump. If electric, turn on the ignition. If manual, find the pump lever ②. The engine may need to be turned over a half revolution to get the manual pump working.
3. Move "upstream" from the lift pump (i.e., toward the point of fuel injection on the engine) to the first bleed nipple in the system, which is normally on the secondary fuel filter, and unscrew the nipple a couple of turns ③.

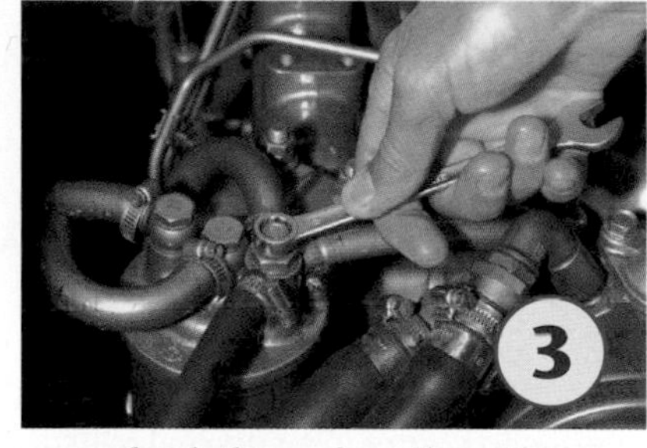


4. Operate the lift pump until fuel free of air bubbles flows out, catching spilled fuel. Then close the nipple. If the air bubbles don't clear, either the tank is low on fuel or there is an air leak on the suction side of the pump; check the seal on the primary filter first, especially if it has been changed recently.
5. Move upstream in the fuel system to the next bleed nipple, which is normally on the injection pump, and repeat.
6. Once finished, open the throttle wide and crank 10 to 15 seconds.
7. If the engine does not fire, loosen the injector nuts (see page 183), open the throttle wide, crank until fuel spurts from each loosened connection, and then tighten.

*CAUTION: You must never loosen an injector nut on one of the new generation of diesel engines with a common rail fuel injection system.*

The engine should fire. Note: You can also bleed a newer engine after a fuel filter change in order to avoid the prolonged cranking that may otherwise be necessary to fill the new filter element with fuel.

## Winterizing (or Annual Maintenance)

1. In freezing climates all raw-water systems must either be drained or filled with nontoxic (propylene glycol) antifreeze. If draining, remove the raw-water pump cover and pull out the impeller. If adding antifreeze, remove the raw-water hose from its seacock, dip into a bucket of antifreeze solution, and run the engine until the solution comes out the exhaust.
2. Inspect the raw-water pump impeller for signs of wear or cracking. Replace as necessary or at the specified intervals.
3. At least every two years, drain the freshwater side and refill with a fresh ethylene glycol antifreeze solution to restore the corrosion inhibitors.
4. Wash the valves on any vented loops in warm water to clean out salt crystals.
5. Change the engine oil at the end of the season rather than the beginning of the next (this removes corrosive acids from the crankcase).
6. Change the transmission oil.
7. Pump a sample from the base of the fuel tank (as on page 186) and remove any water or sediment. Fill the tank to minimize condensation.
8. Break loose the exhaust hose at the water lift muffler and check for carbon buildup (there should be no more than a light film) (page 185). If present, review the operating practices to prevent long-term damage to the engine.
9. Spray WD-40 or a similar penetrating fluid into the air inlet, then seal the inlet to prevent moisture entry. Place a note in a conspicuous place to remind yourself to unseal this before cranking the engine!
10. Remove the battery from the boat or ensure that it gets charged periodically (once a month for wet-cells; every few months for gels and AGMs).
11. Check the wiring harness and all electrical connections for signs of abrasion or corrosion and rectify as necessary. Spray with a corrosion inhibitor.
12. Check all hoses for signs of softening, bulging, kinking, or abrasion, and all hose clamps for signs of corrosion. Replace as necessary.
13. Every couple of years, or if confronted with unexplained vibration, check the engine alignment.

## Recommissioning

1. Unseal the air inlet.
2. Replace the raw-water pump impeller (if removed).
3. Pump a sample from the base of the fuel tank and remove any water or sediment.
4. Replace the battery (if removed).
5. If the engine has a "stop" lever, activate this to prevent the engine from starting, then crank 10 to 15 seconds to initiate oil lubrication. Let the starter motor cool 2 minutes, then crank.

CHAPTER 12

# Emergencies On Board

John Rousmaniere

Boating is a remarkably safe sport, yet emergencies can and do occur. According to Coast Guard statistics, the most frequent accidents include collisions, falls on deck or in the cabin, groundings, flooding, and fire. We won't talk about collisions here except to say that, like all accidents, they are often caused by alcohol abuse, operator inattention, or ignorance of basic rules. Neither will we address first aid.

Here the subject is onboard emergencies that can damage the boat or cause injury or even death. We'll interject some cautionary words about preventing emergencies.

# Crew Overboard (COB) Rescue

If someone (the COB) goes over the side, you have six tasks, none requiring much more than basic boating skills.

**1. Organize the remaining crew.** Strong, decisive, positive leadership is needed. Note your geographical position. Nobody goes into the water as a rescuer without permission (the only reason to dive in is if the COB is unconscious; the rescuer must wear a PFD and be tethered to the boat).

**2. Get buoyancy to the COB.** Throw cushions, life rings, or the Lifesling—a retrieval system consisting of a buoyant yoke at the end of a long line tied to the boat. (The boat drags the line and yoke to the swimmer, who gets into the yoke and is hauled to the stopped boat and then out of the water.)

**3. Keep the COB in sight.** Stay nearby and instruct someone to point continuously at the COB, shouting encouragement.

**4. Make a rescue maneuver.** You must stay near the COB and get back quickly. There are three simple options:

- **Under power or sail.** ***The quick stop:*** When the COB goes over, turn the boat into the wind, then circle the COB slowly. Drag the Lifesling or its line into his or her hand, or

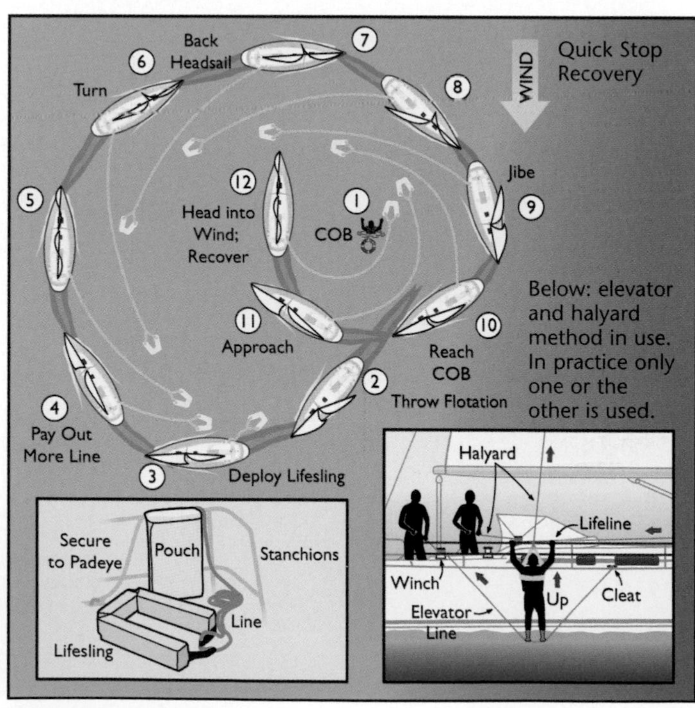

throw a line when the boat stops. If under sail, trim the sails tight and *don't cast off the jibsheet when tacking or jibing.* This keeps the boom from banging around, and the backed jib (headsail) slows the boat and allows quick turns.

- **Under power.** Several yards from the COB, take the engine out of gear and throw a line to the COB or let the Lifesling down to the COB.
  ***OR (large boat),* the Williamson Turn:** alter course 60 degrees to one side, then turn 240 degrees in the other direction to come back to the COB. Follow the directions above.
- **Under sail.** ***The figure eight (reach-and-reach) (useful in strong winds because there is no jibe):*** When the COB goes over, get on a beam reach and sail for a few seconds. Tack, reach back below the COB, and head up to the COB, dragging the Lifesling or throwing a line.

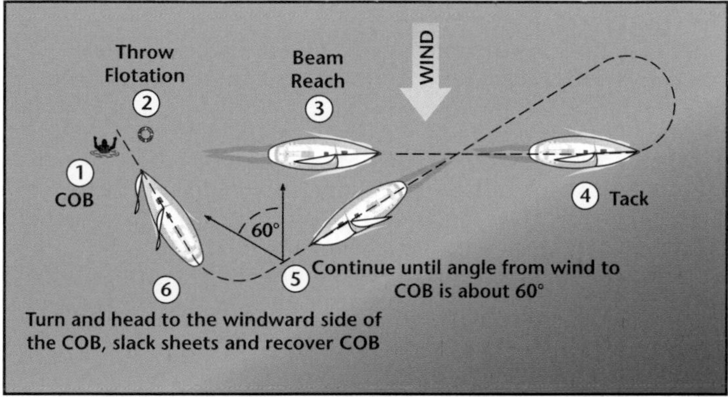


***OR heave-to after returning to COB:*** This leaves the boat jogging along very slowly and, in most cases, self-steering so nobody is needed at the helm. On a close reach, trim the jib flat on the windward side and adjust the mainsheet and traveler so the boat self-steers. In a variation called the Rod stop (named for seaman Rod Stephens), sail on a beam reach, roll up the jib (or let it luff), and push the mainsail all the way out, securing it there with a line.

**5. Make physical contact.** When the COB has hold of the Lifesling or line, stop the boat by taking the engine out of gear or luffing and lowering sails. Pull the COB to the boat.

**6. Retrieve the COB.** You usually can pull the COB over either side. But if the boat is rapidly sliding downwind, it may be best to retrieve over the upwind side so as not to drift over the COB. If the COB is in the Lifesling, clip a halyard to it, lead the halyard to a winch, and hoist the victim on deck. (You may need a block and tackle.) Without the Lifesling, the COB can be lifted by strong crewmembers or helped up a swim platform or ladder. Or drape a line over the side, lead the line to a winch, have the COB kneel or stand on it, and use the elevator method to hoist the COB. *Do not try to lift the COB by the boom,* which will likely swing and hit someone, and may be too low.

## If You Fall Overboard

Do not try to swim. You won't be able to catch the boat, and you'll wear yourself out. Get rid of objects that weigh you down and assume a fetal-type position—arms folded, knees drawn to chest—to reduce loss of body heat. Blow a whistle, shine a light, or make splashes to attract attention.

# Fire

To use a fire extinguisher, aim it at the base of the fire, pull the trigger, and apply with a sweeping motion, side to side.

Three types of fires are typical on boats: combustible materials (Class A), liquids (Class B), and electrical (Class C). The label on the fire extinguisher indicates the type(s) it can handle.

**Class A—Combustible material fires (wood, trash, cloth, etc.):** Use water or an extinguisher suitable for Class A fires, such as a dry chemical or aqueous foam device. (Halon has been banned.)

Label for a fire extinguisher that can handle three different types of fires.

**Class B—Flammable liquid fires (cooking fuel, engine fuel, grease, etc.):** Immediately cut off the flow of fuel by turning off the stove or engine *and* the fuel supply at the tank. Do not spray or dump water on the fire (this may spread it). Extinguish a liquid fire with an extinguisher suitable for Class B fires, such as a $CO_2$, dry chemical, or aqueous foam extinguisher, or cover the fire with a wet towel. Dampen combustible objects to prevent the fire from spreading.

**Class C—Live electrical fires:** Immediately turn off the power source. Extinguish the fire with an extinguisher suitable for a Class C fire, such as a $CO_2$, dry chemical, or aqueous foam. Do not use water.

Since a dry chemical or aqueous foam extinguisher will put out all three types of fires, one of these should be your first choice. Smaller bottles are easier to handle than big ones. Dry chemical extinguishers are effective at ranges from 5 to 15 feet.

# Taking on Water

If the bilge fills, use all your manual and electric pumps while energetically applying a bucket brigade until you have gotten ahead of the leak. Check the deck, anchor locker, ventilators, hatches, mast, rudder post, propeller shaft, and other gear for major leaks. Water can come from all directions. Also check the bilge, seacocks, and hoses. If a hose is leaking, shut the seacock and replace the hose or tighten or replace the hose clamp. If the seacock or its through-hull fitting is missing or damaged, drive a plug into the hole with a hammer.

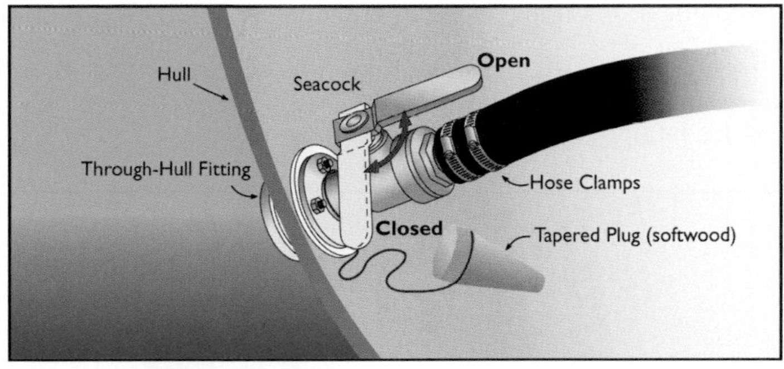


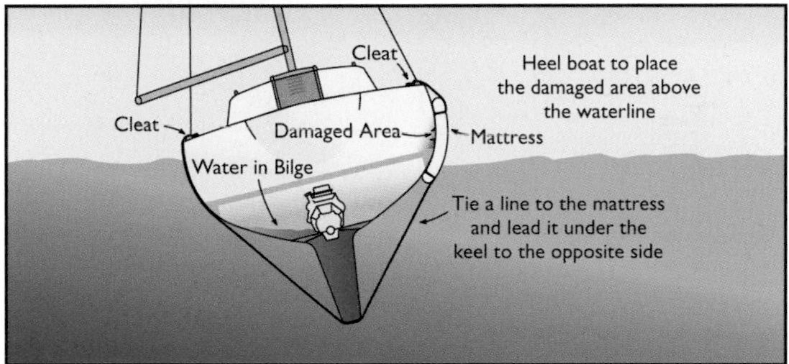


If the water is still coming in, there probably is a hole in the bottom. Heel the boat so the hole is as far out of the water as possible and cover it from the outside with a sail or mattress or fill it from the inside with a mattress. Keep pumping and bailing.

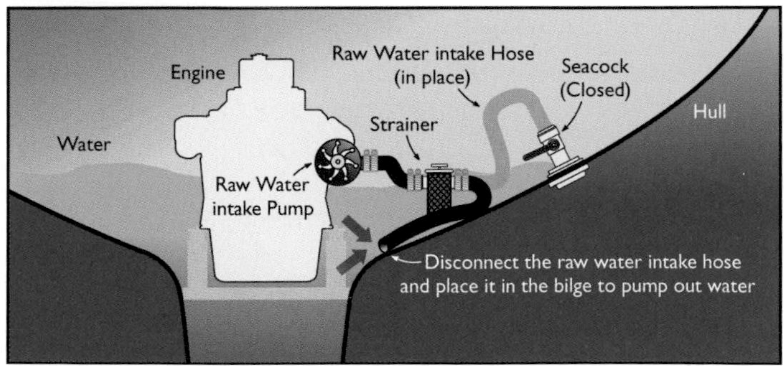


An emergency bilge pump may be improvised from the engine's water cooling system. Close the seacock for the water intake and move the hose from the seacock into the bilge.

# Running Aground

First, study the situation. Is the boat leaking? What part of the boat is aground? Can you see a safe channel? Check the tide tables. If the tide is flooding, you may float off. If ebbing, move fast!

**Back off.** Go out the way you came in—carefully, for the rudder may be damaged by a rock. In mud or sand, it may help to rock the boat to break the hold on the boat's keel.

**Set out an anchor in a dinghy or by wading.** Take a strain on the rode to pull the stern or bow off.

**Heel the boat to decrease draft.** Put the crew's weight at one side (for example, on the boom) and try to sail or power off.

**If the tide is going out,** put fenders under the lower side to prevent hull damage and lead a halyard to shore to keep the boat from flopping over in the wrong direction.

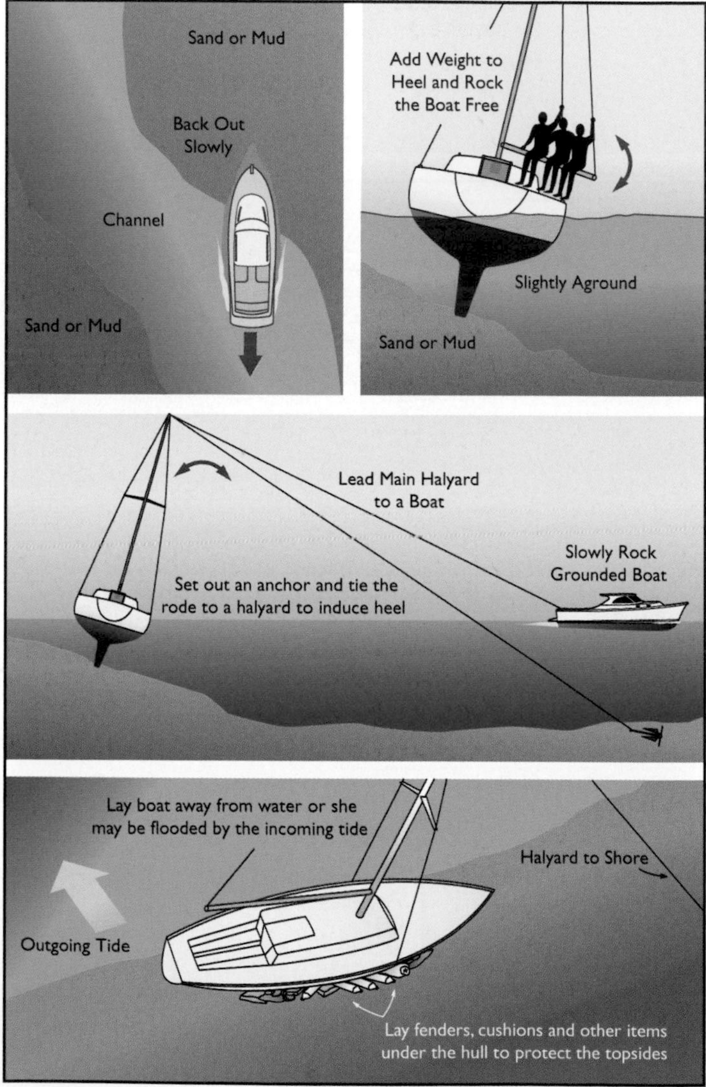

# Towing

If offered a tow:

**1. Settle terms.** Agree on a fee, destination, hand signals, and radio frequency. Avoid a dispute about salvage rights by leaving a crew on your boat and giving the tow boat your line. Be sure to establish a safe towing speed so your boat is not pulled apart or towed under water.

**2. Use a nylon line.** It stretches and absorbs jerks. Secure it to the largest through-bolted fitting on deck, like a bow cleat, a winch, or the mast. Back up this fitting with another line, pulled taut, or create a bridle as in the illustration. Make sure lines run fair, without rubbing against fittings. A fairlead may have to be improvised on the bow from a sail stop or a short length of line and a block.

**3. Start towing slowly.** Increase speed and adjust the towline length until your boat is riding in the trough of a wave well behind the tow boat.

**4. Shorten the tow line in crowded waters, or tow alongside for maximum control.**

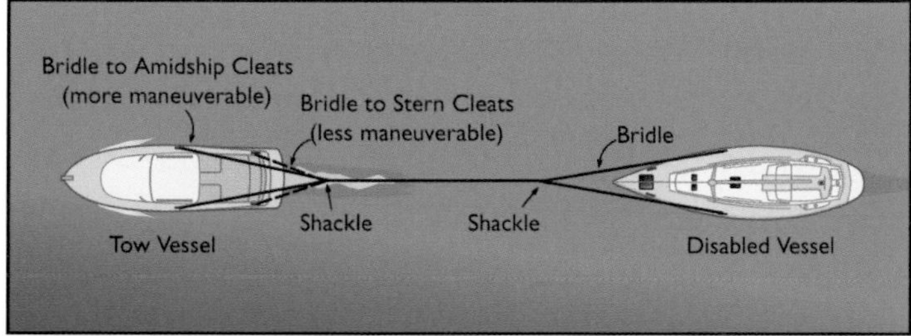


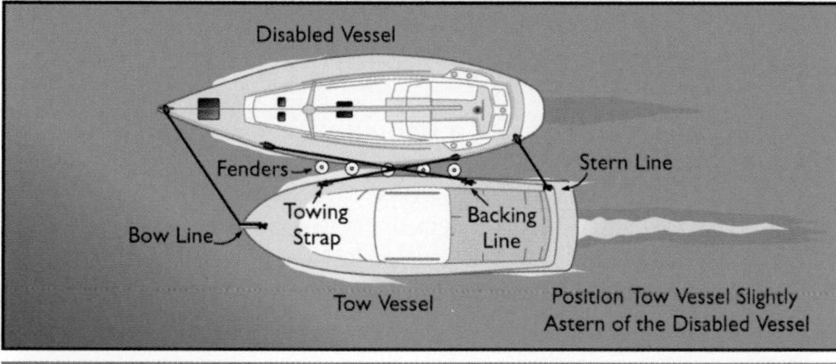

# Steering Failure

If the steering system breaks, stop the boat and inspect for damage that can be repaired with spare wire, bulldog clamps, shackles, or other fittings. If repair is impossible, call for a tow, attempt to self-steer, or jury-rig a rudder. When the steering cable breaks in a wheel-steered sailboat, you may find a post atop the steering quadrant on which to bolt an emergency tiller.

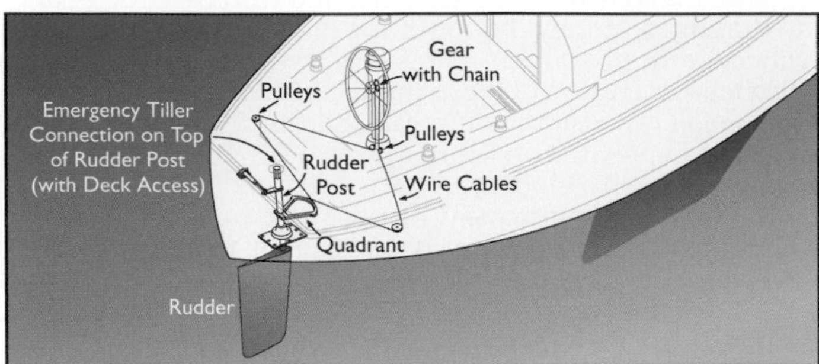


## Self-Steering

**Powerboats.** A twin-prop boat might be steered by balancing the force of the two engines. Single-prop boats usually cannot be steered without a rudder.

**Sailboats.** Many boats can be self-steered by trimming the sails and finding the right balance between the jib (pulling the bow down) and the mainsail or mizzen (pushing the bow up). A ketch or yawl usually self-steers most effectively because the mizzen balances the jib.

## Jury-Rigged Rudders

On powerboats and sailboats, a temporary rudder can be jury-rigged (improvised) by dragging a paddle-like object, some fenders, or another substantial object over the stern and adjusting it with lines to swing the stern. Because the loads are large, the system will break unless it is flexible. In this possible solution, the hinge at the stern must have plenty of give or the jury-rigged rudder will snap; make it from a loose assembly of rope.

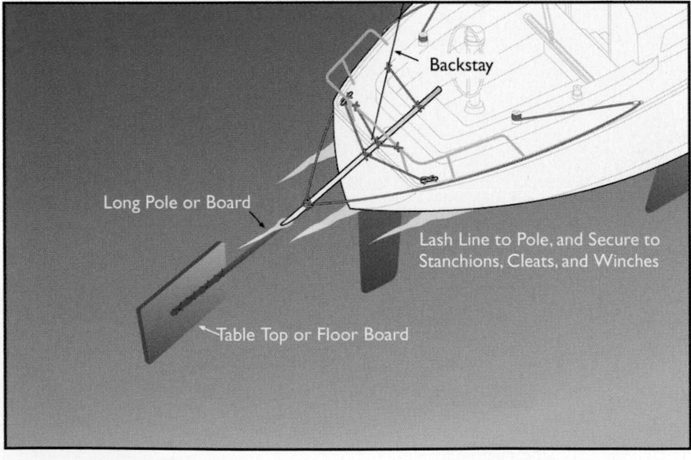

# Broken Rigging

**If a shroud breaks.** Immediately luff the sails and tack the boat to put the load on the other side. If the headstay breaks, immediately bear off downwind. If the backstay breaks, luff up and get the sails down. A stay can be repaired using spare wire and bulldog clamps, or a substitute stay can be rigged using a halyard. Someone may have to go aloft in a bosun's chair.

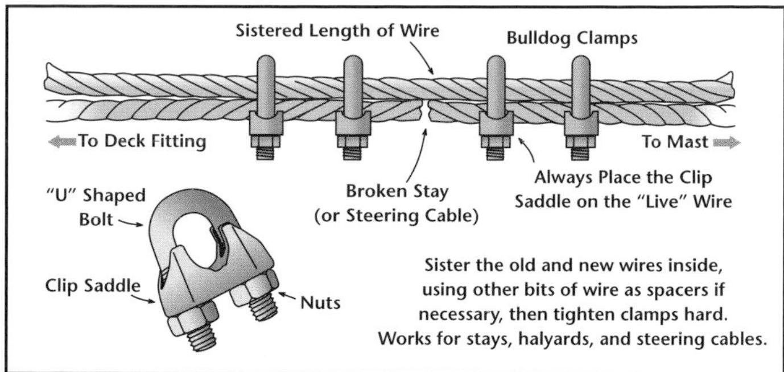


**If the mast breaks.** Clear away the mess before it holes the hull by pulling the cotter and clevis pins in the turnbuckles. Wire stays usually cannot be cut. A dismasted boat rolls and pitches violently, so wear and hook on safety harnesses and crawl on deck. A new mast can be jury-rigged by lashing together the remains of sails and spars with line.

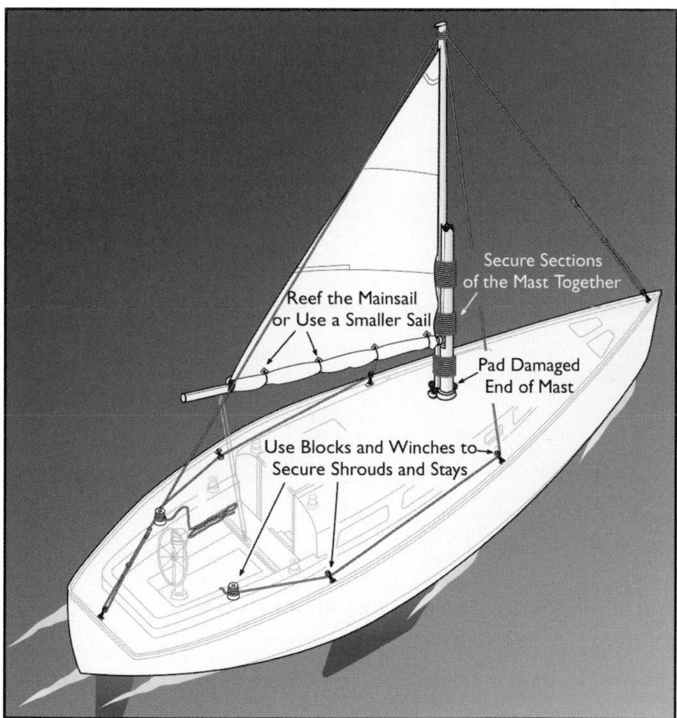


Only a few of the many possible jury-rig possibilities are shown here. Necessity is the mother of invention. Can you use a spinnaker pole as a gin pole to help erect a mast section? Use what you have!

# Losing Power
## (see also Chapter 11)

Engine shutdowns are often caused by problems with fuel, with the cooling system, or with the electrical system.

**Fuel problems** cause most engine troubles. If the engine stalls, the fuel may be dirty. Replace the fuel filters. If the engine is still balky, there may be an airlock in the fuel line. Remove it following the instructions in the engine manual.

**Cooling problems** cause the engine temperature to rise dangerously. Stop the engine and inspect the raw-water intake. The seacock may be closed or the system may be clogged by weed. One sign of a damaged cooling system is that water is not spitting out of the exhaust pipe.

**Electrical problems** may prevent the engine from starting or running smoothly. No engine will start with a dead battery. Reserve one battery for starting. With a gasoline engine, clean or replace the spark plugs.

### Engine Troubleshooting Guide

| SYMPTOM | POSSIBLE CAUSE | REMEDY |
|---|---|---|
| Engine won't crank. | Starter switches not turned on properly. | Turn on proper switches (consult your owner's manual). |
| | Battery discharged. | Charge battery or turn battery switches to include house batteries in charging battery. If you get engine started, find out why battery was discharged. |
| | Starter solenoid or starter defective. | Listen to starter motor when someone else turns ignition switch. If you hear a click and nothing happens, tap side of starter motor once with hammer while trying to start. The starter may start (this is only a temporary fix). Be ready to shut off emergency engine electricity if you hear a loud whirring hum, however. Call a professional. |
| | Loud, whirring hum. | Severe problem in starter. Turn off power to engine start circuit; use emergency switch if you have one. Don't use starter. Call a professional. |
| Engine cranks, but won't start. | Out of fuel. | Add fuel and bleed fuel lines if necessary. |
| | Fuel line valve closed. | Open valve. |
| | Fuel shutoff cable is shutting off fuel. | Move shutoff cable to ON position. |
| | Air in fuel line. | Bleed fuel lines. |
| | Blockage in fuel line. | Clear blockage. |
| | Very dirty fuel filters. | Change fuel filters. |
| No water exiting exhaust. | Water intake closed. | Open seawater intake seacock, fast! |
| | Blockage in seawater intake line. | Clear blockage. |
| | Defective impeller pump. | Replace impeller. |
| Engine runs ragged. | Dirty fuel. | Change fuel filters, change to different fuel tank if possible. Have professional clean tanks. |
| | Dirty fuel filters. | Change fuel filters. |
| | Blockage in fuel line. | Clear blockage. |
| | Fuel lift pump defective. | Replace fuel lift pump. |
| Engine smokes. | Defective injectors. | Replace injectors. |
| | Serious engine problem. | Call professional. |
| | Too much oil in engine. | Stop engine; pump excess oil out. Do not run engine in an excess-oil state: Very dangerous! |

### Additional Possibilities for Gasoline Engines

| SYMPTOM | POSSIBLE CAUSE | REMEDY |
|---|---|---|
| Engine cranks, but won't start | Defective spark plugs. | Replace spark plugs. |
| | Carburetor problem. | Call a professional. |
| | Engine timing problem. | Call a professional. |
| Engine runs ragged. | Defective spark plugs. | Replace spark plugs. |
| | Carburetor problem. | Call a professional. |
| | Engine timing problem. | Call a professional. |

(Chart courtesy David Kroenke, *Know Your Boat*)

# Preventing Accidents

A few simple routines can keep emergencies from occurring in

**Be careful with alcohol.** It spoils good judgment, makes you unsteady on your feet, and causes seasickness.

**Know your boat.** Have a diagram showing where all important gear is stowed.

**Wear a PFD.** Almost 75% of all reported recreational boating fatalities are caused by drowning. In almost 90% of these tragedies, the victims were not wearing life jackets or other personal flotation devices (PFDs).

**Wear a safety harness.** It prevents people from falling overboard in the first place. According to the Coast Guard, 38% of reported boating deaths are due to falls overboard, and when someone goes over the side the chances of a fatality are one in three. There are some excellent combination PFD-safety harnesses on the market. Put on the harness before you come on deck, and hook it in the cockpit before you step out of the companionway. Hook the safety harness tether into sturdy jacklines or through-bolted fittings. Keep the tether short so any fall won't be long. Clip on whenever you're unsteady, and especially when doing a two-handed job—like steering, coming in or out of the companionway, trimming sails, or hoisting sails.

**Prevent falls.** One of the main causes of injuries in a boat is a fall on deck or in the cabin. Everybody should wear nonskid shoes. When you feel unsteady on your feet, use grab rails and lifelines or crawl on deck (the best sailors do it).

**Tame the boom.** A flying boom can cause serious, even fatal, head injuries. Even in light wind, hold it out with a preventer—a line leading from the boom forward to the deck, through a block, and back to the cockpit.

**Stay dry and warm.** A dry body is a warm body—and also an effective body, because symptoms of hypothermia include slow thinking and loss of agility. Wear good foul-weather clothing as soon as the spray begins to fly. Underneath, wear layers of fleece clothing.

# Getting Lost

If you don't know where you are, stop the boat (a sailboat can heave-to), take a deep breath, calm down, and think. Using the chart, methodically examine your surroundings as you try to re-create your recent course or courses. Have people with fresh eyes search for landmarks or buoys. Take bearings to any landmarks or buoys you can see or identify. In poor visibility, if you can't fix your position with GPS, either stay where you are or proceed slowly in a direction you know to be safe—toward open water, a bold shore without off-lying hazards, or an aid to navigation that produces a distinctive sound signal and is not close to a reef or other hazard.

# Emergency Calls and Signals

Before signaling a Mayday or SOS, ask yourself, "Is this truly a life-threatening emergency? Can I get home on my own?" Every distress call puts at least one other boat at risk.

## VHF-FM Radio: Avoiding Collision

Even when you have the right of way under the Navigation Rules, if you feel the slightest concern about a possible collision, talk to the other vessel on VHF Channel 13 (the bridge-to-bridge channel) or Channel 16 (the emergency channel). Even if your message is simply, "I'm the blue sailing vessel on your port bow. Do you see me?," the other captain will appreciate it. When near or crossing shipping lanes in poor visibility, announce your boat's type, position, speed, and heading on Channel 13 or 16. Ask nearby vessels to do the same and say you're standing by on Channel 16. Even if you don't hear a response, you will get the attention of the other vessel's crew.

## VHF-FM Radio: Distress Alerts

**BY VOICE:** Tune the radio to Channel 16, the international distress frequency. (Because VHF has a range of only about 50 miles or less from a typical small or medium-size boat, it may not be helpful at sea unless nearby boats relay your call.) Then *slowly and clearly:*

**1. Say, "Mayday, Mayday, Mayday."**

**2. Say your boat's name three times, followed by your radio call sign.**

**3. Say "Mayday" and your boat's name again, then your geographical position.** Preferably, give your position in latitude and longitude (read it off the GPS or chart). But it can be a bearing and distance to or from a buoy, a point of land, or other charted object. (For instance, "We're two miles northeast of gong number 1 off Oyster Bay.")

**4. Briefly describe your situation, your distress, and the assistance you require.**

**5. Describe your boat by type, color, and size.**

**6. Say how many people are aboard, and if they need medical attention.**

**7. Sign off (say "over").**

*Repeat the above until someone acknowledges.*

When USCG or law enforcement officials respond to your call, they will follow a set procedure that you may find frustrating because some questions may not seem relevant to your situation. Try not to be impatient. These professional men and women are doing the job they were trained for. The quicker you provide answers, the quicker the officials will get to the specifics of your problems

**BY DIGITAL SELECTIVE CALLING (DSC) VHF-FM RADIO:** If your boat's VHF radio is equipped with Digital Selective Calling (DSC), and it is properly installed and registered *(see below)*, distress calls are almost automated.

**1-A. Lift the cover and press the DISTRESS button. If the display reads "Undesignated," press the button for three to five seconds.** The radio transmits a simple "Mayday" alert in a digital signal containing your identity and location over Channel 70 to the Coast Guard and other ships.

**1-B. If the display provides a choice between "Undesignated" and "Designated,"** selecting "Designated" calls up a menu that allows you to specify the type of trouble you are in. Then press the button for three to five seconds to send the signal.

**2. When the call is acknowledged digitally by another DSC-equipped radio,** you will hear a tone.

**3. If the radio does not switch automatically to Channel 16 for voice transmission, press the CANCEL/CLEAR button.**

**4. On Channel 16, send a voice message concerning your situation (see above) and talk to rescuers and other vessels.**

*DSC installation and registration.* In order to send complete distress calls, a DSC-equipped VHF radio (1) must be connected to the boat's GPS navigation system receiver; *and* (2) the boat's unique Maritime Mobile Service Identity (MMSI) number must be registered with the Coast Guard; *and* (3) the radio must be formatted with the MMSIs of radios you wish to call. The U.S. Coast Guard's group MMSI is 003669999. Local U.S. and Canadian Guard Guard stations have MMSIs available from local authorities.

## Visual Distress Signals

Most boats 16 feet or longer must carry distress signals for use by day. If out at night, they must carry night signals.

**Day distress signals.** Ignite an orange smoke signal, show an orange flag with a black square or circle, wave hands or honk horns aggressively, or reflect sun with a mirror.

**Night distress signal.** With a bright flashlight signal SOS (dot-dot-dot, dash-dash-dash, dot-dot-dot).

**Day/night distress signal.** Fire off a red flare (rocket or hand-held). (White flares are intended to identify a boat when a collision threatens.)

***Note: Smoke signals and flares must be replaced by their expiration dates.***

Smoke Flare

Flare Gun

Gun shots

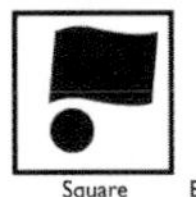

Square over ball

Black square and ball on a field of orange

Inverted flag

Morse code SOS

Parachute flare

Waving of hands

Dye in water

Radio MAYDAY

Loud horn

Fire

Smoke canister in water

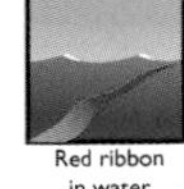

Red ribbon in water

# Evacuating Crew by Helicopter

**1. Wear PFDs and safety harnesses.** The boat will roll violently in the helicopter downdraft.

**2. The pilot is in charge.** He and the rescue crew will communicate by radio, hand signals, or signs.

**3. Jog along slowly.** Unless otherwise ordered, keep the wind on the port side.

**4. Prepare to put the injured crew in a dinghy or a life raft tethered to your boat.** Direct evacuation from a low powerboat may be possible, but superstructures and masts will tangle the rescue equipment. (Uninjured evacuees may be instructed to jump into the water.)

**5. Don't touch the litter basket or cable before they are grounded in the water or on deck.** They carry a violent static electric shock.

**6. Leave a written medical report with the person being evacuated.**

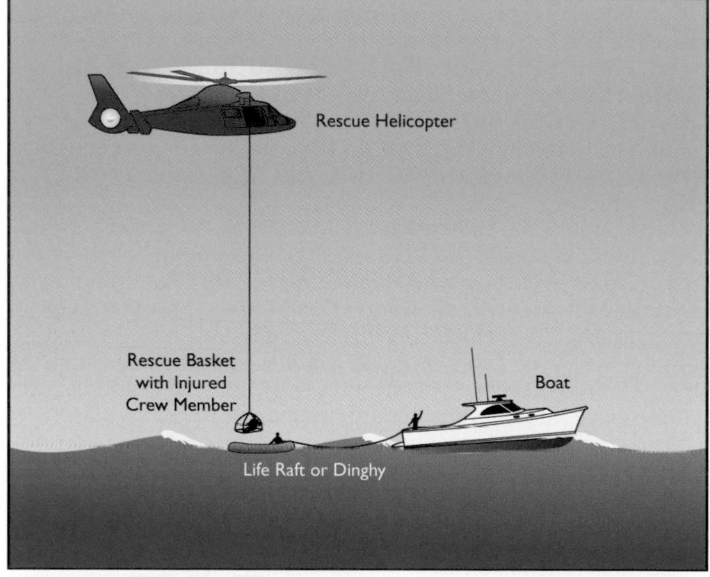

# Abandoning Ship

This is absolutely the last resort. Resist the temptation to get off the boat simply because you are seasick, wet, bruised, and miserable. As the saying goes, "The only time to step into a life raft is when your first step is *up*." No matter how bad the situation may seem, the boat often survives. The crew may be in more danger when abandoning the boat than on board. A life raft is an extremely unseaworthy vessel, a helicopter rescue is hazardous, and it's always risky to bring boats alongside in rough weather. But if the boat is obviously going down, or if there is a serious fire, you have good cause to abandon ship.

**1. Bring the life raft on deck and tie its tether to the boat.** Or prepare the boat's dinghy.

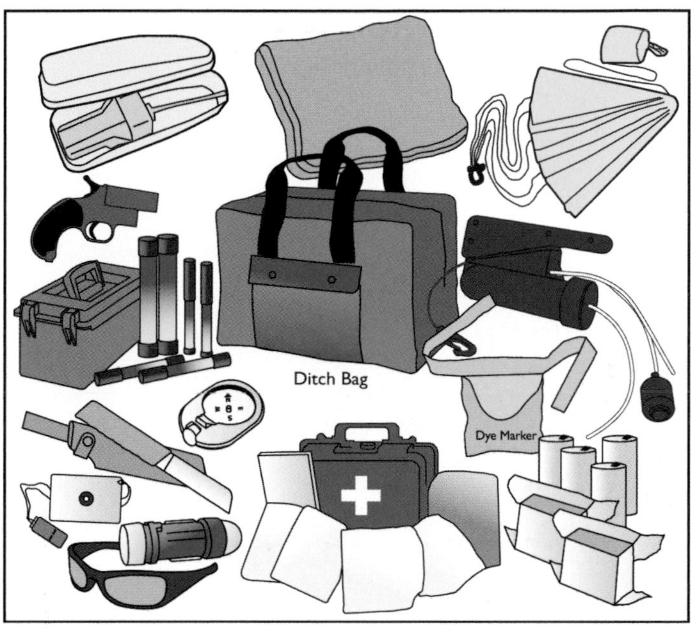


**2. Prepare an abandon ship bag ("ditch bag").** This collection of gear and rations should address the problems of thirst, cold, hunger, wet, and signaling rescuers. Take water (and, ideally, a hand-operated membrane desalinator with which to make more), paddles, food, a knife, a handheld VHF-FM radio, flares, a signal mirror, an EPIRB (satellite radio beacon), a sea anchor, seasickness medication, fleece clothing, foul-weather clothing, blankets, waterproof containers, a small bilge pump, a sponge, etc.

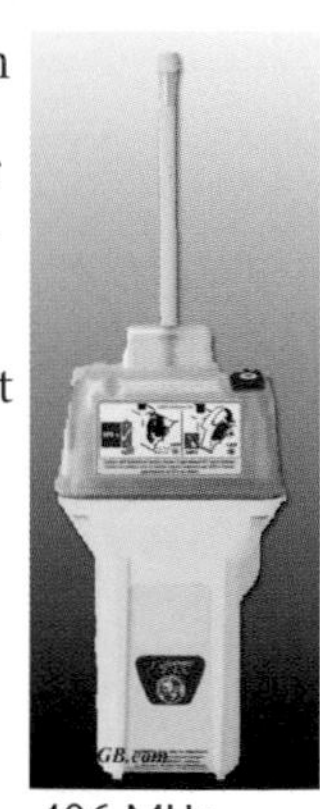

406 MHz EPIRB

**3. Inflate the life raft.** Tie tether to boat, throw raft downwind, and pull on tether until raft inflates. It may inflate upside down and have to be righted.

**4. Notify others.** Using the radio and leaving a note, identify the boat and yourself and say you will return.

**5. Abandon ship.** Put the gear in the life raft, climb in, turn on the EPIRB, and cut the tether to the boat.

CHAPTER 13

# Emergency First Aid On Board

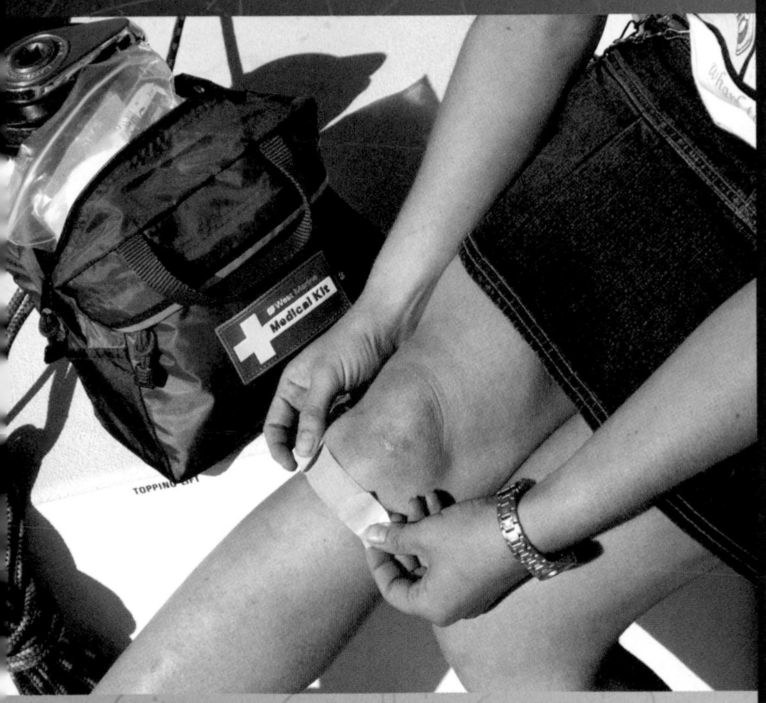


Richard Clinchy

# What to Do First

## Get the Big Picture

**How many people are ill or injured?** If more than one, make all as comfortable as possible and treat the most serious first.

**Think about causes.** Suspect burns after a fire or explosion, wounds after a collision, etc. If victim is diabetic or has history of heart trouble, suspect these causes.

**Any risk to others on board?** If the boat is taking on water, get life jackets on everyone. If there is a fire on board, maneuver boat to keep smoke and flames downwind.

**Know your limits.** This chapter focuses solely on the immediate care of emergencies that present an imminent threat to life or risk of serious permanent disability. Do the best you can, and do not be afraid to act, but get professional medical help for the victim as soon as possible.

## Injury

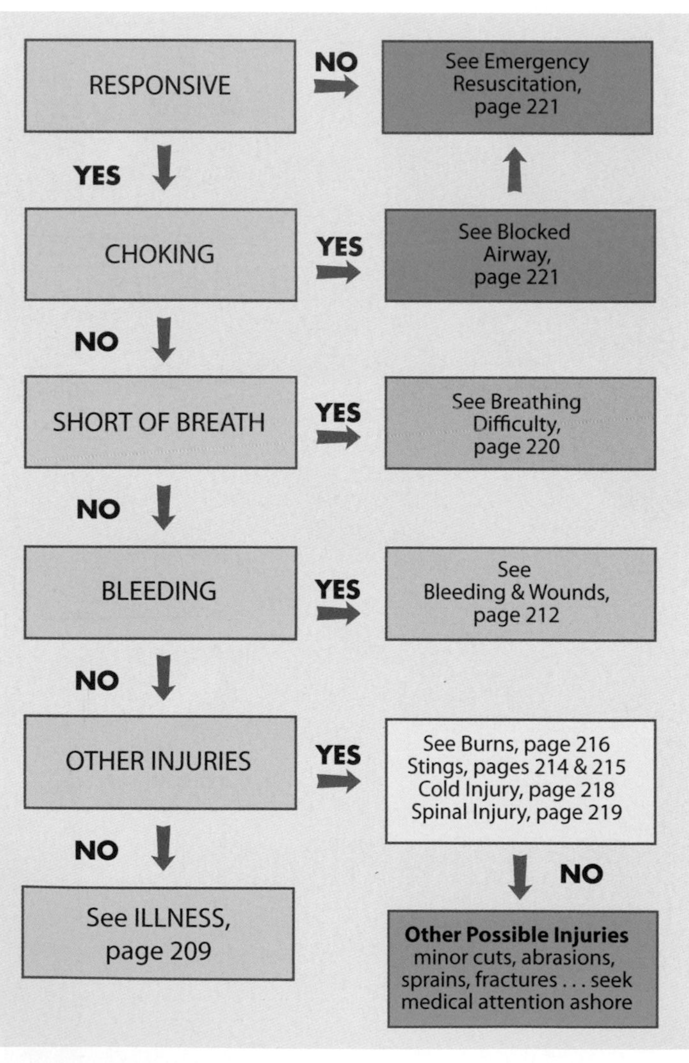

## Get Help

**Where are you?** Write it down. GPS can give you latitude and longitude, or you can note distance and direction from the nearest nav aid or landmark.

**If you have a marine radio on board, use it on Channel 16.** It is more reliable than a cell phone. For a life-threatening illness or injury or possible loss of the boat, start your transmission stating, "Mayday-Mayday-Mayday." If your radio has digital selective calling (DSC) capability and is linked to GPS, press the distress button. If you call the Coast Guard by radio, describe in as much detail as possible what is occurring on the boat, what emergency action has been taken thus far, and your location.

**If you can't get help by radio, use your cell phone and call 911.**

**When talking to a 911 operator, don't disconnect first.** Let the emergency operator control the call.

## Illness

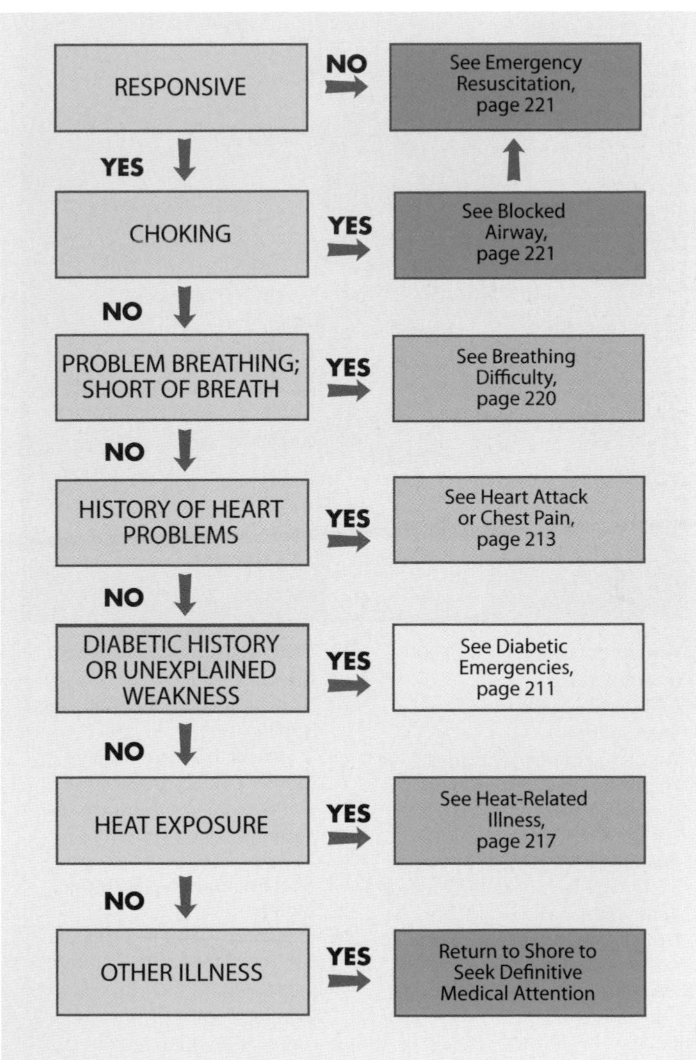

# Recommended First-Aid Kit

Your onboard first-aid kit should contain these items at a minimum:

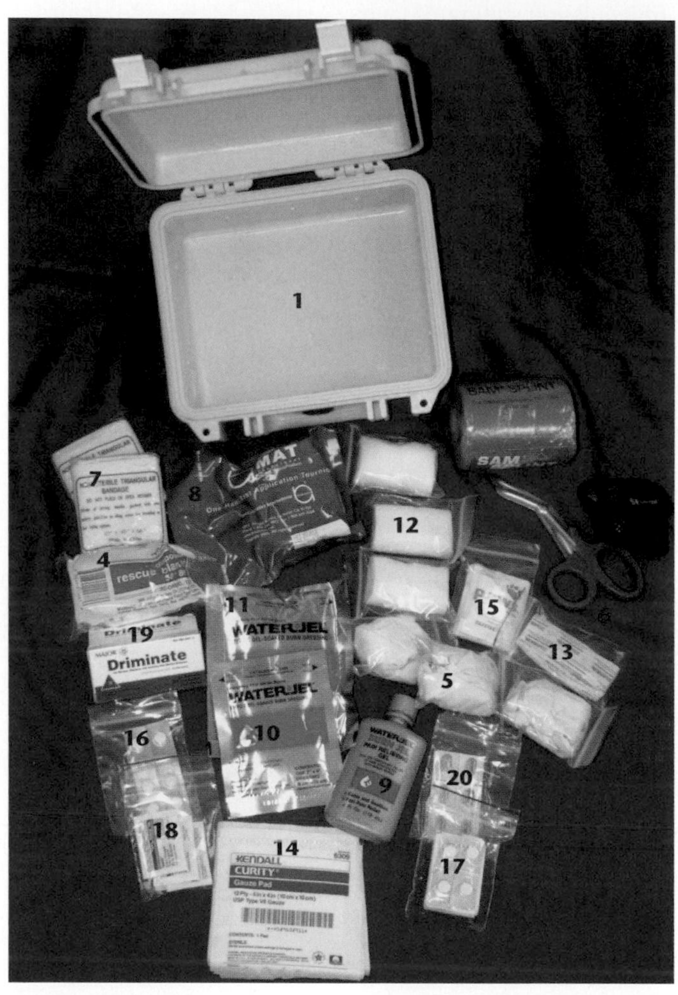


1. Waterproof case (Pelican 1300 recommended)
2. CPR barrier mask—1
3. SAM Splint—1
4. Warming emergency blanket—1
5. Hypoallergenic disposable gloves—3 pairs
6. EMS utility shears—1
7. Triangular bandage—2
8. 1″ MAT (Mechanical Advantage Tourniquet)—1
9. Cool Jel treatment for minor burns—small bottle
10. Water-Jel sterile 4″ x 4″ burn dressing—1
11. Water-Jel sterile 4″ x 16″ burn dressing—1
12. 3″ conforming gauze bandage—3 rolls
13. 1″ plastic bandage—25
14. Sterile 4″ x 4″ dressing—4
15. Germacidal wound wipes—4
16. Aspirin—325 mg buffered tablets
17. Acetaminophen—500 mg tablets
18. Ibuprofen—200 mg capsules
19. Motion sickness medication
20. Diphenhydramine (Benadryl)—25 mg capsules

A kit that precisely matches these specifications can be purchased from the author at Boating Good Samaritan Kit (phone: 850-939-0840; web: www.boating-good-samaritan.com). Equivalent kits are available from West Marine at prices ranging from $80 to $300 (see www.westmarine.com) and from other retailers.

## Diabetic Emergencies

1. Most diabetics adequately manage the disease and maintain stable blood sugar levels.
2. The onset of a diabetic coma from insufficient insulin—leaving cells unable to absorb glucose from the blood—is usually gradual and therefore unlikely to reach crisis stage. Blood sugar levels elevate as the condition progresses, leading to severe *hyperglycemia*. Early symptoms include thirst and frequent urination, followed later by nausea, vomiting, shortness of breath, and ultimately coma.
3. *Hypoglycemia*, or low blood sugar—whether from taking too much insulin, skipping food, or excessive stress, exercise, or alcohol consumption—can develop more rapidly and usually without warning (except that the victim is usually aware that he or she is diabetic). Possible symptoms include:
   - Weakness
   - Dizziness
   - Excessive sweating
   - Pale, cold, and moist skin
   - Rapid pulse
   - Headache
   - Poor coordination
   - Shakes or trembling
   - Changes in behavior or mood
   - Seizures
   - Eventual coma
4. The treatment of a victim with low blood sugar is simple and quickly effective if initiated soon enough. Give the victim any food or drink that contains sugar, including soda, fruit juice, ice cream, candy bars, or spoonfuls of table sugar dissolved in water. If the victim loses consciousness, place sugar, cake icing, or similar under his or her tongue.
5. Do not let a recovering victim resume normal activity too quickly. He or she should rest and should be allowed to eat some food that will provide a longer-acting release of sugars into the blood.

*DISCLAIMER: This chapter augments but does not replace appropriate training in first aid and CPR. Boaters are encouraged to supplement and confirm information in this chapter with other sources, including recognized training agencies. The author and publisher assume no liability with respect to the accuracy, completeness, or application of information contained in this chapter.*

# Bleeding and Wounds

1. Don disposable gloves.
2. Press a 4" x 4" sterile dressing on the site of the bleeding.
3. If blood seeps through, add more dressings.
4. Once bleeding is stopped, wrap wound with a conforming dressing.
5. Stop bleeding with pressure and elevation as necessary. If this fails to stop bleeding from an arm or leg, apply a tourniquet and arrange for rapid transport of the patient to a hospital. Any flat, nonstretch bandage, sail tie, belt, or similar can be used as a tourniquet. Wrap tightly, as closely above wound as possible. Damage to the arm or leg is possible after a few hours, but this is preferable to having the patient bleed to death.

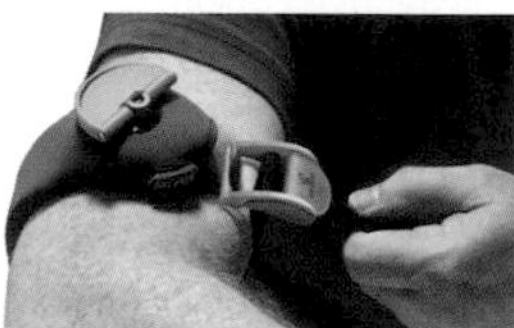

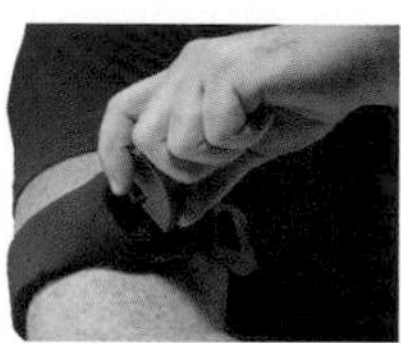

Use of the MAT tourniquet. After clipping around limb above wound, cinch strap tight, then tighten further by turning key clockwise. Release by pressing red release button and then lifting the clip.

If professional medical care cannot be reached within 24 hours, it is a good idea to clean the wound daily or whenever a dressing gets wet or dirty in order to minimize infection. Use the following steps:

1. Remove dressings.
2. Wash the wound using soap and clean water. Bleeding may restart. If so, repeat steps 1–5 above.
3. Flush wound with clean or sterile water.
4. Apply fresh, sterile dressings and bandage.

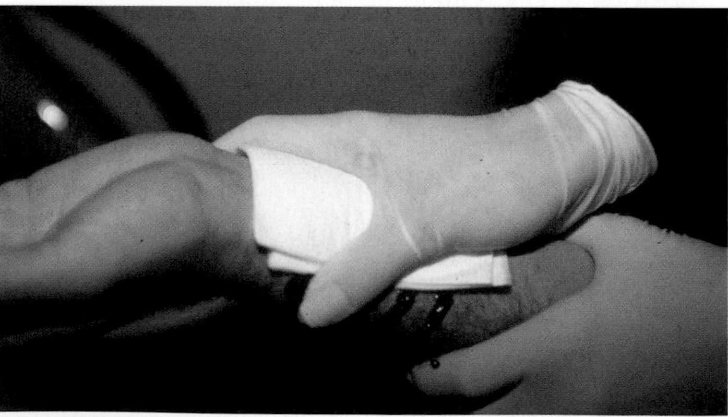

Applying a dressing to a wound.

When an object is impaled in the victim, do not remove it. Instead, stabilize the object using additional dressings or anything else at hand.

If part of the victim's body has been removed as a result of the wound, take the following additional steps:

1. Rinse the removed part in clean water to remove dirt and debris. Do not scrub.
2. Wrap the part in a sterile dressing.
3. Place the wrapped part in a plastic bag or wrap to keep it from getting wet in the following step.
4. Immerse the wrapped part in ice water, but avoid direct contact with ice.
5. Transport the removed part to the hospital with the victim.

## Heart Attack/ Chest Pain

1. Common signs and symptoms:
   - Anxiety
   - History of high blood pressure, angina, or heart disease
   - Recent significant exertion before onset of chest pain
   - Chest pain that does not change with the victim's position or breathing
   - Pain that radiates up the sides of the neck or down the victim's arm or arms
   - Complaint of indigestion that is not consistent with recent food consumed
   - Rapid or irregular pulse or complaint of "palpitations"
   - Pale, cool, moist skin
   - Noticeable increase in breathing rate.
2. Place victim in a comfortable position, usually semi-sitting.
3. If the victim has a history of angina and carries nitroglycerin, have the victim self-administer the nitroglycerin. Assist as necessary. Nitroglycerin can be taken at least two more times at 3-minute intervals if pain is not relieved with the first dose.
4. If the pain persists 15 minutes after nitroglycerin, suspect a heart attack. Rapid transport to medical care is vital.
5. If you suspect a heart attack, allow the victim to take one adult aspirin tablet, but give no fluids other than a swallow of water with the aspirin.
6. If there is oxygen on the boat, administer oxygen to the victim at a high flow.
7. Getting a heart attack victim to medical care quickly is critical.

# Insect Stings

Insect stings can be painful but are usually not life-threatening unless there is a severe allergic reaction.

1. Insect stings will show redness and swelling at the site of the sting. Pain may be intense initially but then subside to a dull pain.
2. First and foremost, observe for signs of an allergic reaction. What to watch for:
   - Numbness or itching around the mouth and the face
   - Difficulty breathing
   - Tightness in the throat or chest
   - Agitation and anxiety
   - Diminished level of consciousness
3. If an allergic reaction appears to have occurred, determine if the victim carries an anaphylaxis (allergic reaction) kit, typically called an Ana-Kit, which includes epinephrine (EpiPen) as well as Benadryl.
4. If so, administer both the oral and self-injected medication as quickly as possible. Time is of the essence.
5. Reassure the victim while preparing to support the victim's breathing and circulation as described on page 221.
6. A large local reaction to a sting does not indicate an allergic reaction but simply that the victim is highly sensitive. Administer a single dose of Benadryl.
7. Absent an allergic reaction, make the victim more comfortable and relieve pain with the following steps.
8. Apply an ice pack to the sting site for up to 20 minutes or until the pain is relieved.
9. If you have acetaminophen or ibuprofen on board, give the victim the normal adult dose.
10. Your onboard first-aid kit should contain some form of sting-relief swabs. Use one directly on the sting site.
11. Continue to watch the victim for at least an hour to be certain that no signs of an allergic reaction (see #2 above) develop.

Note on CPR (see page 221): This chapter provides a quick overview for performing CPR (cardiopulmonary resuscitation) on an adult. Most emergency medical personnel recommend modified chest-compression and rescue-breathing techniques for children and infants. To be fully prepared for medical emergencies, take a nationally recognized course in CPR. Such courses are readily available in all communities and can be completed with an investment of only several hours of time.

# Marine Stings

If someone on your boat comes out of the water with welts or severe itching, it's likely that he or she has been stung by some marine organism such as a jellyfish, anemone, or fire coral.

1. Watch carefully for the signs and symptoms of an allergic reaction as explained on page 214.
2. If you see obvious signs of tentacles or debris on the victim, do not touch this material with your hands as you might get stung too.
3. Rinse visible tentacles or debris from the victim's skin surface using salt water. Do not use fresh water, since this will cause additional stinging.
4. If shaving cream and a razor are on board, lather the affected area and shave the skin surface. Discard the removed shaving cream, since it contains stinging cells.
5. Since most marine venoms break down in the presence of heat, put hot packs on the injured area or expose the area to the hottest water that the victim can tolerate for as long as possible.
6. If you have white vinegar or ammonia on board, pour full-strength vinegar or diluted ammonia (1 part household ammonia mixed with 3 parts water) on the injured area to neutralize the toxin. Pour as much as can be tolerated.
7. As with insect stings, acetaminophen or ibuprofen may relieve some of the pain.
8. If the patient can tolerate it, Benadryl (diphenhydramine) may also be useful to relieve the itching that typically follows the initial burning and pain.

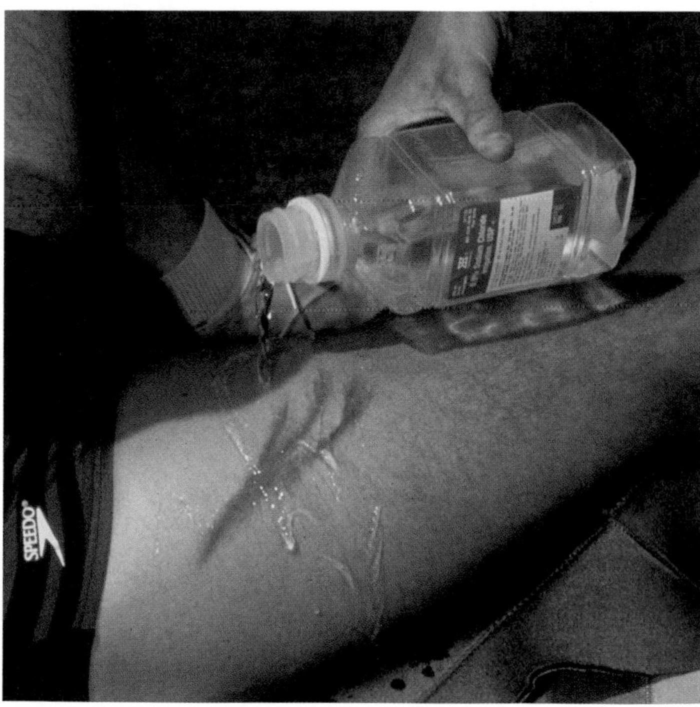


Rinsing a jellyfish sting with diluted ammonia.

# Burns

1. Most burns on a boat will be contact burns. If burning clothing or other material is involved, make sure it has been removed from the victim.
2. Do not manage burns long-term on a boat.
3. Critical burns that require immediate medical attention and are true emergencies include:
   - Electrical burns
   - Burns around the face
   - Burns covering more than 20% of the body
   - Burns around the genitals
   - Burns involving the fingers and/or toes
   - Significant chemical burns
4. The first step in treatment is to stop the burning. Pour cool, clean water over the burned area to cool the tissues.
5. Remove jewelry, watches, belts, and clothing from the burned area.
6. Cover the burned area with a Water-Jel dressing, or apply Cool Jel to a minor burn before applying a sterile dressing.
7. Protect any blisters that develop in the burned area from bursting.
8. Bandage appropriately and immobilize the burned part.
9. If fingers or toes are involved in the burned area, place small nonstick gauze pads between the involved fingers and toes before bandaging. This will prevent the burned fingers and toes from sticking together.
10. Carefully monitor the victim's breathing and overall condition while waiting for help or returning to the dock.
11. Giving fluids by mouth is a good idea, but do not overdo this to the point that vomiting might take place.

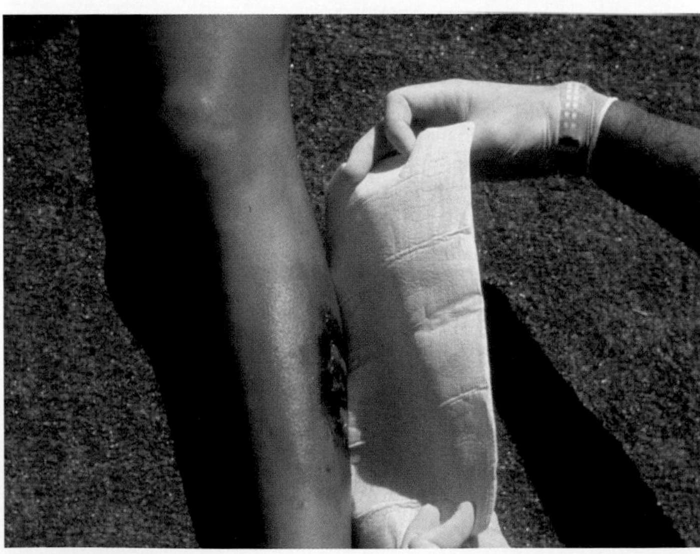

Applying a burn dressing.

# Heat-Related Illness

Differentiating between non-life-threatening heat exhaustion and life-threatening heatstroke is difficult even for professionals, so treat any heat illness as an emergency.

1. Anyone who begins to experience even the most minor symptoms of heat illness should drink water and be taken to shore immediately.
2. Early symptoms include:
   - Headache, weakness, nausea, and/or dizziness
   - Elevated body temperature
3. Progressive symptoms include:
   - Skin cool and clammy (still sweating) or hot and dry (no longer sweating)
   - Body temperature above 104°F.
   - Confusion, disorientation, or diminished consciousness
4. Shelter the victim from the heat and initiate emergency cooling.
5. Remove excess clothing from the victim.
6. Immerse the victim in cool water or cover with ice water–soaked towels or cloths.
7. Victim should sip cool water or diluted (50-50) electrolyte drinks if possible.
8. Monitor the victim carefully. If you see any signs of deterioration, apply ice around the neck, scalp, in the armpits, to the flanks, and to the groin area.
9. PREVENTION is the best treatment. Drink plenty of water *before* getting underway. Continue to drink water underway—as much as 2 pints per hour. Intersperse electrolyte drinks such as Gatorade. Avoid beverages containing alcohol or caffeine, both of which increase dehydration.
10. Clear or light-colored urine indicates adequate hydration.
11. Do not overhydrate. Relieve thirst but do not cause bloating.

# Cold-Related Injuries

The most serious cold-related injury encountered by boaters is cold-water immersion. Get the victim out of the water quickly. Extended immersion can lead to hypothermia if death does not occur first.

1. Progressive signs and symptoms of hypothermia may include:
   - Shivering or difficulty moving body parts
   - Poor judgment or confusion
   - Apathy
   - Lack of coordination
   - Rapid breathing and/or heartbeat
   - Stupor
   - In extreme cold there will be a loss of the ability to shiver
   - Unconsciousness
   - Slowed breathing and heart rate
2. Handle the victim carefully, since in severe cases the heart may be susceptible to heartbeat abnormalities that can be fatal.
3. Get the victim out of the wind and remove all wet clothing.
4. Dry the victim and do whatever you can to warm the victim without rough handling. Wrap the victim in dry clothing and blankets, use the metallic warming blanket from your first-aid kit, or use another dry person's body warmth.
5. Make sure the victim's body *and head* are covered with dry clothing or wrapped in a heat-conserving blanket.
6. If the victim is capable of swallowing safely, have him or her drink warm, sweet liquids. DO NOT permit alcoholic beverages of any kind.
7. Do not leave the victim alone. It is important to continue to monitor his or her condition.

The HELP (Heat Escape Lessening Position) posture will slow a swimmer's loss of body heat, but the most critical survival factor for a person overboard is wearing a PFD (personal flotation device). The victim's first reaction when falling into cold water is to gasp and then aspirate water. He or she may lose the ability to swim, and only a PFD will keep him afloat.

# Spinal Injuries

A serious fall or impact may cause injury to the spinal cord. There is little you can do to treat such an injury, but appropriate management is critical.

1. Suspect injury to the spinal cord and surrounding bony structures if the victim exhibits any of the following:
   - Significant pain or tenderness at any point along the spine, including the bones in the neck
   - Loss of ability to move arms or legs
   - Loss of feeling in arms or legs
   - A complaint of weakness in arms or legs after a fall or being struck by a sailboat boom
   - Loss of feeling or a complaint of pins and needles in any part of the body below the neck following an injury
2. Lay the victim flat on the boat's deck for stability. If he or she must be moved, one rescuer should immobilize the head and neck while others lift the body as a unit.
3. Manually stabilize the victim's head and neck, getting additional help from a cervical collar, life jackets, clothing, towels, etc., as available and necessary.
4. If you need to manually maintain the victim's breathing, use the jaw-thrust maneuver to open the airway. Do not employ the head-tilt, chin-lift procedure.
5. If the spinal cord injury is severe enough, it may be necessary to support the breathing of a fully conscious victim, since the muscles used to breathe may not work properly.
6. Minimize pounding or disturbance of the boat. Focus on a smooth transport rather than speed.
7. Do not allow any handling of the patient that will in any way disturb the immobilization of the victim's body.

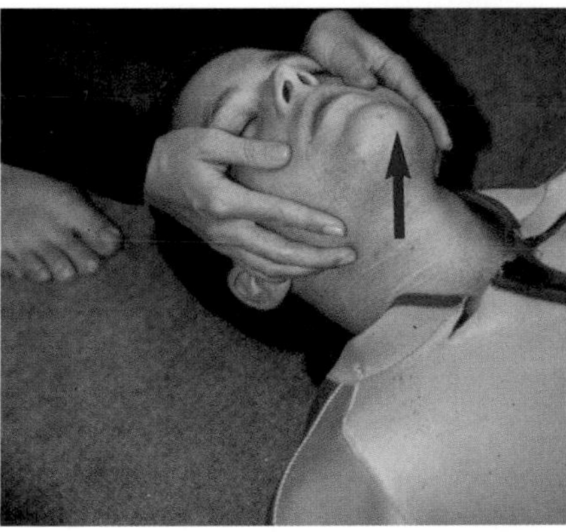

**Jaw thrust.** To open a victim's airway with this technique, put your fingers under each side of the jaw and lift it up *without* tilting the head back. Use this technique when you suspect a neck or spinal injury.

# Breathing Difficulty

1. The victim will typically complain that he or she can't catch his breath or is short of breath.
2. First ascertain whether the victim has a chronic disease such as asthma, chronic bronchitis, or emphysema. If not, shortness of breath may be a sign that the victim is suffering from a heart attack (page 213) or sting (pages 214 and 215).
3. Get the victim in a comfortable position—usually a sitting or semi-sitting position.
4. Reassure the victim that help is coming or will be waiting when the boat returns to the shore.
5. Loosen any clothing that might restrict breathing. This includes any tight upper-body undergarment of a woman.
6. If oxygen is on board and someone is trained to use it, administer it to the victim.
7. If the victim's breathing stops, go to page 221 and follow the steps you will find there.

**Ventilating** with barrier mask. In CPR, give two breaths sufficient to cause the chest to rise, about 1 second each, then do chest compressions. Your first-aid kit should include a barrier mask.

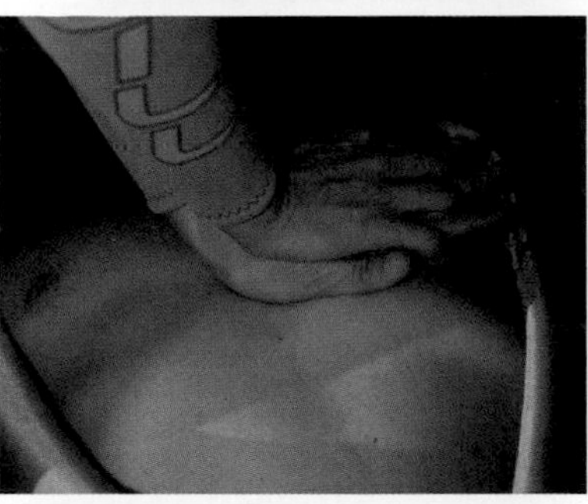

**Chest compressions.** In CPR, follow ventilations with 30 compressions at a rate of 100 per minute. Then repeat ventilating/chest compression sequence.

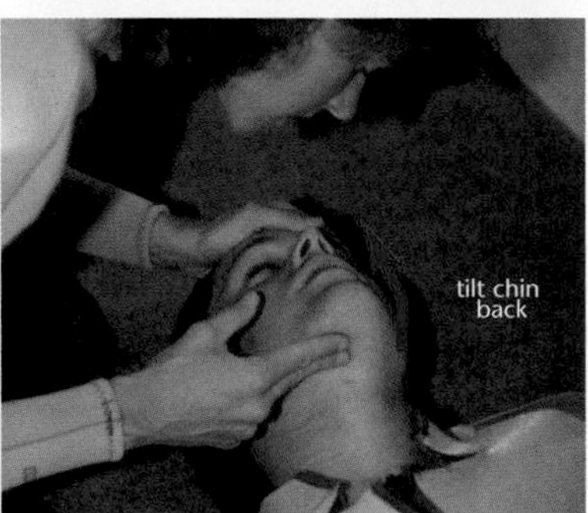


**Head-tilt, chin-lift procedure.** Use this to open the airway prior to rescue breathing when you are sure there is no neck or spinal injury. If such injury is possible, use jaw-thrust technique (page 219).

# Emergency Resuscitation

## CPR

1. If a victim has collapsed and is seemingly unresponsive and you have someone else on board, contact the Coast Guard or 911 for emergency help. If you're alone, start from Step 2 before summoning help.
2. Shake the victim and shout, "Are you OK?"
3. If no response, DO NOT DELAY… DO NOT CHECK FOR PULSE. (See page 214 for note on children.)
4. Open the victim's airway using the head-tilt, chin-lift procedure (see page 220). If you suspect a neck or spinal injury, use the jaw-thrust procedure (see page 219). Give two breaths sufficient to cause the chest to rise (see page 220). Breaths are about 1 second each. Have the person who is contacting the Coast Guard or 911 say that CPR is in progress.
5. Begin chest compressions with hands placed in the middle of the chest at the nipple line (see page 220). Compressions should be administered at a rate of 100 compressions per minute. Give 30 compressions and then 2 more ventilations as in Step 4. Watch for the chest to rise. Continue this 30:2 compression-ventilation series for about 2 minutes.
6. If you're alone, call the Coast Guard or 911 after your first 2 minutes of CPR.
7. If the victim has not responded and an automated defibrillator is on board, connect it to the victim and activate it now.
8. Continue compressions and breaths until no one on board is physically capable of continuing or help has arrived.

## Choking—Blocked Airway

1. If the victim CAN make noise, don't do anything. Air is moving.
2. If the victim makes no noise or only nods "yes" when asked, "Are you choking?" act immediately.
3. Give abdominal thrusts until the victim breathes or becomes unconscious. If abdominal thrusts don't work, give the victim chest compressions.

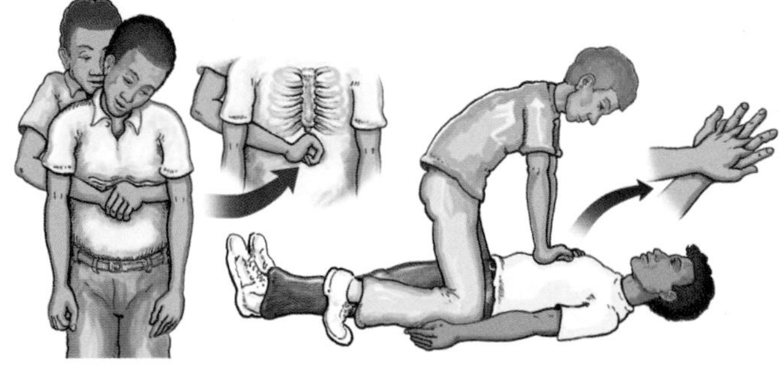

**Abdominal thrust** (Heimlich maneuver) on standing (left) or unconscious (right) victim. For hand position for chest compressions, see page 220.

## CONTRIBUTORS

**Nigel Calder**, a diesel mechanic, boatbuilder, and marine technical writer, is the internationally acclaimed author of *Boatowner's Mechanical and Electrical Manual*, universally recommended as the first and most essential book to carry aboard for assessing and maintaining your boat's systems. He is also the author of *Marine Diesel Engines*, *Nigel Calder's Cruising Handbook*, and *How to Read a Nautical Chart*, among other nautical books.

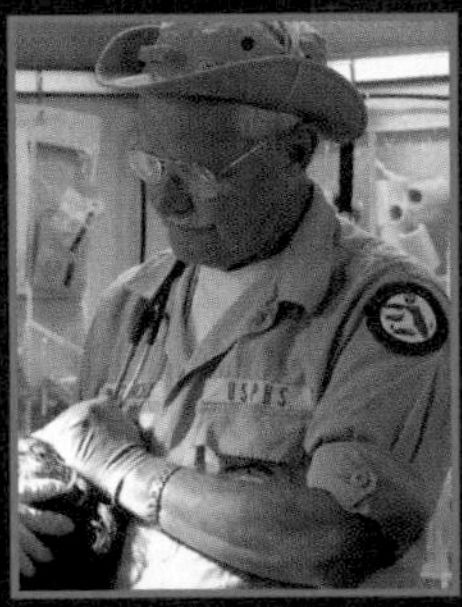

**Richard Clinchy**, PhD, is a paramedic and military and EMS medical equipment consultant with nearly 50 years of prehospital emergency medical care experience and over 35 years as an emergency medical care educator. Formerly chairman of the American College of Prehospital Medicine, he is the author of the Dive/First Responder text and training program and has written or edited seven books on diving and emergency medical care. He is the former Chief, Department of Education, United States Coast Guard Auxiliary.

**Bill Gladstone** is the Director of Education for North Sails and author of the North U *TRIM*, *Tactics*, and *Cruising* books and CDs. Bill has been teaching sailing for over 30 years. He is the former Commodore of the Yale Corinthian Yacht Club. Graduates of his seminars and clinics are racing and cruising worldwide.

**Peter Nielsen** is the editor of *SAIL* Magazine and was previously an editor at *Yachting Monthly* in the UK. An experienced mariner who has cruised, raced, and anchored worldwide, he is also the author of *Sailpower*.

# CONTRIBUTORS

**John Rousmaniere** is the author of the bestselling *Annapolis Book of Seamanship*—widely hailed as the best book available on seamanship under sail—as well as *Fastnet, Force 10*; *After the Storm*; and a dozen other nautical books. He lectures widely on seamanship and safety, and won the Captain Fred E. Lawton Boating Safety Award for outstanding contribution to boating safety through the media. He has sailed more than 35,000 bluewater miles.

**Bob Sweet** is the author of *GPS for Mariners*, *The Weekend Navigator*, and *Powerboat Handling Illustrated*. A former radar and communications system engineer and executive manager of a corporate business unit that helped develop GPS for the U.S. Air Force, he is the Assistant National Education Officer for the United States Power Squadrons. Bob is also a navigation instructor and an avid boater with more than 30 years' experience on the water.

**Charlie Wing**, author of *One-Minute Guide to the Nautical Rules of the Road*, received his PhD in oceanography from the Massachusetts Institute of Technology. He lived aboard a cruising sailboat for 6 years, during which time he earned a U.S. Coast Guard Captain's license. His frustration with available license study guides led him to create International Marine's bestselling *Get Your Captain's License*, now in its third edition. He is also the author of *Boatowner's Illustrated Electrical Handbook* and *How Boat Things Work: An Illustrated Guide*.

# INDEX

Index